I am
an
X kid!

Backyard Bible Club 2006

Family funstuff
BIBLE STORIES
Elementary

Faith Kids

Faith Kids® and Godprints™ are imprints of
Cook Communications Ministries, Colorado Springs, CO 80918
Cook Communications, Paris, Ontario
Kingsway Communications, Eastbourne, England

FAMILY FUNSTUFF BIBLE STORIES (ELEMENTARY)
©2001 by Cook Communications Ministries

First printing, 2001
Printed in Singapore

1 2 3 4 5 6 7 8 9 10 (printing/year) 05 04 03 02 01

Edited by: Lois Keffer and Susan Martins Miller

Written by: Mary Grace Becker, Annette Brashler Bourland, Sharon Bryant,
Jeanne Gowen Dennis, Elisabeth Hendricks, Marianne K. Hering, Jodi Hoch,
Dana Hood, Lois Keffer, Susan Martins Miller, Amy Nappa, Mike Nappa,
Faye Spieker, Dawn Renee Weary, Peggy Wilber, Jennifer Root Wilger

Cover and Interior Design: Chuck Haas Designs

Cover Illustration: Todd Marsh

Interior Illustration: Scott Angle, Kris Cartwright, Georgia Cawley, Bob de la Peña,
Jesse Clay, Rob Collinet, Corbin Hilam, Pamela Johnson, Lois Keffer, Benton Mahan,
Todd Marsh, Kevin McCain, Donna Kae Nelson, Kay Salem

ISBN: 0-7814-3547-1

Table of Contents

Go for the Godprint

The Bible was meant to be shared. By people of all ages for all time. By kids. By moms and dads and whole families.

The Bible is more than a collection of great stories—it's God's truth. For people of all ages for all time. For kids. For moms and dads and whole families. This treasury of Bible stories features a rich variety of masterful storytelling— dramas, eyewitness accounts, humorous poems—even games and riddles! Each turn of the page reveals something new and exciting.

The Bible was meant to be taken to heart and lived out. By kids. By moms and dads and whole families. So we've followed each Bible story with a Go for the Godprint section that helps kids and families do just that. In the Go for the Godprint pages you'll find:

• The **Godprint:** What characteristic does God want to give kids that's illustrated in this story? This section presents the Godprint in language that's clear and challenging to kids.

• **What Digby Dug Up:** Fun Bible factoids and interesting cultural tidbits that lead to a clearer understanding of the story.

• A fun activity, craft or game that helps put feet on the Bible truth. It's great when kids learn Bible stories and think about them. It's better yet when kids live out what they've read! If your kids are learning from **Godprints** curriculum at church, they'll recognize the friendly characters from Potterfield who host each activity.

Jake's Mirth Quake: Lively games.
Mo's Fab Lab: Great science stuff.
Izzy's Art Cart: Creative art and craft projects.
PJ's Good to Go: Simple ways to serve others.
Herbie's Hideaway: Activities for thoughtful reflection.
Café de Click: Food fun to celebrate what God does for us.
GP Theater Company: Imaginative ways to relive the story.
Wally's Walkabout: Whole-body ways to learn.

• **God Talk:** Creative, family-involving ways to pray.

Enjoy these pages of Bible adventure with your kids. And don't be surprised when Godprints start popping out all over your family!

How Everything Came to Be

In the beginning, before time began, there was nothing. No sound. No light. No form.

Nothing but God—the great I Am who always was, still is, and forever will be. The Spirit of God hovered over the deep, dark mists of space.

Then God spoke. "Let there be light." Radiant spears of light shattered the darkness. The Lord called the light "day" and the darkness "night."

God spoke. "Let there be an expanse between the waters to separate water from water." The waters split in two, and God called the sparkling blue space above, "sky."

God spoke. "Let the water under the sky be gathered together, and let dry ground appear." The waters rushed together and God called them "seas." Dry ground rose and mountains pierced the sky. God called the dry ground "land."

By God's word, their emptiness took form and became the world we know. God saw that it was good.

God spoke. "Let the land produce vegetation: seed-bearing plants and trees on the land that bear fruit with seed in it, according to their various kinds." Trees spread their leafy branches. Flowers blossomed, luscious fruit ripened, and vines twisted and twirled. God saw that it was good.

God spoke. "Let there be lights in the expanse of sky to separate the day from the night, and let them serve as signs to mark seasons and days and years, and let them be lights in the expanse of sky to give light on the earth." The sun warmed the freshly formed world. The moon glowed in the night sky, and stars scattered their twinkling light across the universe.

By God's word
our whole universe
came to be. And God saw that
it was good.

God spoke. "Let the waters teem with
living creatures, and let birds fly above
the earth across the expanse of sky."
The creatures of the sea frolicked in
the water. Octopusses stretched
their tentacles, whales spouted,
and dolphins danced in the
waves. Mighty eagles took flight
and tiny sparrows built their
nests. God blessed the birds
and fish and told them to
multiply.

By God's word the sky and seas
filled with living creatures. And
God saw that it was good.

God spoke. "Let the land
produce living creatures
according to their
kinds: livestock,
creatures that
move along the
ground, and
wild
animals,
each
according to
its kind." And
it was so.

9

Lions roared, giraffes stretched their necks, and ooey-gooey worms burrowed into the ground.

God spoke. "Let us make man in our image, in our likeness, and let them rule over the fish of the sea and the birds of the air, over the livestock, over all the earth and over all the creatures that move along the ground." God told them to have children and fill the earth. And it was so.

By God's word animals and people inhabited the land. God saw that it was very good!

Then God rested from his work. He blessed the day he rested and made it holy.

God spoke our world into existence, and all the life that fills it. Nothing happened by chance or accident. God's world shows us his awesome power, his love for variety and his wisdom.

We honor God when we care for our amazing world. We can't make things happen just by speaking. Taken care of God's world can be hard work. It's a beautiful planet and God made it to give us everything we need.

The world is your home. Take good care of it.

Go for the Godprint

Stewardship: God created the world, then put the first two people in charge of taking care of it all. That job passes on to us. Think of the world as God's wonderful gift—a precious jewel he hung in space. It's ours to care for. When we show respect for the things God made, we honor God. You're a trusted steward of God's resources. Enjoy the job!

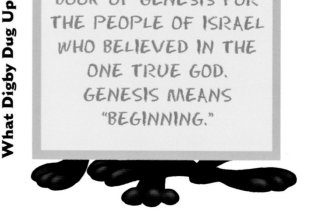

What Digby Dug Up

MOSES WROTE THE BOOK OF GENESIS FOR THE PEOPLE OF ISRAEL WHO BELIEVED IN THE ONE TRUE GOD. GENESIS MEANS "BEGINNING."

Mo's Fab Lab:

Create a crystal garden to remind you of the beautiful, secret places in God's world that you can explore someday. Have Mom or Dad help you mix the following ingredients in a bowl.

6 tablespoons salt	6 tablespoons liquid bluing
6 tablespoons water	1 tablespoon ammonia

Place small pebbles in a shallow glass dish. Pour the mixture over the rocks, then drip food coloring on top. Crystals will begin to grow soon! Add water occasionally to keep the crystals growing. Place the glass bowl on an old tray, because the crystals will grow over the sides of the dish!

God Talk

Walk with your family
to a beautiful spot in God's creation.
Read Psalm 104,
then read the following excerpts as a prayer.
How many are your works, O Lord!
In wisdom you made them all; the earth is full of your creatures.
When you send your Spirit, they are created, and you renew the face of the earth.
May your glory, Lord, endure forever, may you rejoice in your works!
I will sing to you, Lord, all of my life; I will sing praise to my God as long as I live.
May my meditations be pleasing to you, as I rejoice in you, Lord.

Just Dust?

If you were going to make a person, how would you begin? With eyes? A nose? Ten toes? What would you use? A crayon? A marker? Modeling clay?

When God made the first person, he began with dust. Just dust from the ground. Then he formed all the parts that are parts of you.

Run your fingers around your ears and feel all the little ridges and fleshy parts. God knew all the wonderful things the first people would hear. He knew all the wonderful things you would hear, too: bird songs, a fresh burst of rainfall, the loving words of the people who care for you.

God made two strong feet with five toes apiece. Wiggle all your toes. Sometimes toes seem silly and they really hurt when you stub them. But God knew that people would need toes for balance. He knew they would help us jump and turn and spin. He knew how good it would feel to wriggle them in warm sand.

God made arms that could hug and lift and carry. And fingers that could put food in our mouths and play instruments and write letters and run through the soft fur of animals. What's your favorite way to use your fingers?

God made eyes that could take in all the amazing colors of creation. Look out your window. How many shades of green can you see? How would you describe the color of the sky? God knew that when we saw with our eyes all the wonderful things he made, we would remember that he is the great Creator who made it all.

God gave the first people amazing brains. Brains that reason and make good decisions. Brains that know feelings like love and anger, contentment and silliness.

God stretched skin over the first person he named. Have you ever thought about how wonderful your skin is? It's elastic so you can stretch in any direction. It's a waterproof barrier that keeps everything that's supposed to be inside inside and everything that's supposed to be outside outside. If you rip it up, it grows back together. And it does other incredible things like goosebumps and freckles.

God finished up all the details like hair and fingernails and teeth.

But the best was yet to come.

God breathed into the nostrils of the first person and gave him life. And in that moment God changed him from a pile of dust into Adam, a human being made in God's own image. Adam had the ability to love, to make good choices, to manage the garden and to know God himself. There was no other creature like Adam. Then God made Eve to be Adam's companion and helper.

Adam and Eve are your ancestors. If you go way, way, way back in time, you're related! Is that cool or what?

But in all the time between Adam and Eve and you, there's never been another person just like you. Never. Not even one. You are a completely unique creation. When God put you together inside your mother, he knew all about you. And he loved you. He had great hopes for you, and he still does.

God's greatest hope for you is that you will love him and learn to be like him. That's the best thing anyone can do. Because people are a lot more than just dust.

When God made people, he thought, "Very good!" That means you, son of Adam or daughter of Eve. You are made in God's very image. You are precious and unique. And don't you forget it!

Go for the Godprint

Preciousness: Is it ever hard for you to be happy about the way God made you? People who are not happy with themselves may spend a lot of time trying to be someone else. The greatest secret to being happy is knowing that God loves you just the way you are. Celebrate the way God made you. God does!

What Digby Dug Up
God made everything else in the world before he made people. He made people for a special reason—

TO TAKE CARE OF THE EARTH AND TO HAVE A RELATIONSHIP WITH GOD THAT THE REST OF CREATION DOES NOT HAVE.

GP Theater Company

Gather some socks that have lost their mates and an assortment of decorative craft items, such as ribbons, buttons, yarn, wiggle eyes, fabric and felt scraps, plastic jewels, glue, needle and thread. Work together to make sock puppets that represent all the members of your family.

Then use your sock puppets with fun voices to tell each other things that you appreciate about each other. You might tell kind things that another person does for you, or how someone makes you laugh, or why you like to spend time with another person in your family.

Then talk about:

- **Why are these puppets special to us?**

- **Why are we special to God?**

God Talk

Put a picture of yourself
up on your bedroom wall.
Write six things that you like
about yourself on sticky notes.
Tape the notes around your picture.
Whenever you see your picture, say to God,
"Thank you for making me…" and thank God
for the six things you wrote down.

A Serpent Comes A-Calling

Adam and Eve lived in a garden designed just for them. They were carefree. They were loved by God. And best of all God would come and talk to them. Sometimes he came in the evening when the breeze was cool and the air felt wonderfully fresh.

One day someone else entered the garden. He was not invited, but he came anyway. Satan hated God. He would do everything in his power to destroy the perfect peace God had created.

Satan knew that the Tree of Knowledge of Good and Evil was off-limits to Adam and Eve. God was very clear about that. Adam and Eve understood. They would not touch the tree. So what would Satan do that would tempt Eve to do the thing she said she would not do? He took the shape of a serpent and caught Eve on a stroll through the garden.

"Did God really say, 'You must not eat from any tree in the garden'?" Satan asked.

Eve answered plainly. "We may eat fruit from the trees in the garden, but God did say, 'You must not eat fruit from the tree that is in the middle of the garden, and you must not touch it, or you will die.'"

Satan was ready with a reply. "You will not surely die, for God knows that when you eat of it your eyes will be opened, and you will be like God, knowing good and evil."

Eve took a bite. She waited for the ground to shake or the sky to fall; but nothing happened. Then she offered some to her husband, Adam, and he ate too. Satan was delighted. He had won. Adam and Eve suddenly felt naked and ashamed. They ran to hide.

"Where are you? Where are you?" God called to Adam. God looked for the man he loved so much.

Adam heard God calling. He knew he could not hide forever. Adam and Eve came out of their hiding place and stood before God. They told God what they had done. Adam blamed Eve. "She gave me the fruit. It's her fault."

And Eve blamed the serpent. "The serpent tricked me, so I ate." God called the serpent and cursed him. "Cursed are you above all the livestock and all the wild animals! You will crawl on your belly and you will eat dust all the days of your life."

But God was not done. Eve would now have pain with the birth of her children. And Adam would have to work very hard to provide a home and food for his family. There would be weeds to pull and thorns and nettles to prick his feet. The beautiful garden filled with good things was closed forever. Even the animals became wild. Banished from the Garden of Eden, Adam and Eve fell into a life of worry and work. God sent an angel with a swift and flashing sword to guard the garden entrance. The remarkable garden was closed.

Sadly, God no longer came to talk with Adam and Eve. Their disobedience put an end to their closeness. God still loved Adam and Eve. He would care for them. But things were not the same.

Go for the Godprint

Fairness. Does it seem like Adam and Eve's punishment was too hard? Sometimes our choices have tough consequences, either for ourselves or other people. Adam and Eve learned that. God wants us to be honest and fair in our relationships with family and friends. What can you do to treat the kids you know fairly?

What Digby Dug Up
The Garden of Eden was a beautiful place. In Hebrew, *Eden* means "paradise." It can also mean "bliss" or "delight."

Izzy's Art Cart

GET LIST: 8"X8" SQUARE OF SANDPAPER, YARN, MARKER

Do you ever want time on the TV or computer but someone else is using it…again? Make a "Tic-Tac-Know!" board using an 8"X8" square of sandpaper. Place two vertical pieces of 8-inch yarn on the sandpaper. Cross with three horizontal pieces of 8-inch yarn.

Use a thin-tipped marker to write blocks of time in each box. Place it next to the computer or TV. Let everyone pick a different colored button. Now, have each person pick a time and put his or her button in that square. Make your choice and live with the fair (and square!) consequences by sticking to the plan.

God Talk

Set aside time after a long day to talk to God. Ask him to help you make responsible choices. Make a Toothbrush Reminder to make sure you don't forget! Using craft foam (a color that matches your toothbrush would be neat!) and a small cookie-cutter, trace the shape of the cutter on the foam and then cut out. With permanent marker write the words "Pray Today!" on the foam. Cut a small x in the center and push your toothbrush through.

Noah's Diary

God's Command

As I begin this diary, I am over 500 years old. I have a good wife and three sons named Shem, Ham and Japheth. And I have a wonderful God who cares for those who love him. But most people hate him. The earth is filled with sin and violence, even among my relatives. Why don't they listen to reason and obey God? Now he's going to destroy them all, but save my family. We have to build an ark, a huge boat, out of wood. I wonder if I can find some beavers to help cut down the trees.

In the Middle of Our Work

The ark has been a monumental task—and I mean monumental! I feel like an ant beside it. We divided the decks into rooms to hold all the different animals God is sending with us. We'll have only one door, but we'll leave space at the top for fresh air to come in. We're covering the whole thing, inside and out, with sticky, stinky pitch to keep the water out. We're building exactly the way God commanded. Everyone thinks we're crazy, but it doesn't matter. I love God, so I'll obey him.

It's Finished!

I am now 600 years old and our task is complete. In seven days, God will send a flood to destroy everything that breathes, people and animals alike. My family has already stored food onboard. Now we're watching a parade. Two-by-two, male and female animals of every kind are marching up the ramp into the ark. What an amazing creation each one is!

The Deluge Begins

My wife, sons, their wives, and our little zoo have been in the ark for seven days. God closed the door, and now we hear water coming from the sky and bursting from the ground below us. The animals are restless. They seem to understand what's happening. There will be thirty-nine more days and nights of rain, but God promised to take care of us. All these wonderful creatures will keep us busy. Uh-oh! One of the monkey's is riding a horse!

Forty Days Tomorrow

The wind is roaring and waves are crashing against the ark. This boat that seemed so huge before feels tiny in this vast ocean. There's one more day of rain to go. We're floating high above mountains now, the only eight people left alive on earth. So much has been destroyed—all because of sin. I'm grateful God chose to rescue us. Just think…if I had not obeyed him!

Five Months

God sent strong winds, and the floodwaters are draining away. I know, because we hit something and stopped moving. I think we're lodged on a mountain. I can't wait to trade animal smells and noises for fresh air and gentle breezes. Now that monkey is throwing fruit at the elephants!

Nine months

Last week I opened the window at the top of the ark. I sent out a raven to see if he could find a place to land, but he's still circling. I sent a dove, too, but she returned to me. Today, I sent her out again. When she returned, she had an olive leaf in her beak! The earth is coming alive again!

One week later

Today I sent the dove out again, but she has not returned. She must have found a place to land!

We Come Out

Today, after over a year on the ark, God called us out. All the animals followed. The earth looks so different, but it's wonderful to be out in the sunshine again. I built an altar and we sacrificed burnt offerings to the Lord. He promised never to destroy the whole earth again with water. As long as earth lasts, we'll have planting and harvest times, summer and winter, day and night. I'm so grateful God told me to build the ark. And I'm glad the monkey now has a tree of his own. I hope my children and grandchildren never forget that God takes care of those who love him!

Go for the Godprint

Preciousness: When you put your heart into making something, you love it. Although God loves all his creatures, he values people as his special creation. That's because he made us in his own image. His love for us never ends—even when we sin. That's why he provided an ark to save Noah's family. Centuries later, he sent Jesus to save all of us.

What Digby Dug Up

The ark was 450 feet long, 75 feet wide and 45 feet high. That means it was longer than a dozen big school buses and taller than a four-story building!

Wally's Walkabout

Get your family together for a scavenger hunt. Set your kitchen timer for ten minutes. Then scurry around and try to find ten things that come in pairs. Line everything up on a table like pairs of animals going into the ark. Give everyone a chance to tell about what they found. Talk about:

- *Why are these things important to us?*
- *What do we do to take care of these things?*
- *How is that like the way God takes care of us?*

God Talk
Set out a chair for each family member.
Run a rope around the chairs in the shape of an ark.
Set the stage by putting on a CD of ocean sounds.
Then make "rain" by patting your legs.
Take turns thanking God for times he has taken care of your family.
After each prayer, shout this cheer together: "Rain or shine, God is there. He will keep us in his care!"

A Choice for Peace

Dear Journal,

It's been a while since I wrote last, so let me catch you up. I'm living in Haran and working as a servant for a man named Abraham and his wife Sarah. Their whole family lives here—Grandma, Grandpa, aunts, uncles, nieces and nephews. I think it's going to be a good place to stay!

Dear Journal,

Remember that I said this was a good place to stay? Well, guess what? We're moving! Abraham told me to pack the camels and get ready to go. I asked him where we were going and you'll never believe this! He doesn't know! He said God told him to leave and will tell him where to stop. He doesn't even have a map. All he has is the word of this God! He thinks that's enough.

Dear Journal,

Everything's packed and we're heading out today. I still don't know where. Abraham and Sarah gathered their animals and all of us servants and said goodbye to their family—except for Abraham's nephew, Lot. Lot decided to come along. And of course, there were Lot's family, his servants, and sheep and camels, too. You've never seen so many animals and people all traveling to…who knows where?

Dear Journal,

It seems like we've been traveling forever, but we've finally settled in Bethel. Abraham's nephew Lot is still with us, and (just between you and me) this could become a problem. With all of our sheep and all of his sheep, there are not enough land and water to go around. If you ask me, we're headed for trouble.

24

Dear Journal,

Well, it happened! A terrible argument broke out today between Lot's herdsmen and ours. It wasn't a pretty sight! Yelling and screaming, fussing and fighting! Wait until Abraham hears about this. After all, if Abraham is right, God promised this land to him and not to Lot. I'll bet Abraham will send him packing. All of his sheep and herdsmen, too. I certainly won't be sad to see them go. I just wish he'd hurry and do what has to be done. Maybe I should tell him what's going on.

Dear Journal,

I just don't understand Abraham! I told him about Lot's herdsmen and how much trouble they've been. I told him there wasn't enough room for all of us! You'll never believe what he did. He went over to see Lot, and I thought he was really going to let him have it. Imagine my surprise when he said, "Lot, we're family. We follow a God of peace. He wouldn't want us to be arguing and fighting." Then he told Lot, "We need to split up." I thought, "Yeah, this is it! Now he's going to get it!" But instead,

he told Lot to look at the land. He said, "You choose first. If you take the land to the left, I'll take the land to the right. After you pick, I'll take what's left over." And wouldn't you know it, Lot chose the prettiest land—trees, water and lots of good grass for his sheep. Abraham didn't even argue. He just hugged his nephew and said goodbye. Not a fuss. Not a fight. It was all settled, just like that!

Dear Journal,

Most people would say it was crazy to let Lot choose first. That's what I thought, too. But not Abraham. He knew it was more important to follow God than to get his own way. And guess what! God blessed him. God gave Abraham more land than you can imagine! The next time I have an argument, I hope I have the courage that Abraham had to choose peace instead of fighting.

Go for the Godprint

Respectful: Have you ever shouted "Me first!" or made sure you got the biggest piece of cake? Being respectful means thinking about what others need and not just about what you want. Abraham showed respect for Lot when he let him choose first. How can you show respect to the people you know?

What Digby Dug Up

ABRAHAM AND LOT GREW UP IN UR, A VERY BUSY ANCIENT CITY. AS THEY TRAVELED TO THEIR NEW HOME IN CANAAN, THEY WENT THROUGH THE "FERTILE CRESCENT," AN AREA OF LAND WITH RICH SOIL AND PLENTY OF WATER.

Herbie's Hideaway

Think about how many times each week you have the chance to choose between peace and fighting, or between respecting others and looking out for yourself. Make a family "AFTER YOU!" journal. Fold three pieces of paper in half together to create a small book. You can staple the folded edge, or punch holes and tie your book together with ribbon or yarn. Have fun decorating the cover. Find a time each day for a week to talk together about times that family members chose to say, "AFTER YOU!" and put others first. Record these things in your journal. Have some silly family fun using the words, "AFTER YOU!" with each other. Make it a game. Who knows? It might just stick!

God Talk

Choose someone in your family
to read this verse:
"If it is possible, as far as it depends on you,
live at peace with everyone" (Romans 12:18).
Take turns saying this simple prayer,
filling in the blank with a name:
Dear God, help me to live at peace with _____.
In Jesus' name, amen.

God's Laughter Surprise

H is for Heir. An heir is a child who will inherit what belongs to the parents when they die. Abraham was sad because he didn't have an heir. He didn't have any children at all. Abraham talked to God about this problem. He said, "Lord, I don't have any children. When I die I would like to give all my belongings to my child. Since you haven't given me a child, I will have to give everything to one of my servants. I guess my servant Eliezer will inherit my home and belongings."

O is for Old. Abraham and his wife Sarah were getting older and older. Most people have children between the ages of 20 and 40. Abraham and Sarah were much older than this. They were getting close to being 100 years old. That's way too old to have a baby. They knew they would never have any children. They wouldn't have an heir.

P is for Promise. After Abraham talked to God about how sad he was about not having an heir, God made a promise to Abraham. God said, "You will have a son."

God took Abraham outside and told him to look up at the sky. God said, "Count the stars, Abraham." Have you ever tried to

28

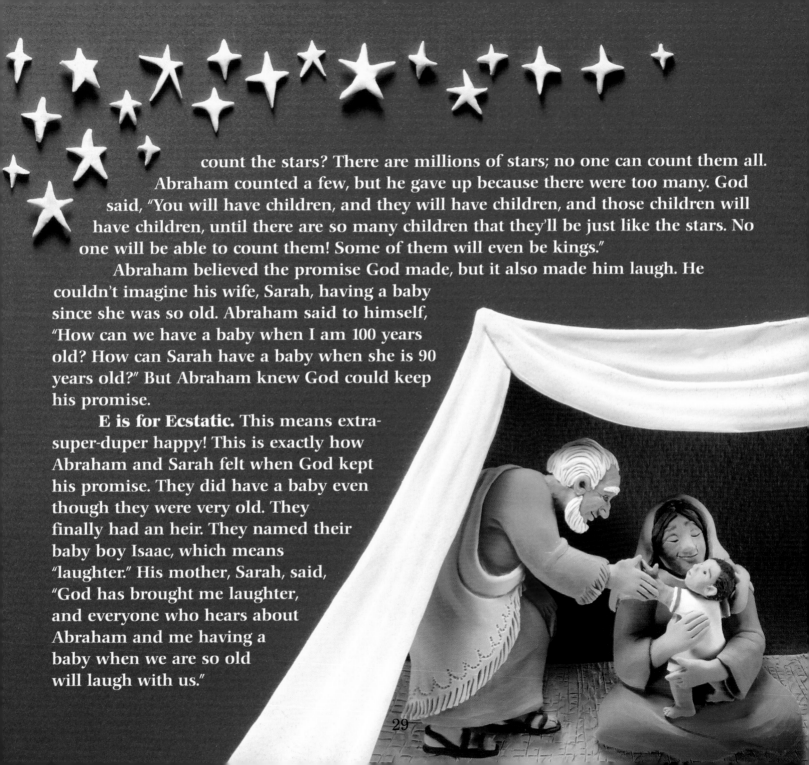

count the stars? There are millions of stars; no one can count them all. Abraham counted a few, but he gave up because there were too many. God said, "You will have children, and they will have children, and those children will have children, until there are so many children that they'll be just like the stars. No one will be able to count them! Some of them will even be kings."

Abraham believed the promise God made, but it also made him laugh. He couldn't imagine his wife, Sarah, having a baby since she was so old. Abraham said to himself, "How can we have a baby when I am 100 years old? How can Sarah have a baby when she is 90 years old?" But Abraham knew God could keep his promise.

E is for Ecstatic. This means extra-super-duper happy! This is exactly how Abraham and Sarah felt when God kept his promise. They did have a baby even though they were very old. They finally had an heir. They named their baby boy Isaac, which means "laughter." His mother, Sarah, said, "God has brought me laughter, and everyone who hears about Abraham and me having a baby when we are so old will laugh with us."

29

H-O-P-E spells hope. Hope means being sure that God will do what he says he'll do. Abraham and Sarah wanted an Heir. They were getting Old. God made a Promise. And when God kept his promise, they felt Ecstatic. Sometimes it was hard for Abraham and Sarah to have hope that God would keep his promise. Some days they tried to think of other ways to solve their problem. But none of their ideas worked. They had to keep waiting and trusting that God would keep his promise. And God did!

We can be like Abraham and Sarah, too. Because God keeps his promises we can have hope while we wait for those promises to come true!

Go for the Godprint

Hope: Have you ever had to wait a long, long time for someone to keep a promise? Were you sure that the promise would come true, like Abraham and Sarah were? God never loses control of our lives. He can make good things happen even from bad things. When you think about the future, what good things do you think God wants to make happen for you?

What Digby Dug Up

Abraham was originally named "Abram," which means "father." While he waited for God's promise to come true, God told Abram to change his name to Abraham, which means "father of a multitude." This change was another way God told Abraham he would be the father of many descendents.

Café de Click

Go to the store and buy a cake mix and frosting ingredients. Look at the picture on the box and talk about what you hope the cake will look like. Then follow the instructions on the box to mix the batter and bake the cake. While you wait for the cake to bake, talk about:

- **How do you hope the cake tastes?**

- **How does the time you spend looking forward to the cake help you enjoy it?**

- **How can waiting for God to do something good for you help you be thankful for what he does?**

Frost and decorate your cake, then enjoy it together. Before your first bite, say something that reminds you that God is in control of what happens to you.

God Talk

Read Psalm 33:22 aloud together
as a prayer of hope and blessing.
*May your unfailing love rest upon us,
O LORD, even as we put our hope in you.*

If Camels Could Talk

Camel 2: All right, all right. We're getting up.

Camel 3: So what's so terrific about this trip?

Camel 1: We're going wife hunting.

Camels 2 and 3: What?

Camel 1: Not for us! For Master Isaac.

Camel 2: Why would they send us to get a wife for Master Isaac?

Camel 3: There are plenty of girls around here.

Camel 1: Last night I overhead Master Abraham tell the head servant to go find a wife for Master Isaac.

Camel 2: So?

Camel 3: There are plenty of girls around here.

Camel 1: He said she had to be from the native land.

Camel 3: The native land?!

Camel 1: Right! So she would worship the true God. The girls around here all worship idols.

Camel 2: Well, why didn't you say so?

Camel 3: I'm there, man. Get me a saddle bag. Let's shake a leg!

Camels 1 and 2: Groan!

Abraham's camp, early in the morning.

Camel 1: Guys, guys, wake up!

Camel 2: Huh? What time is it?

Camel 1: Time for the trip.

Camel 3: Which trip? Who tripped? Did I trip?

Camel 1: Come on, come on, come on! This is it! This is the trip!

Camel 3: Hooves and humps! What's the big deal with a trip?

Camel 2: It's what we do. We're camels.

Camel 1: But this is the top trip of our careers. Come on—get your legs underneath you and push!

32

Nearing the end of the journey. Approaching Laban's camp.

Camel 2: Are we there yet? My feet are killing me.

Camel 3: There's a bump on my hump. What a load!

Camel 1: Gifts, gifts, gifts for the wife, wife, wife.

Camel 2: If we don't find her soon they're gonna land in the sand. I'm draggin'.

Camel 3: You're not a dragon, you're a camel.

Camel 2: Very funny.

Camel 1: Keep your chin up, boys. You know what they say: Neither rain nor snow nor dark of night will keep us…

Camel 2: What's snow?

Camel 1: Never mind. Look—there's a well! Let's kneel down. Maybe somebody will feel sorry for us and bring us water.

Camel 2: Hey, the servant's kneeling too. What's he doing?

Camel 3: And if he's kneeling, who's gonna bring the water?

Camel 1: Shh. Don't you guys know anything? He's praying! Listen.

Camel 2: He's asking God to help him find the wife.

Camel 3: He's asking for a sign.

Camel 1: The girl who gives water to him—and to his camels—will be the one.

Camel 2: Water? Did somebody mention water? Are we there yet?

Camel 1: Look! There's a girl with a water jar.

Camel 2: She's going to the spring.

Camel 3: She's coming back with water.

Camel 2: The servant is talking to her.

Camel 3: He's asking for a drink!

Camel 2: He's drinking!

Camel 3: She's going back for more!

Camel 1: Oh, she's definitely the one all right. Did you hear what she said? She'll draw water for us until we've finished drinking!

Camel 3: Drink up, fellas. Master Abraham's servant is going inside to talk to the relatives. It's time to celebrate.

33

Laban's camp, the next morning.

Camel 1: Guys! Guys, wake up!

Camel 2: Yawn! Let me guess. We're tripping again.

Camel 3: Nothing, absolutely nothing, will get me off this bed of straw.

Camel 1: Just get up. Look! Rebekah is coming this way.

Camel 2: Hey. How do you know her name?

Camel 1: Somebody had to keep a lookout while you guys were snoozing in the straw.

Camel 3: Let me guess. And you just happened to overhear that Rebekah is the bride we came looking for?

Camel 1: Yep, yep, yep. Her family didn't want to let her go right away, but she said she was ready.

Camel 2: Then we'd better get ready.

Camel 3: Check it out! She's got her own camels. A girl with her own camels can't be all bad.

Camel 1: Here's more good news. The servant gave gifts, gifts gifts to the family, family, family.

Camel 2: So our loads will be light, light, light!

Camel 3: Right, right, right! Let's hit the road, boys.

Camel 1: Maybe I can give the bride a ride!

Camel 2: Are we there yet?

Go for the Godprint

Integrity: Abraham sent his servant hundreds of miles back to his homeland to find his son a wife who believed in God. Abraham's servant wisely waited for God to show him just the right wife for Isaac. It will be a while before you look for a husband or wife, but you can trust God right now to guide you into the friendships that please him. Will you ask God to help you choose friends who will encourage your faith?

What Digby Dug Up

Abraham's servant gave gifts of gold and silver jewelry to Rebekah's family. These expensive gifts showed the "in-laws" that Rebekah's new husband would take good care of her.

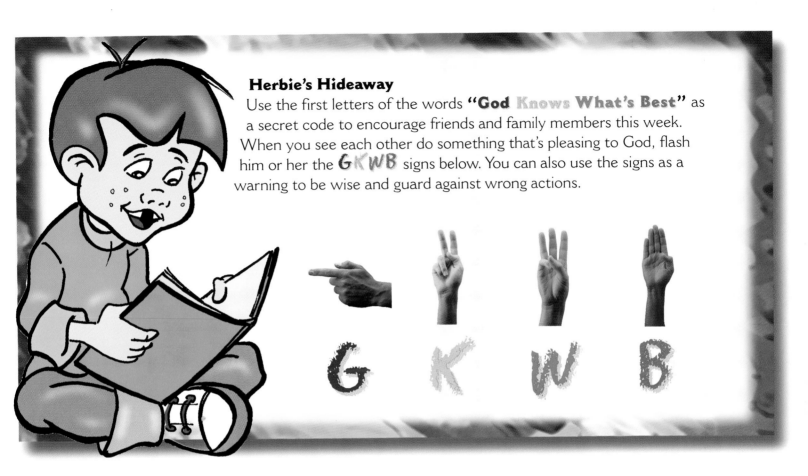

Herbie's Hideaway

Use the first letters of the words **"God Knows What's Best"** as a secret code to encourage friends and family members this week. When you see each other do something that's pleasing to God, flash him or her the **GKWB** signs below. You can also use the signs as a warning to be wise and guard against wrong actions.

G K W B

God Talk

Write the names of some of your best friends
in fun letters and decorate them with glitter glue.
Put the names in a special spot—
the inside of your closet door,
in a friendship folder, or on a poster.
Pick a special day of the week to pray for your friends.
Ask your family to join you.
Touch each friend's name and pray that your friendship will honor God.

Forgiveness Wins Out

Round 1: Esau vs. Jacob

Esau and Jacob were twins. Their father, Old Isaac, was blind. In Bible times, before a father died he gave the oldest son a blessing. That was Esau. When Old Isaac was about to die, he wanted to give Esau his blessing. Esau was a hairy hunter and prepared special meals for Old Issac, which pleased Old Isaac very much.

Jacob found out Old Issac was going to give Esau the blessing. He didn't like being left out. Jacob decided to trick his dad into giving the blessing to him instead. The problem was Jacob had smooth skin and wasn't much of a cook. But he had some ideas. Jacob dressed in Esau's clothes and even wore sheepskin to pretend he was hairy like his brother. His mother helped him cook some food. Guess what? The trick worked. Jacob fooled his father and stole the blessing from Esau.

At first Esau was very sad that Jacob had stolen his blessing. But then his sadness turned into anger. Esau's anger flamed out of control. Esau wanted to kill Jacob. But Jacob found out about Esau's plan and ran away to let his brother cool off. Jacob stayed away for 20 years. He got married and had children. But he didn't forget his twin brother.

When Jacob decided to try to see his brother, he wasn't sure if Esau was still angry or not. Would you still have been angry? What if Esau was still flaming mad at him for what he had done?

What do you think happened when they met each other?

36

Round 2: Take It to God!

When Jacob ran away from Esau, he was all by himself. Now he had a big family and a lot of servants and hundreds of animals to take care of. He sent some of his servants ahead with a message for Esau. The messengers also took gifts for Esau: sheep, cattle, camels and a lot of other things that Jacob thought Esau would like.

Finally the brothers saw each other from a distance. Esau ran to meet Jacob and threw his arms around Jacob's neck and kissed him. They both cried. There was no fighting or anger at all. Instead, the two brothers had a joyful reunion. Can you believe it? Esau was excited to meet Jacob's family. He didn't care about the gifts Jacob sent. He was happy with what God had already given him.

What happened to these guys? God knocked out their anger. God changed their hearts and healed their hurts. Esau forgave Jacob for doing such a mean thing to him. Esau decided not to get even with Jacob, but to let God do all the work.

Ding!

Round 3: How About You?

Have you ever been in a fight with someone at school or a brother or sister? Have you ever been treated unfairly? When you feel this way, it's easy to get stomping mad. But if your angry actions get out of control, someone could get hurt. Esau and Jacob help us learn that God can knock out your anger before anyone gets hurt. Esau didn't try to get even. He waited for God to make Jacob feel sorry for what he had done. And then Esau was ready to forgive. He was happy with his life, even if he didn't get Old Isaac's blessing.

Ding!

Go for the Godprint

Forgiveness: When people hurt us, it's natural to want to get even. To forgive someone is to say, "I will not get even." We forgive others because God forgives us. Can you think of someone you need to forgive?

What Digby Dug Up

Why didn't Esau and Jacob's father just say he had been tricked and change what he had done? Back in Bible times, a person's word was a contract. When a father gave his son a blessing, it could not be changed.

Herbie's Hideaway

When you're angry, God can help you knock out anger. Fill a shoe box with things that help you calm down—things like balloons, bubble wrap, jump rope, clay, squishy ball, favorite music, or art materials. Decorate the outside of your box with pictures of the story of Esau and Jacob. This will help you remember how God can help you knock out your anger. Whenever you get angry, grab your knock-out box and get busy doing things that will knock out your anger!

God Talk

Sing this song to the tune of "I'm a Little Teapot."
When I'm a little angry, I pout and shout,
I try my best not to have a blowout.
When I get all steamed up, I just shout,
"God, help me knock my anger out!"

Joe's No Good Very Bad Day

Choose the ending for each section, then read on and see if you're right.

1

Joseph was 17 and his father's favorite child. His dad gave him a gift that made his ten older brothers jealous. What do you think it was?

a) A colorful coat? b) A feast with his friends? c) A new pet lamb?

a) Tear his coat to pieces and make him wear rags.
b) Kill him and pretend an animal did it.
c) Drop him in a well to cool off because he was hot and sweaty.

3

Everyone was upset because Joseph dreamed he was so great that even the sun, moon and stars would bow down to him. His brothers went away to graze their sheep. Their father sent Joseph to them to find out how they were doing. When they saw him coming in his fancy coat, what did they decide to do?

2

Joseph's new coat wasn't all that made his brothers angry. He told them about two dreams he had. In one, his brothers' bundles of grain bowed down to his. In the other, what do you think happened?

a) He was a king and his brothers were his slaves.
b) The sun, moon and eleven stars bowed down to him.
c) His sheep grew huge and trampled all his brothers' puny ones.

4

The oldest brother, Reuben, didn't want to kill Joseph even though the others did. He said to throw Joseph into a dry well. He planned to rescue him later and take him back to his father. The brothers dropped Joseph into the well. Joseph didn't get discouraged and he didn't give up. When Reuben came back, what did he find?

a) Joseph was gone.
b) Joseph was dead.
c) Joseph had climbed out and was joking with his brothers.

5 Joseph was gone when Reuben returned. Judah had talked his brothers into selling Joseph as a slave to people in a passing caravan. Joseph didn't get discouraged and he didn't give up. Where do you think the caravan went?

a) To the Mediterranean beach for a vacation.
b) To Africa to buy camels.
c) To Egypt to sell spices.

a) Seven fat cows came from the Nile and then seven skinny cows came out and ate them up.
b) Seven fat cows trampled Pharaoh and Joseph became Pharaoh.
c) Seven pyramids rose in the desert and people came from all over the world to see them.

6 After Joseph left for Egypt, the brothers killed a goat and dipped his colorful coat in its blood. They told their father they found the coat. He thought Joseph was dead and mourned for him a long time. Meanwhile, Joseph was sold as a slave to Potiphar, the captain of Pharaoh's guard. Then someone lied about Joseph and he got thrown in prison. But Joseph didn't get discouraged and he didn't give up. Two years passed. Then Pharaoh had a strange dream. What do you think it was?

8 It was a big responsibility to tell Pharaoh what the dreams meant. But Joseph didn't get discouraged and he didn't give up. He knew that God would help him. After Joseph heard the dreams, he told Pharaoh that God was showing what would happen. The two dreams had the same meaning. The seven fat cows and seven heads of good grain stood for seven good years in Egypt with lots of food. What did the seven skinny cows and heads of grain mean?

a) Pharaoh was going to get fat and have to go on a diet for seven years.
b) There would be seven years of famine.
c) Fat cows were going to have to eat skinny grain for seven years.

a) I had a dream that you, Pharaoh, bowed down to me.
b) I have power to tell you what your dreams mean.
c) I can't interpret your dreams, but God can, and he'll tell you what you need to know.

7 After Pharaoh's dream about the fat and skinny cows, he had another dream about seven healthy heads of grain. Seven thin, dry heads of grain sprouted and swallowed up the good ones. Pharaoh asked all his wise men and magicians to tell him what the dreams meant, but no one could do it. One of the servants, a cupbearer, remembered that Joseph had explained dreams, and that what Joseph told them came true. So Pharaoh sent for Joseph. What did Joseph tell him?

Joseph told Pharaoh that he should put someone in charge of saving food during the seven years of plenty so they would have food during the seven years of famine. Pharaoh thought that was a great idea. He said nobody was wiser than Joseph, because God's spirit was in him. What did Pharaoh do next?

a) Put Joseph in charge of all of Egypt, over everyone but Pharaoh.
b) Bowed down to Joseph and made him Pharaoh, king of all Egypt.
c) Sent him back home as a reward.

So Joseph was put over all of Egypt, first after Pharaoh. Find out what happened to his brothers in the next story.

Answers:
1a, 2b, 3b,
4a, 5c, 6a,
7c, 8b, 9a

Go for the Godprint

Perseverance: It's hard to keep doing what's right when it seems that everyone around us is doing wrong or making fun of us for being different. God wants us to keep doing the work he gives us to do. We don't have to be discouraged and we don't have to give up! Ask God for strength, and he will help you keep going.

What Digby Dug Up

In Joseph's time, most people used their coats as a pillow or a blanket, or to carry things in. But the colors in the coat Joseph's father gave him made it too fancy for ordinary work. That's what made his brothers jealous.

Mo's Fab Lab

Find several old, dull pennies. Rub them with a paper towel and see if you can get them clean. If you don't succeed, place them in a small glass jar with

✓ **3 tablespoons vinegar**

✓ **2 tablespoons salt**

✓ **1 heaping teaspoon baking soda.**

Shake! How long does it take to make the pennies shiny and new looking? Amaze your parents with this cool trick. Then talk about:

• **What was it like to try to clean the penny yourself?**

• **How was using the vinegar solution like getting God's help?**

• **What kinds of jobs seem impossible without God's help?**

• **How can you encourage each other to hang in there when everything seems to go wrong?**

Give each person in your family a shiny penny to keep as a reminder that God is in control and you can trust him to help you with hard things.

God Talk

There may be times in your life
when things seem out of control.
Get a grip with God
by grabbing a paper plate and a marker.
On one side write down things you are in control of
and on the other side write down things you are not in control of.
Then, tell God everything you wrote about.
Hang your plate on a fun-colored shoelace in your room
to remind you to "hang in there," because God is in control of everything on our plates.

Joe's Bro's

Joseph's brothers sold him as a slave years and years before our story begins. Little did they know he had risen to be the second in command of all Egypt! Start reading in the sack where the alphabet ends. Then follow the clues to find where the story continues.

Issachar

Joseph turned away and started to cry, but he didn't tell his brothers who he was. To make sure they'd come back, he kept Simeon in prison. Joseph's servants filled the brothers' bags with grain and secretly put their silver into the bags too. The brothers loaded their donkeys and left. That night one brother found the silver in his bag. They panicked. Would the Egyptian leader think they'd stolen the silver? *It's not a pair of jeans.*

Asher

They hadn't gone far when the manager who worked for Joseph caught them. He accused them of stealing Joseph's silver cup. They denied it and promised that if anyone had the cup, he would become a slave. The manager found the cup in Benjamin's sack. They all returned to the city. Judah pleaded with Joseph to let him take Benjamin's place. He said his father would die if Benjamin didn't return home. *Go to the sack starting with the third letter in the word describing how Jacob felt.*

Simeon

When the brothers arrived to buy grain, they were taken to Joseph's house. What did this mean? Simeon got out of prison to join the rest of the brothers. Joseph asked about their father. They gave him Jacob's gifts. When Joseph saw Benjamin, he went to his room to weep. At lunch, Benjamin received five times as much food as anyone else. When they left, their sacks were brimming with grain. They didn't know their silver was there, too. And Joseph's silver cup was hidden in Ben's sack! *Go to the sack starting with the second letter in the word from the last clue.*

Zebulon

People were starving, so Jacob told his sons to go buy food in Egypt. The 10 oldest went. Benjamin stayed home because his father was afraid to lose him. In Egypt the brothers asked to buy grain and bowed down to Joseph just as his dreams predicted. They didn't recognize Joseph, but he recognized them! He pretended to think they were spies. *The next one rhymes with Dad.*

Naphtali

Finally their father agreed that the brothers should go back to Egypt and buy more grain. They promised to keep Benjamin safe. Jacob sent gifts to Joseph with double the silver. When Benjamin left, his father mourned. *The next three sacks' initials spell a word that tells how Jacob felt when his sons left.*

Benjamin

Pharaoh heard about Joseph's family reunion. He was pleased and told Joseph to send carts and supplies so his brothers could bring their families to Egypt. Joseph sent them off with new clothes, money and donkeys loaded with gifts for their father.

Rhymes with Cuban.

Gad

"No! We came to buy food," they said. "We were 12 brothers. The youngest is with our father and another is dead." To prove their innocence, Joseph told them to bring the youngest brother to him. "We're being punished for what we did to Joseph so long ago," they said to each other. The brothers didn't know that Joseph understood every word.

"It's a car?"
Or is it someone's name?

Reuben

Old father Jacob didn't believe Joseph was alive until he saw the carts loaded with gifts and food. He took his whole family and everything he owned and left for Egypt. God told him in a vision that his family would become a great nation there.

Willing to be a slave in Benjamin's place.

Levi

They told their father that the Egyptian leader wanted to see Benjamin, the youngest brother. Then they emptied their sacks and found the silver Joseph had slipped into their bags. It frightened them and upset Jacob. "I've lost Joseph and Simeon. Now you want to take Benjamin away!" They promised to bring Benjamin back, but their father said it would kill him if Benjamin left. So they stayed…until they ran out of grain.

Sleeping in the daytime is called a _____.

Dan

When the brothers came back, Joseph cried and said, "I'm Joseph—your brother! Is my father still alive?" Joseph comforted his terrified brothers. "I'm the brother you sold into Egypt. Don't worry or be angry with yourselves. God sent me here to protect our people. Hurry home and get our father. I'll provide for you and your families here, because there are five years of famine left." He cried and hugged them all.

First syllable rhymes with "hen."

45

Judah

Anxious to see his father, Joseph rushed in his chariot to Goshen. He threw his arms around Jacob and cried for a long time. Pharaoh let Joseph's relatives settle in Goshen. Jacob lived for 17 more years and all his family had plenty to eat during the famine.

Read the story in this order: Zebulon, Gad, Issachar, Levi, Naphtali, Simeon, Asher, Dan, Benjamin, Reuben, Judah.

Go for the Godprint

Resourcefulness: When it seems like everything goes wrong, there are always ways to make it better! For example, if you plan an outdoor party for a friend and it rains, you change it to a Noah's Ark party. When we follow God's plan, he gives us imagination and tools to help us finish the work he wants us to do.

What Digby Dug Up

Joseph was 17 years old when his brothers sold him into slavery. He spent the next 11 years as an Egyptian slave. He spent two years in prison. He became the governor of Egypt at the age of 30.

PJ'S Good to Go

Have you ever tried to make something great out of stuff around the house—without buying anything new? Gather up a collection of things from the recycling bin, the kitchen junk drawer or a craft tub. Find things like: colored paper, old greetings cards, strings and ribbons, small toys, interesting containers, fabric scraps, cardboard pieces. Brainstorm a unique gift that you could make from your odds and ends to give to a friend or neighbor who needs encouragement. A bird feeder? A vase? A sculpture? A wind chime? Work together and use your resourcefulness to make something fun and wonderful. Then plan a time to deliver the gift and let God use you to encourage someone else.

God Talk

God gave Joseph an interesting life
and moved him to lots of different places.
Make a map of your family's life together.
On a large sheet of paper,
draw pictures of where you have lived,
special events in your life and the people
who have been important to your family. Then pray:
Thank you, God, for the places you have taken us.
Thank you, God, for the people you have given us.
Thank you, God, for being with us when we didn't understand your plan.
Keep the map of life in the same place you keep other maps.
Whenever someone in the family uses a map to find a destination,
remember your map of life and pray again.

47

A Miniature Ark

Mother hurried at her work. At any minute, soldiers could break in, snatch my baby brother, and throw him into the Nile River to drown. Hebrew slaves in Egypt weren't allowed to keep boy babies. Pharaoh wanted them all killed. For three months my mother hid my brother, but he had grown too big to hide.

I held him close and cried. He was so beautiful! Why would anyone want to kill him? I didn't understand his cooing, but his eyes told me that he trusted me. Only God could help him now.

My mother covered a basket with tar and pitch to keep the water out. Then she took the baby from my arms, kissed him and laid him in the basket. We slipped outside and walked casually toward the river. The baby whimpered, but the people around us were too busy to notice. In my heart, I asked God to keep him quiet.

My mother stepped into the shallow water of the Nile and set the basket among the tall reeds. The river gurgled against the little ark, but the reeds held it safely in place. Mom checked inside for leaks and kissed her baby once more. As she closed the lid and left, she asked me to watch from a distance to see what would happen to him.

I hid in the tall grass and waited for what seemed like hours. Then I heard voices. Some young ladies were coming to the river to bathe. One of them was Pharaoh's daughter! What would she do if she found my brother? Her father wanted him dead. I hoped she wouldn't find him.

Pharaoh's daughter stepped into the quiet water near the reeds as her maids walked near the river's edge. Then she saw the basket and asked her maid to bring it to her. I held my breath and prayed. As the princess opened the ark, I heard pitiful crying. The baby must have been hungry after all that time.

"This is a Hebrew child," the princess said.

I had to do something to help my baby brother! I ran right up to Pharaoh's daughter. Before I knew it, I had offered to find a Hebrew woman to feed the baby for her. And she said yes.

It was amazing! A miracle really. The daughter of Pharaoh, the baby murderer, was going to save my baby brother!

I ran to find my mother. My heart pounded and my feet kicked up dust on the path. I ran so fast that I almost tripped myself. When I told my mother who found the baby, she could hardly believe it.

Pharaoh's daughter asked my mother to take care of the baby. She even offered to pay her! Little did she know that she was paying my mother to care for her own baby. When he was older, my mother took him to the princess. Now he's being raised as the son of Pharaoh's daughter. That means he's Pharaoh's *grandson*! Isn't it amazing the way God saved my brother?

Because she drew him out of the water, the princess calls my brother "Moses." I guess God must have something important for him to do when he grows up. I'll just stand at a distance and wait to see what happens, just as I did when he was in the tiny ark among the reeds.

Go for the Godprint

Preciousness: God saved Moses for important work, and he has great things in store for you, too. You are very special to God. He made you in his image, a little bit like himself. God does good work, and he'll help you do good work, too. Will you depend on him?

What Digby Dug Up

Maybe hearing about her ancestor Noah gave Moses' mother the idea to build her son a tiny ark. Noah coated his ark with pitch to keep the floodwaters out. Pitch is thick and sticky, so Moses' mother used it to change a basket full of holes into a waterproof boat for her baby.

Mo's Fab Lab

Fill a large bowl with water. Lay a tissue on top. Does it float? How long does it stay up? What would happen if you made a boat out of tissue? Like the basket Moses' mother used, a tissue is full of holes. So how can you make a waterproof boat out of tissue?

Experiment with different coatings to see what works best. Melted wax in a mold or waterproof tape might work, but an easier way is to simply wrap aluminum foil around the tissue. The foil will help the boat keep its shape, too. Make a waterproof tissue boat and place something special in it like a flower, a small toy or a favorite food. As your boat floats in the bowl, remember that God knows how to protect what is precious to him. And that includes *you!*

God Talk

Have one person read the first part
and everyone say the second part of this prayer.
Each time you say the second part,
throw a flower petal (or something else that floats)
into a bowl or sink full of water to remind you that
God took care of baby Moses and he will take care of you.
You know the number of hairs on my head.
I trust your plan for me.
You know every thought I have.
I trust your plan for me.
You know my weaknesses and strengths.
I trust your plan for me.
You know what makes me glad, sad or mad.
I trust your plan for me.
You know my future and my past.
I trust your plan for me.
You know my deepest secret dreams.
I trust your plan for me.

51

Excuses, Excuses

I'm Seamus O'Sheep and I've come here to say
That God can use you in a fantastic way.
No matter your height or the size of your shoe,
God's planned an incredible job just for you.

52

But first, listen closely as I tell the story
Of how my great-grandpappy sheep saw God's glory.
He followed his shepherd, a fellow named Moses,
Out into the desert (to graze, I supposes).

He had just settled down in the grass for a nap
When he heard a sharp sound like a crackly-snap.
A bush was on fire. Its branches were blazing!
But it didn't burn up—this plant was amazing.

The minute that Moses looked into the flame
The voice of the Lord began calling his name.
When God called his name, Moses perked up his ears.
When God called again, he called back, "I am here."

When God called, my grandpappy's ears perked up too.
He wondered what God wanted Moses to do.
God said, "My people in Egypt are working intensely.
I've heard their cries, and they're suffering immensely.

It's time now to free them from their cruel king
And give them a new land that's full of good things.
Here is the way this will all come about:
Moses, it's your job to go lead them out."

"But, who am I, Lord? Must you choose me?
It takes more than a shepherd to set people free."
"Excuses, excuses," my grandpappy thought.
God can use anyone, shepherd or not.

If God gives you a job, he'll help you do it.
Just trust him and ask him to help you snap to it.
"I will be with you," the Lord God replied.
When you leave Egypt, come to this mountainside."

Moses just frowned. "Will they know God?" he wondered.
"What if they ask me your name, God?" he blundered.
My grandpappy baa-ed with a shake of his head.
Hadn't Moses been listening to one word God said?

"The people of Israel—will they know you by name?
And just what should I say if they ask why I came?"
Then God said to Moses, "I am who I am—
God of Jacob and Isaac and wise Abraham.

"Tell them the God of their fathers has sent you
And never forget that I'll always be with you."
Moses still wasn't sure, so he picked up his rod.
Then he wrinkled his brow as he called back to God.

"Your people, O Lord, do deserve to be free.
But what if the people won't listen to me?
They may not believe me that I've seen the Lord.
They may not accept that I'm speaking your word."

Excuses, excuses, my grandpappy fumed.
If Israel's counting on this guy, they're doomed!
"What's that in your hand?" asked the Lord. "Throw it down."
Just then Moses' rod started slithering around!

One minute a staff, the next second a snake.
It was almost more than grandpappy could take.
And when the Lord said, "Pick it up by the tail."
It was all poor old Grandpap could do not to wail.

Excuses, excuses, he thought with a shiver.
(The sight of that snake made him shudder and quiver.)
But when Moses stood up with the snake in his hand
His staff reappeared. Now wasn't that grand?

My grandpappy marveled—these signs were amazing.
And it all started out with a bush that was blazing.
Then God said, "If they don't believe you, don't worry.
Once you show them these signs, they'll believe in a hurry.

"Please Lord," begged Moses. "I'm not the one.
You need a good speaker to get this job done."
Excuses, excuses, my grandpappy muttered.
It sure doesn't matter to God if you stutter.

Now God was angry. "Didn't I give you speech?
Didn't I give you sight? Can't you trust me to teach?
I'll put words in your mouth. I'll be with you too,
And I'll show you everything you need to do."

So when you think God has a job for you, pray!
Remember my grandpappy's story, then say:
"Excuses, excuses won't get in my way—
If God wants to use me, then he'll find a way!"

Go for the Godprint

Perseverance: Have you ever felt the way Moses did—like you wanted to give up because doing things God's way just seemed too hard? Following God can be hard—if you try to do it alone. But if you let God help you, you can do it! God won't ever give up on you. Will you persevere in following God?

What Digby Dug Up

IN THE OLD TESTAMENT, GOD OFTEN USED FIRE TO LET HIS PEOPLE KNOW HE WAS WITH THEM. AFTER MOSES LED THE PEOPLE OUT OF EGYPT, GOD APPEARED IN A PILLAR OF FIRE TO GUIDE THEM THROUGH THE DESERT (EXODUS 13:21-22).

Herbie's Hideaway

Catch yourself saying "I CAN'T..."?

You'll have to pay the Can't Can.

Cover an empty can with tissue or construction paper.
Write the words "Can't Can" on it.
Each time a family member is overheard saying "I can't..." or any other excuse, that person must contribute a coin to the Can't Can and repeat Philippians 4:13: "I can do all things through him who gives me strength." Donate the money you collect to your church.

God Talk
Make a burning bush snack to help you pray.
You'll need a zucchini, a vegetable peeler,
cheddar cheese, and pretzel sticks.
Cut zucchini into two-inch chunks.
Use the vegetable peeler to peel strips of cheese.
Poke pretzel stick branches into the zucchini.
Hang the cheese strip "flames" from the pretzel stick branches.
For extra hot "flames," add salsa or hot sauce.
For each bite you take, ask God to help you stick with something hard he wants you to do.

Frogs, Insects and Hail, Oh My!

There are too many Israelites here! Oh, my!

Pharaoh was worried as he looked at his land.
"These Israelite people could get out of hand.
I'll make them my slaves and they'll work just for me.
I'll build a grand city for the whole world to see."
So he put them to work every day in the sun.
They stomped mud and straw to make bricks by the ton.

What will become of God's people? Oh, my!

God heard his people and he had a plan.
Moses would lead them out of that land.
So he went to the king and said, "Let us go!"
But Pharaoh just sneered, shook his head and said, "No!"
He thought he had power, but soon he would see
That God's mighty power would set his people free!

What will God do to this Pharaoh? Oh, my!

So God said to Moses, "Stretch out your hand.
And the Nile will turn to blood by my command."
Even then Pharaoh said, "These slaves are mine!"
Then Moses said, "Pharaoh, tomorrow you'll find
Frogs everywhere! In the houses and streets,
In your pots and your pans, in your clothes and your sheets.

Frogs everywhere that you look! Oh, my!

Still Pharaoh was stubborn and would not give in,
So God tried to teach him again and again.
First gnats and then flies were buzzing around.
Sick cattle, sick people; hail fell to the ground.
Then locusts came down and ate every crop.
Three days dark as night. Oh, when would it stop?

Plague after plague came to Egypt! Oh, my!

While all of these plagues came upon Pharaoh's land
God protected his people with his mighty hand.
No locusts or frogs, flies or gnats could be found
In the houses and streets on their side of town.
Though they were protected, they still were not free,
But God had a plan, and soon they would be.

The last plague is coming to Egypt! Oh, my!

Through all of the plagues Pharaoh's mind was still set,
Then came the last one he'd never forget.
Though Moses warned him, he did not believe.
Because of his choice, all of Egypt would grieve.
When they saw what had happened, all Egypt wept.
Each firstborn had died while they quietly slept.

Even the son of the Pharaoh! Oh, my!

Again God protected the ones who believed
And he told his people, "Tomorrow, we leave!"
Pharaoh called Moses to see him and said,
"What have you done? My firstborn is dead.
So gather your people and take them away.
I want all of them out of Egypt today!"

We have to leave quickly! Let's go! Oh, my!

All of God's people left Egypt that day.
They gathered their things; Moses led them away.
When they left, Pharaoh said, "What have I done?"
He ordered his soldiers, "Bring back every one!
Without them my great plans are ruined, you see.
I need slaves for building my city for me."

The soldiers are chasing God's people! Oh, my!

The Israelites came to the Red Sea, and wondered,
"How will we cross?" Then behind them it thundered.
They turned and the sight they saw filled them with fear.
"Moses!" they cried, "Why'd you bring us out here?
The soldiers are coming, there is no way out!
Where is this God that you told us about?"

"We're all going to die in this desert! Oh, my!"

Then Moses lifted the staff in his hand.
God parted the sea so that there was dry land.
The Israelites walked through to the other side
The soldiers said, "Follow them quickly! Let's ride!"
But with chariots there in the midst of the sea,
God moved his hand and the waters flowed free!

The soldiers have been washed away! Oh, my!
Our God has saved us today! Oh, my!

Go for the Godprint

Confidence: To have confidence means to be sure of something. You can be absolutely, positively, completely sure of one thing: you can always count on God! That's what confidence is all about. Where does your confidence come from?

What Digby Dug Up

In the Egypt of Bible times, not only was Pharaoh a king, but the Egyptian people believed he was a god. When God sent the plagues to Egypt, he was saying, "Pharaoh is not a god. I am the only true God."

Mo's Fab Lab

GET LIST:
PAN, WATER, PEPPER, DISHWASHING LIQUID

Here's a fun way to think about what it must have been like to watch as the waters of the Red Sea parted. Fill a pie pan with about half an inch of water. Generously sprinkle pepper on the water to cover the surface. Squeeze one tiny drop of dishwashing liquid in the middle of the pepper, and watch what happens. The pepper will move outward to the edge of the pan. This will happen very quickly, so be sure everyone is looking. Just for fun, try to separate the water with your hands and hold it back. We can't even hold back this tiny bit of water, but God held back the waters of the sea!

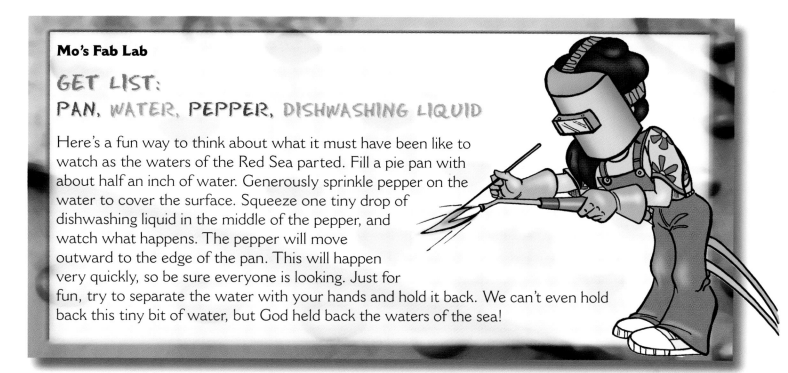

God Talk

Moses sang a song of praise
when God saved the Israelites from the Egyptians.
This song is found in Exodus 15.
Use the following words from Moses' song as a family prayer.
One person can read each line aloud,
and the rest of the family can repeat it together.

Leader: The Lord is my strength and my song;
All: The Lord is my strength and my song;
Leader: He has become my salvation.
All: He has become my salvation.
Leader: He is my God, and I will praise him,
All: He is my God, and I will praise him,
Leader: My father's God, and I will exalt him.
All: My father's God, and I will exalt him.

Mumble, Grumble, Gripe and Groan

Mumble, grumble, gripe and groan.
Whine and wail and cry and moan.
Every day we get more manna.
Never figs or ripe bananas.
Gimme dates or mutton stew.
Anything unique would do.
No–more–manna!

Manna dumplings, manna pie.
Manna muffins, my oh my!
Nothing else around to buy.
Manna stir-fried, manna boiled
Manna baked and flaked and broiled.
And overnight the manna's spoiled!
No–more–manna!

Manna salad, manna cake.
The thought gives me a stomachache.
How much more can one kid take?
I've even had some manna tea
Though we're quite far from the sea.
(A little joke there–pardon me.) *
No–more–manna!

60

The manna menu's such a bore
I can't take it any more.
I wish we had a grocery store.
What's a kid like me to do
When the options are so few?
I'd like a steak to barbecue.
No-more-manna!

BUT:

Back before the manna fell
Things weren't going all that well.
Every day our stomachs growled
Toddlers fussed and babies howled.
We would starve—that's what we feared.
We prayed and then this food appeared!

The Lord Jehovah heard our prayer.
Then—manna, manna everywhere.
Every day each family takes
Baskets full of frosted flakes
"It tastes like honey-flavored bread!"
That's what Uncle Eli said.

It's God who makes the manna fall
Or else we'd have no food at all.
That would be ca-TAS-trophal!
Trusting God's the thing to do
He sends flocks of quail, too.
Perhaps I'll have some manna stew.
Thank you, Lord, for manna.

A few days later:

Mumble, grumble, gripe and groan.
Whine and wail and cry and moan.
What a huge no-water zone!
I want a drink!

We thought Egypt was the worst
But now we're scared we'll die of thirst.
We'll get rid of Moses first.
I want a drink!

I'm so thirsty I could choke.
I know I'll shrivel up and croak.
This Moses guy is such a joke!
I want a drink!

He led us through the sea, it's true
And washed up Pharaoh's army, too.
It was an awesome thing to do, but
I want a drink!

Life right now is no big treat.
Sweaty people, tired feet.
Dragging through the desert heat.
I want a drink!

Where is God? What is his plan?
This desert's like a frying pan!
I thought Moses was the man.
I want a drink!

He's our leader. It's his task.
To give me water for my flask;
Is that so very much to ask?
I want a drink!

Moses has his miracle rod,
The very one he got from God.
The one that left old Pharaoh awed.
Will I get a drink?

He's using it to hit a rock.
Water's gushing! What a shock!
This is not the time to talk.
God sent a drink!

Glug, glug, ahhh.

I'm beginning to understand
That God has everything all planned
As we cross this barren land.
Thanks for the drink.

God wants us to travel light
Knowing things will be all right
Because he's with us day and night.
I'll trust you, Lord. (I think.)

A "manatee" is a sea cow.

Go for the Godprint

Trust: "Just trust me." Did anyone ever tell you that? Trust is exactly what God expected from the Israelites. After all, he'd created ten plagues, parted the Red Sea and drowned Pharaoh's army—just to mention a few things. But the Israelites still fussed and grumbled about day-to-day details. God sent manna every day except the Sabbath so the Israelites would learn to trust him. That same manna-maker caretaker is looking out for you. Will you trust him?

What Digby Dug Up
In the Hebrew language, manna means "what is it?" Look up Exodus 16:31 to find out what manna tasted like.

62

Jake's Mirth Quake

Want to have a manna-gathering experience? Set a popcorn popper in the middle of a clean sheet or plastic tablecloth. Turn on the popper but leave the lid off. When it starts to pop, "manna" will fall from the sky! Give everyone a plastic bowl and see who can gather the most in 15 seconds. Before you enjoy the popcorn, talk about reasons you have to keep trusting God.

God Talk

Make yourself a "Trust Crust"—
a piece of toast with honey.
With every bite you take,
thank God for one way he's shown
that you can put your trust in him.

From Exodus 19-20

To the Mountain on Eagles' Wings

Three months. Three long months of trekking through the desert. God's people were slaves no more. It was time to find out what God planned for them next. God called Moses up to the mountain, while the people waited in the desert. God told Moses exactly what he wanted the people to know.

God said, "You yourselves have seen what I did to Egypt, and how I carried you on eagles' wings and brought you to myself. Now if you obey me fully and keep my covenant, then out of all nations you will be my treasured possession."

Imagine being carried on the wings of eagles! God's strong protection was around his special people. It was time for the people to understand how to show their love and gratitude to God.

God gave four commands about how the people should show that they worshiped the true God.

1

YOU SHALL HAVE
NO OTHER GODS
BEFORE ME.

2

YOU SHALL NOT
MAKE FOR YOURSELF
AN IDOL
IN THE FORM
OF ANYTHING.

3

YOU SHALL NOT
MISUSE THE NAME
OF THE LORD
YOUR GOD.

4

REMEMBER
THE SABBATH DAY
BY KEEPING IT
HOLY.

What do these commandments mean?
Match one of the answers on the next page with each of these commandments.

God doesn't have a form we can see. So to make a statue or a picture and say that it's God is wrong. And since no other gods are real gods, making statues or pictures of them is wrong, too.

Nothing else in our lives should ever take the place of God in our hearts. Not work, not money, not even other people.

After six days of creation, God rested on the seventh day. He knows that we need to rest from our work, too. We honor God when we save one day each week to rest and remember how God cares for us.

Don't use God's name in wrong ways. Don't make promises with God's name or blurt it out in anger. Use God's name in ways that honor him. That shows how you really feel about God.

Go for the Godprint

Submissiveness: Have you ever broken a rule? Sure. Probably you thought what you wanted was more important than the rule. Submissiveness means choosing to obey God, even when you want to do something else. The Ten Commandments help us know how God wants us to live. When we choose to obey them we show we're grateful for how God cares for us.

What Digby Dug Up

God gave Moses the Ten Commandments in Exodus 20. However, the Bible doesn't mention the actual tablets of the Ten Commandments until Exodus 32:15. God wrote on the tablets himself, and Moses carried them down the mountain to the people.

Café de Click

GET LIST: 1/2 CUP BROWN SUGAR, 1/2 CUP PEANUT BUTTER, 1 TABLESPOON GRANOLA OR WHEAT GERM.

Make edible tablets. Mix the brown sugar, peanut butter and granola. Add more peanut butter if the mixture is too dry, or more sugar if it is too sticky. Imagine what the stone tablets Moses carried might have looked like and form the dough into that shape. Use a toothpick to draw squiggly lines to represent God's writing on the tablets. As you eat your tasty tablets, talk about why you think God gave the Ten Commandments and how your family can make them a part of your life.

God Talk

Choose a special hour every Sunday
that your family can set aside to honor God together.
Work together to write a short prayer that you can all memorize.
Use this prayer to begin your special honor hour each Sunday.

EVERYDAY LIVING

INDEPENDENCE WITH HONOR

I think I'm old enough to make my own decisions! I want to choose what to eat, what to do, who my friends are. But my parents still want to tell me what to do. I hate to admit it, but their ideas are not so bad. When I do what makes them happy, I know I please God, too. Even when we disagree, I can be polite and respectful. I don't want to hurt them on purpose. So I guess I'll listen when they have something to say.

LIFE IS PRECIOUS

I was so mad that I wished he were dead! I picked up the biggest rock I could find, and I was ready to throw it right at his head. But I let the rock fall to the ground. And I walked away to cool off. No matter how much someone else hurts me, what I was thinking about is wrong. God doesn't want me even to think about things like that.

ONE AND ONLY

I've been married a long time. Years and years. Some of my friends think I've been married too long. They think it must be boring to love the same person for so long. But I don't think so. We have our days when we don't get along. But I hang in there. I don't even think about anybody else. Just her. That's the way God wants it.

NEIGHBORLY CONTENTMENT

I could stand here at the fence and look out at that land forever. It's great land. And the house! It's a gorgeous house, with stables and champion horses and a full staff of servants. I used to think that I would give everything I have if I could own land and a house like that. But now I'm happy with what God gives me. I still admire my neighbor's land, because it is beautiful, but I don't have to be jealous of what someone else has.

EASIER THAN YOU THINK

My friend got a great new outfit. When I said I liked it a lot, she said I could get one, too. It was really easy, she said. There was only one clerk in the shop. He couldn't watch everything all the time. If I just waited until he was busy with another customer, I could just take it. My friend even said she would help. But I turned around and walked away. I was not going to take something that doesn't belong to me.

TRUTH TRIUMPHS

Why would I say something like that? Some kids at school don't like the new boy. They figured out a way to get him in trouble. But they wanted me to say something that wasn't true. They thought the teachers would believe me instead of the new boy. It wasn't a big lie. It just wasn't the whole truth. So I didn't do it. Why would I say something like that?

God gave his people six commandments about how they should treat each other. Can you match the commandments to the stories you just read?

5
HONOR YOUR FATHER AND YOUR MOTHER.
6
YOU SHALL NOT MURDER.
7
YOU SHALL NOT COMMIT ADULTERY.
8
YOU SHALL NOT STEAL.
9
YOU SHALL NOT GIVE FALSE TESTIMONY AGAINST YOUR NEIGHBOR.
10
YOU SHALL NOT COVET YOUR NEIGHBOR'S HOUSE, WIFE, SERVANT, ANIMAL OR ANYTHING.

Go for the Godprint

Self-control: Can you remember a time when you said something to a friend and you knew it was wrong? Maybe the words just slipped out of your mouth before you could stop yourself. Self-control means not doing what we selfishly want to do, but instead choosing to treat other people in a way that honors God.

What Digby Dug Up

When God gave the Ten Commandments, the people saw thunder and lightning on the mountain and they were frightened. Moses knew that the fear of God would help the people keep from sinning.

Herbie's Hideaway

GET LIST: PAPER, INK PADS

As a family, choose one word that describes how you want to treat other people. Some words you might choose are: fair; respect; honest; love. Press your fingers onto the ink pads and then onto the paper to spell out the word with your fingerprints. Put the fingerprint word up on the refrigerator or a wall where everyone can see it. When you look at the fingerprints of the whole family, remember that God cares about how we treat other people, including the ones whose fingerprints you have. After a few days, talk about how well you've done treating each other with the word you chose.

God Talk
Choose a prayer leader to read the light print.
Everyone else reads the dark print.
With my family,
Lord, help me show respect.
With my friends,
Lord, help me show kindness.
With new people I meet,
Lord, help me show your love.

From
Numbers
13:1-2, 17-30;
14:6-9

Wise Spies and Spies' Lies

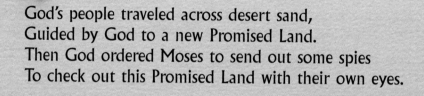

God's people traveled across desert sand,
Guided by God to a new Promised Land.
Then God ordered Moses to send out some spies
To check out this Promised Land with their own eyes.

Moses chose twelve to go, one from each tribe,
Instructing them all to come back and describe
The place God would give them—a land good or bad,
The people, the cities, the trees that it had.

The next forty days they explored all the sights,
Found figs, pomegranates and other delights.
They cut a huge cluster of grapes from a vine.
It took two to carry it. That land was fine!

They told their own people, "We have to conclude
This land is amazing with lots of good food."
But ten of the spies started making a fuss.
They said, "This great Promised Land isn't for us.

72

"Their men are gigantic; their cities are strong.
They'll eat us alive! We can't go. It's wrong."

"Hey, stop that," said Caleb, "and listen to me.
Of course we'll defeat them with God, easily."
But nobody listened. They joined in the chant
The ten spies had started, the chant of "I can't."

"Their men are gigantic; their cities are strong.
They'll eat us alive! We can't go. It's wrong."

Joshua joined in with Caleb just then.
They stood up alone against ten other men.
"Please don't rebel against God here today.
We can be faithful. Let him lead the way."

They said to the people, "It's such a good land.
Let's go in and claim it. You must understand,
We have God's protection, while they will have none.
Don't give up before we have even begun.

"Don't be afraid. We will swallow them whole."
But the lies of the ten spies had taken their toll.
The people were angry repeating the chant
The ten spies had started, the chant of "I can't."

Their men are gigantic; their cities are strong.
They'll eat us alive! We can't go. It's wrong."

They stayed in the desert because of their sin.
God opened the way, but they wouldn't go in.
So next time God wants you to do something tough
Remember that his strength is always enough.

Go for the Godprint

Faithfulness: Does God care about the choices you make? Whether you wear a green or blue shirt doesn't matter, but lying or telling the truth matters a lot. God is faithful. Showing love and loyalty to him means trying to please him and do what he wants you to do—even when it's hard or scary.

What Digby Dug Up

The Promised Land was called Canaan, a rich and fertile country. It was approximately 150 miles long and 60 miles wide, about the size of the state of Vermont. It was the land God had promised to Abraham, Isaac and Jacob.

Café de Click

The Promised Land was rich in foods the people weren't used to. The "new" land was lush and filled with vegetation and fresh fruits. In the rows of letters below, strike out the names of fruits and find the secret message.

GODGRAPESLEADSDATETHEAPPLEWAYAPRICOTSYOUW
ATERMELONCANLEMONBEFIGSFAITHFULPOMEGRANATE.

As a reward, make Promised Land Fruit salad. With your family, shop for fruit you don't usually buy. You might try some listed in the code above! Remove the seeds and cut the fruit into bite-sized pieces. Squeeze lemon juice over the cut fruit to keep it from turning brown. Try a little honey or orange juice concentrate to sweeten it. Stir and enjoy!

Answer to code: God leads the way. You can be faithful.

God Talk

Joshua and Caleb weren't afraid to trust God
and stand against the crowd.
Let each family member tell
when it's hard to take a stand for God.
Then pray this prayer together:
God, give us courage when we need to face the crowd.
Help us take a stand for you, and say it right out loud.
In Jesus' name, amen.

Joshua's River Walk

Joshua **People** **River** **Ark** **Stones**

 and the Israelites were camped near the Jordan . Just on the other side of the

was the land God had promised. The needed to get to the other side of the , but the

water was too wide to cross. "How will we get to the other side?" the wondered.

Then God told what to do. "God is about to do an amazing thing for us," said to the .

The were excited to see what God would do.

 told the priests, "Pick up the of the Lord. Stand at the edge of the ."

When the priests were standing by the ,  gathered the together. "Look,"

said. "The  of the Lord is crossing the ▭ ahead of you. This will be a sign that God is with us. When the priests' feet touch the water in the ▭, it will stop flowing."

The ▭ watched as the priests stepped into the ▭. Right away, the water stopped flowing and piled up in a great heap! The priests stood still with the ▭ of the Lord and all the ▭ crossed on dry land.

It was a big job to get all those ▭ across the ▭. Moms and dads, babies and kids, grandmas and grandpas all walked through, and no one even got wet! ▭ and the priests waited patiently until everyone made it across.

After all the ▭ had crossed the ▭, ▭ told them, "Choose one man from each tribe. Tell them to pick up ▭ from the dry ground in the ▭." So the men took the ▭ from the ▭ and carried them to the camp.

After all the ▭ had crossed, ▭ told the priests to bring the ▭ of the Lord out.

Right away, the  started flowing again.

and the set up the 12

near their camp in a place called Gilgal.

told the , "When your

children ask you about these , tell them

how God stopped the so we could

cross on dry land. These stones will remind

everyone who sees them that God will always help

his .

Go for the Godprint

Diligence: How long would it take for your whole family to walk across a bridge over a river or stream? Your whole neighborhood? Your whole church? Your whole town? Joshua and the priests waited patiently while thousands of people crossed the Jordan and stepped into the promised land. Even though they must have been tired, they kept a steady watch until every last person made it across. Because of their diligence, God's plan was accomplished. Will you work steadily to do the things God asks you to do?

What Digby Dug Up

Why didn't the people just swim across the river? Because of spring rains and snow melting, the Jordan River often overflowed its banks at harvest time. When the people approached it, it was probably more like a huge marsh-like swamp.

Café de Click

Mix up a blue jello "river" according to the package instructions.
Pour the liquid jello into a bowl. Before you refrigerate the jello,
place 12 grape "stones" in it. When the jello sets, the "stones" will settle
in the "river." As you enjoy your cool, fruity treat, talk about these questions.

• **How do you think the people felt when they reached
  the river but couldn't get across? Have you ever felt like that?**

• **The stones reminded the people of the way God helped them
  cross the river. What reminds you that God will always help you?**

God Talk
Go on a hunt for prayer stones.
Each family member should find three or four stones.
Look for different types of rocks to make your collection interesting.
Wash the prayer stones and sit with them in a circle.
Place a tray in the middle of the circle.
Take turns placing a stone on the tray and thanking God for a time he helped you.
Your pile of stones, like Joshua's, will remind you that you can depend on God!

Agent J Conquers Jericho

Join secret agent J (Joshua), as he discovers his mission impossible from the master of the possible, God himself!

Can you crack the secret code? Look for the red letters in each section.

Agent J, your mission is to conquer the city of Jericho.

Wow, Lord, you picked me for a mission that would be impossible without you. Jericho is a very well protected city, but you are on our side. Jericho is a really old city. It hasn't been defeated in a very long time. The walls are humongously big. The city walls are 25 feet high and 20 feet thick. These walls are so big that a bulldozer couldn't knock them down. With God's help, we can destroy and take the city of Jericho!

Secret Code #1 :_____

Agent J, your mission is to March.

Okay, Lord, we will march around the city for six days, blow on our trumpets and carry the ark of the Lord. The people in Jericho will surely think that we have lost our minds. They will think we are crazy people. But the Lord will be on our side as we march around the city, blowing our horns and carrying the ark of the Lord. The Lord will help us conquer and avenge this evil city. Sounds like a great battle plan for a mission seems impossible.

Secret code #2_____

Agent J, your mission is to twist and shout!

This is going to be a great adventure. You want us to twist and shout! We can do that. On the seventh day, we will march and twist around the city seven times, blowing our trumpets and carrying the ark of the Lord before us. Then on the seventh lap around Jericho, we won't mumble. We won't pout. We will start to shout. We will win the mighty battle with no swords and no fighting. We know who is on our side! That's right! God is the God of mission impossible.

Secret Code #3_____

80

Agent J, your mission is to watch the walls come tumblin' and rumblin' down. Wow! We did as you said, and sure enough the walls came tumblin' and rumblin' down. It was unbelievable! The impossible happened because God was in charge of the battle. Victory belongs to God and God alone. We did not win the battle of Jericho because we were a grand army or because we're mighty. We positively won the battle of Jericho because we serve a mighty God! God is a God of mission possible!

Secret Code #4_____

Do you ever feel like you are facing the impossible? Remember the secret codes, and you too will experience the God of mission possible.

Secret Codes:

1) Victory is the Lord's.
2) I can depend on God.
3) Nothing is impossible with God.
4) Easy as pie is the Lord's battle cry.

Go for the Godprint

Resourcefulness: Joshua learned that God was going to win the battle by God's design and strength alone. Joshua could have knocked himself out trying to build a huge army, but he knew this was not God's way. God asks us to do the best we can with the abilities he gives us. But God does the rest of the work. There is nothing better than to step back and say "Wow! Look what God did."

What Digby Dug Up

Jericho had huge walls. It was called a "fortified" city because it was strong enough to keep out most enemies. Today it would take a huge bulldozer more than three months to bring down a wall like the one around Jericho, and it would cost a million dollars. God did it in seven days for free.

Café de Click

GET LIST:
   PIE TIN
   INSTANT CHOCOLATE PUDDING
   MILK
   NON-DAIRY WHIPPED TOPPING
   BANANA SLICES
   VANILLA COOKIES

Sometimes when God's way is plain and simple, we have to be careful not to make things harder. Because God can do the impossible, he can make our battles as easy as making this pie. The important thing is to follow his instructions. Make this pie by building layers in this order: instant chocolate pudding mixed with milk according to the directions on the box, whipped topping, banana slices and vanilla cookies. Let the pie set in the refrigerator for about ten minutes before eating it. While you're waiting, say, "Easy as pie is the Lord's battle cry!"

God Talk
Take turns saying things that are scary
or hard to do.
After each one, say together,
"With God's might, we'll be all right."

Might Will Win the Fight!

Gideon was an Israelite
Who led his people out to fight.
His foes would try to muscle in,
But Gideon knew his men could win.

Enemies were as thick as flies.
But he had an army great in size.
Thirty-two thousand standing by
Waited to hear his battle cry.

Gideon would have gone ahead,
But suddenly God spoke up and said,
"Gideon, hold it! Not so fast.
Your mighty army's much too vast.

"Soldiers who win can get swelled heads.
You need to lean on me instead.
Israel's God will save the day
If you send some men away.

"Tell those who tremble in their boots,
Now is the time for them to scoot."
Twenty-two thousand walked away.
Only ten thousand chose to stay.

Gideon's army lost its might
With only ten thousand left to fight.
How could an army small in size
Conquer its foes as thick as flies?

Gideon's army sure had shrunk!
Soldiers who stayed had lots of spunk.
They were courageous, tried and true.
But it became clear that God wasn't through!

God told Gideon, "There's still a crowd,
Too many standing tall and proud.
Tell them to go and take a drink."
God separated them quick as a wink.

"Some of them need to take a trip.
Send away those who kneel to sip.
Those who lap water from a hand
May stay to fight at your command."

Only 300 men that day
Lapped like a dog and got to stay.
Soldiers who left gave them their stuff,
Trumpets and food—more than enough.

How could an army baby-size
Conquer its foes as thick as flies?
Gideon heard God in the night
Telling him, "Now's the time to fight."

Gideon split the group in three
And then he told them, "Follow me."
Each had a torch inside a jar,
A trumpet with sound that carried far.

Quietly his 300 tramped
Out where the foes were all encamped.
Suddenly there were trumpet blasts!
Clay jars crashed and torches flashed!

"A sword for the Lord and Gideon!"
Heard the foes from Midian.
They didn't even try to fight.
They ran away into the night.

How could a few horn-blowing guys
Conquer their foes as thick as flies?
What was the strength that won that fight?
It was the Lord's great power and might!

Go for the Godprint

Confidence: We can get confused and discouraged in hard situations. That's when we need to believe in God's power and trust him to help us. Then our problems and our enemies won't look so big and bad. Like Gideon, we can do what we need to no matter what the odds because we have confidence in the living God!

What Digby Dug Up

The Spring of Harod where Gideon and his army stopped to drink before battling the Midianites is full of leeches. Men who pulled the water up in their hands could check for leeches before they drank. Those who just knelt down and sipped were taking a chance of slurping a leech. Yuck!

GP Theater Company

Play charades with your family. First make sure everyone understands what "confidence" means. Then take turns acting out situations where it is hard to be confident while other family members guess what is being acted out. Think of things like taking a test, jumping off a high dive, trying out new skates or sitting through a scary storm. After each turn, affirm the actor, encouraging him or her to be confident in God's power.

God Talk

Here's a song you can sing
when you find yourself facing
a tough situation or even a bully.
You can sing to the tune of *"Baa, Baa, Black Sheep."*
**Lord of heaven, show me your might.
Be with me always; help me do what's right.
You are faithful, good and true.
Help me keep my trust in you.**

News from Ruth

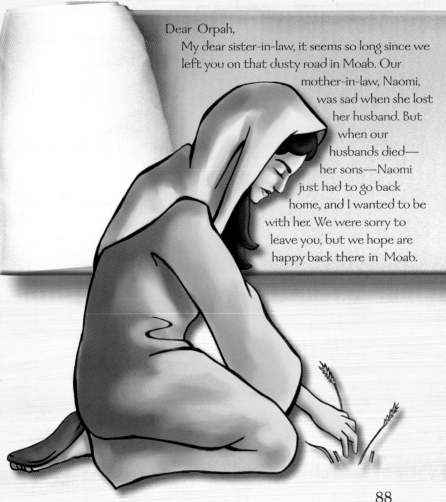

Dear Orpah,

My dear sister-in-law, it seems so long since we left you on that dusty road in Moab. Our mother-in-law, Naomi, was sad when she lost her husband. But when our husbands died— her sons—Naomi just had to go back home, and I wanted to be with her. We were sorry to leave you, but we hope are happy back there in Moab.

When we got to Bethlehem, the people talked about us, because Naomi had lost her family and brought back a foreign daughter-in-law. Naomi thought her life was so bad that she wanted to change her beautiful name meaning "pleasant" to Mara, which means "bitter."

I hated to see her suffer. I did everything I could to help her. The barley harvest was just starting. I went out and collected grain the harvesters dropped so we would have food to eat. While I was working, Boaz, the owner of the land, spoke to me. I

wondered why he was so kind, since I was a foreigner. He said it was because I had been good to Naomi. (She is so wonderful, how could I not be good to her?) He asked God to reward me and said that I had found protection under God's wings. I liked the sound of that. Boaz gave me extra food to eat. I didn't know until later that he also told the harvesters to leave extra grain for me to find.

Naomi realized that someone had helped me because I brought home so much grain. When I told her whose field I'd been in, she got excited. Boaz is one of her husband's relatives—a kinsman-redeemer. That means that he could make sure that our family names would not be forgotten in Israel.

For the rest of the barley and wheat harvests, I gleaned in Boaz's field. Naomi thought it would be safer for me there. One day, she said that she wanted to find a new husband for me— and guess who she picked!

Naomi sent me all bathed and perfumed to the threshing floor one night. Boaz woke to find me lying at his feet. It was so dark that he had to ask who I was. I told him it was Ruth, and asked him to spread the corner of his garment over me. That was a way of telling him that I was willing for him to marry me.

He was really happy about it. He thought I'd be more interested in younger men, but I wasn't. There was one problem, though. Another relative was closer and had the first right to redeem my husband's property and marry me.

I left before it was light. Boaz filled my shawl with grain. What a kind man he is! Then he rushed to the city gate to find the relative he told me about. The way they do things here is interesting. When a person makes an agreement, he takes off his sandal and gives it to the other person in front of witnesses. Boaz gathered ten elders of the town to sit with him and called the relative over. The relative agreed the Boaz should buy my husband's land and marry me. I became Boaz's wife!

That's not the end of our story. This letter is also a birth announcement. Boaz and I had a son! You can imagine the joy I felt laying him on Naomi's lap. Now she has a son again to carry on her family name. And I have a wonderful life in my new home. God has truly been good to me and kept me under his wings.

Love,
Ruth

Go for the Godprint

Love: Jesus gave up everything for us, because God loves us so much. Remembering that helps us show love, too. Loving means doing what's best for others, even if it means we have to give up something ourselves. For instance, we can wash extra dishes, play with a little sister or brother, or give the best seat to someone shorter. How about doing something kind and loving for someone right now?

What Digby Dug Up
According to Jewish law, poor people and widows could follow the harvesters and gather the grain missed or left behind in the fields. This is how Ruth "gleaned" in Boaz's fields.

PJ's Good to Go

Make an "I Love You!" coupon for each member of your family. Decorate index cards or half sheets of paper with markers and glitter. Then write or draw something special you will do for each person. Complete the sentence: "I choose to love you by _____." Some ideas might be: washing the dishes for your sister when it's her turn; reading to your little brother; putting out the trash for your dad; bringing your mom a cold drink and a magazine; extra hugs and kisses for anyone, any time. Then hide the coupons in surprising places for family members to find. Remember, when someone wants to redeem a coupon, show your love gladly!

God Talk

Take turns praying for the people in your family by saying,
"Lord, I love _____ because you love me.
Help me to show _____ my love."

Speak, Lord, I'm Listening!

I'll never forget the first time God called me. I was still a child, just like you. I lived in the temple and worked with the priest, Eli. Eli was an old man then like I am now. His eyes were weak; he could hardly see. Even though I was just a boy, I knew he needed my help.

It may seem odd that God would speak to me; after all, I was just a little boy. In those days, a word from the Lord was rare. He didn't even send special messages to grown-ups very often. There weren't many visions or prophecies, but still God spoke to me.

I remember it like it was yesterday. It had been a long day. Eli and I worked all day in the temple, and we were both tired. Eli went to sleep in his usual place, and I lay down in the temple. I hadn't been sleeping long before I heard someone calling my name. "Samuel, Samuel!" I woke up and I thought, "Something's wrong with Eli." So I ran to see what he wanted. "Here I am, Eli," I said. But Eli said he didn't call me.

I was confused. I knew I had heard my name. It was real and not a dream. But I went back to bed, lay down and went to sleep. I had just nodded off again when I heard the voice a second time. "Samuel, Samuel!" Again I went to Eli. He was the only other person there, so it had to be him calling my name. When I got there, he said the same thing. "Go back to sleep. I didn't call you." Now I was really confused. What was going on? Was he talking in his sleep? I knew someone had called my name. But one more time, I went back to bed.

It took a little longer to fall asleep this time, but as soon as I did, I heard it again, "Samuel, Samuel!" I sat up and thought, "This has to be Eli!" So I went to him and said, "Here I am, Eli. You called me." It was then that Eli understood. He said something to me that seemed impossible. "Samuel," he told me, "The Lord is calling your name. Go back and lie down. If he calls you again, say, 'Speak, Lord. I'm listening.'"

I was a little nervous. Maybe I was even scared. But I went back to my mat and waited. Soon the voice of the Lord came. "Samuel, Samuel!"

"Speak, Lord," I said, "I'm listening."

That was the first time I heard God's voice. He called me many times after that. Even when I was a little boy, God had plans for me. Our holy God chose me to be a prophet. And do you know what? That same holy God who called me on that night has a plan for you, too.

Go for the Godprint

Reverence: Have you ever wondered why we often bow our heads when we pray? It's one way to show reverence for God. We bow to say, "You are a great and mighty God, and I want to obey you." When Samuel heard God's call, he responded with reverence. "Speak, Lord, I'm listening." How will you respond when God calls you?

What Digby Dug Up

The temple in this story was actually the "tabernacle." It was a large tent where the Israelites worshiped God. The Israelites made the tabernacle following God's very special instructions while they were wandering in the wilderness. It was a tent so that it could be moved from place to place as they traveled. King Solomon later built the first temple building.

GP Showtime

Sing this song to the tune of "Are You Sleeping?" Then substitute family names for "Samuel, Samuel" and sing it again. You might like to try writing some verses of your own. After you sing the song together, talk about ways that God might use you. He has a plan for all of us.

Are you sleeping, Are you sleeping,
Samuel, Samuel?
Can you hear God calling? Can you hear God calling?
Samuel, Samuel.

I am listening, I am listening!
Yes, I am! Yes, I am!
I will do your will, Lord; I will do your will, Lord.
Watch and see. Watch and see.

God Talk

Write these three prayer starters
on a piece of paper for each person in your family.
Let everyone take time to think of a way to complete each sentence.
Then you can take turns reading the prayers you have written
aloud in a special time of family praise.

Oh, God, you are so _____.
Lord, I praise you because _____.
Father, because of your great and mighty love, I _____ .
Amen.

Samuel's Search

Saul was the king over Israel, but he hadn't obeyed God. God decided it was time to choose a new king, and he used his prophet, Samuel, to get the job done. You can help decide the best solution—and we'll see what Samuel did too. The first problem to be solved was this. Saul was still the king and he had no plans to step down from the throne. How could Samuel go around the country looking for the man God was going to point out without Saul finding out what was going on? Here's one way to solve the problem:

Samuel could go to a disguise shop and get a costume to make him look like a rock star. Then he could put on concerts all over Israel. In between his concerts he could look for the new king. Or...

Samuel could join the army. Every day while he's out on patrol, he could look through his binoculars to search for the new king. Or...

Samuel could follow God's plan and go to the land of Bethlehem like God directed. He could take along a calf as a gift to God and tell the leaders of that city, "I'm here to make a sacrifice, and I invite Jesse and his sons join me."

Which plan do you think Samuel chose? You're

right! He chose to be loyal to God and follow God's plan. He went out to make a sacrifice, and Saul didn't suspect a thing!

Now here's the next problem. Jesse had eight sons. God had narrowed down the number so Samuel didn't have to search every single house in the land, but Samuel still had to figure out which of these men would be the next king. Here's one way to solve the problem...

Samuel could write down a number and hide it behind his back. Then he could ask each of the sons to pick a number. The son that came closest would be the new king! Or...

Samuel could pick the tallest, or the oldest, or the most handsome. Or...

Samuel could listen to God and let God show him which of the sons was the right one. Which plan do you think Samuel chose? This one is a little tricky because Samuel almost didn't follow God's plan! Jesse's first son was named Eliab. When Samuel saw Eliab he thought, "This is the one! He's tall and handsome!"

But God told Samuel not to look at Eliab just because he was tall and handsome. God could see Eliab's heart and knew that he was not the right man for the job.

So Samuel looked at the next son, Abinadab, and the next son, Shammah. But God told Samuel it wasn't either of them. Samuel looked at seven of

Jesse's sons and still God hadn't said, "This one!" Samuel could have worried, but instead he asked Jesse, "Do you have any more sons around here?"

Jesse answered, "I have one more son, David, who's out taking care of the sheep. He's my youngest son."

Samuel asked them to go get David, and when David came in, Samuel could see he was tan and handsome. But Samuel didn't care what David looked like. He was listening to God, and this time God said, "This is the one." So Samuel poured oil over David's head to show he would be the next king.

David became king of Israel when he was 30, and he ruled for 40 years. That was part of God's plan for his kingdom. God promised David that one of his sons would be the next king, and that he would build a special house for God. And it all happened because Samuel was loyal to God and made the right choices!

Go for the Godprint

Loyalty: If a new kid you really like moves into the neighborhood, will you still keep your old friends too? That's loyalty. What if the new kid wanted you to do things that you knew wouldn't please God? Can you be loyal to God, no matter what?

What Digby Dug Up

The oil Samuel poured over David's head stood for holiness. It meant that David was set apart to serve God. The priests mixed up this special oil with the recipe God gave Moses in Exodus 30:23-25. It contained myrhh, cinnamon, cane, cassia and olive oil.

98

Izzy's Art Cart

GET LIST:
CLEAN WHITE T-SHIRT
FABRIC MARKERS OR PAINTS

Make a **"Team Jesus"** T-shirt. Design a logo that shows that Jesus is the king of your team, and that you want to be loyal to him. Think about what pictures or words you can use to get your message across. Practice drawing your logo on paper first, then carefully draw it on the T-shirt. Use fabric markers or paints to color the design. For even more fun, have everyone in the family make shirts. Wear them to help you stick together when you go to the zoo or on a hike. As you work on the shirts, talk about:

- **How do we show loyalty in our family?**
- **How do we show that we're loyal to Jesus?**

God Talk
Ask your parents about their
favorite "oldies" song.
Make up words to that tune
that show your family's loyalty to Jesus.
Add motions and sing with all the enthusiasm
that you use to show loyalty to your favorite team!
Once a week, sing your song at dinnertime
in place of your usual dinner prayer.

What Goliath Didn't See

Goliath was big. Really big. He was as tall as a kid standing on a grown-up's shoulders. And he was a champion soldier. He liked to stand up tall with all his fighting equipment and dare anyone to fight against him. Goliath was the secret weapon for the Philistines' army. He could stand out in front of the crowd and see everything.

At least he thought he could. Some things he didn't see.

The Philistine army was ready to fight against Israel's army. But they didn't plan a battle for the whole army. Instead, they wanted one man from Israel to come out and fight against Goliath. Just one against one. The loser's country would have to serve the other country. Goliath came out every morning and every night for 40 days and dared anyone to fight him.

No one wanted to do it. Goliath was so big! Even King Saul was terrified.

David wasn't a soldier, but his brothers were. One day his father asked David to take food to his soldier-brothers. David left his sheep, packed up the bread and cheese and went. He got to the army camp just in time to see Goliath come out.

"Choose a man and have him come down to me," Goliath shouted.

No one went. David wondered why. He went to find King Saul.

"I'll fight Goliath," David told the king.

"You're only a boy," King Saul answered, "and he's been a soldier for a long time."

"I'm a shepherd," David told the king.

"Once a lion attacked the sheep, and I killed the lion and saved the sheep. Another time a bear came. I did the same thing. God showed me what to do then, and he'll show me what to do now."

The king decided to let David fight Goliath. But he thought he should at least have some armor and weapons. So he gave David all his own armor and weapons.

David looked ridiculous. Nothing fit right. Everything was too heavy. He couldn't even walk. So he took it all off. But he didn't change his mind about fighting Goliath. He decided to use what God gave him, instead of what King Saul gave him.

What did God give David? A shepherd's staff, a sling shot, a pouch and five smooth stones that he found in a stream. But that's not all.

101

God also gave David great confidence that God had a plan and would show David what to do.

So David went out to meet Goliath. Goliath looked him over. He saw that David was only a boy—a good-looking boy, but still just a boy. He had no armor. He had no weapons. He had no experience as a soldier. He didn't even have any other soldiers ready to help him. Goliath laughed at David and teased him.

Goliath only saw what David didn't have. He didn't see what David did have.

Goliath didn't see David's faith.

Goliath didn't see God's power.

Goliath didn't see God's plan.

But David knew. He stepped forward and called out to Goliath, "You come with a sword and a spear and a javelin, but I come in the name of the Lord Almighty. This day the Lord will hand you over to me. And everyone here will know."

Now Goliath was mad. He ran toward David, ready to attack. David ran right up to meet him. David reached into his pouch, pulled out a stone, put it in the sling shot, slung it and hit Goliath right smack in the forehead.

Whap!

Goliath fell over on his face.

And that was the end of Goliath. David was right about God's power and plan.

Go for the Godprint

Resourcefulness: God didn't ask David to do something hard and then not give him what he needed. God gave David faith, and God made him a good shot with a sling. Like David, we can make the most of what God gives us to honor God. What special abilities has God given you?

What Digby Dug Up

ALL THE PIECES OF GOLIATH'S ARMOR AND WEAPONS PROBABLY WEIGHED 200 POUNDS. HE WORE A HELMET AND SOMETHING TO PROTECT HIS CHEST AND LEGS. EVERYTHING WAS MADE OF BRONZE. HE CARRIED A JAVELIN AND A SPEAR. READ ABOUT IT IN 1 SAMUEL 17:4-7.

Jake's Mirth Quake

Build a tower out of blocks or other things around the house, such as toys that stack or plastic cups. Think of this tower as Goliath, and make it as big and sturdy as you can. Now look for several things you can toss at the tower, such as a bean bag, foam ball or small stuffed toy. Stand back about ten feet and take aim. Can you knock down Goliath with one shot? Let everyone have a turn. Then talk about:

• *What physical abilities did you use to knock down Goliath?* **(Eyes for aiming, muscles for throwing.)**

• *What abilities can you use for the things that God wants you to do?*

God Talk

Set up a step stool.
Take turns standing on the top step,
above the rest of the family, to pray.
Ask God for big faith to do the big jobs
he has planned for you.

Saul's Close Call

Saul learned that David would be the next king.
This made Saul madder than anything!

With three thousand men, Saul went on a hunt.
He planned to kill David. He marched right in front.

While out on the hunt, Saul went into a cave.
Who was hidden inside there? You guessed it—'twas Dave.

He and his men were concealed way in back.
David's men whispered, "It's time to attack!"

Silently David crept up to the king.
He pulled out his sword and then took a swing.

But David did not kill the king on that day,
He just clipped Saul's robe and then sneaked away.

Saul never knew that he'd had a close call.
He didn't know David was in there at all.

So Saul left the cave at a walk—not a run,
But David felt bad for the thing he had done.

He followed and shouted, "My king and my master!
If I were to kill you, it would be a disaster!

God put you in charge as my ruler and king.
I'll never hurt you—it would be the wrong thing.

You want to kill me though I've done no wrong.
I won't fight against you. Let's get along!"

Seeing the piece of his robe David had,
Saul knew his treatment of David was bad.

Saul wept, then answered back with a loud cry,
"David, oh David, you're better than I.

You could have killed me but spared me instead.
Most men would leave all their enemies dead.

May our Lord reward you for what you have done.
I know you'll rule Israel instead of my son."

Saul left with his army, and they went back home.
He promised that he would leave David alone.

But the jealousy Saul felt did not go away.
He mistrusted David 'til his dying day.

David kept waiting and trusting the Lord.
It wasn't his job to chase Saul with a sword.

David knew God was the one to believe in.
It's not up to people to try to get even!

Go for the Godprint

Forgiveness: Everyone knows what it's like to want to "get even" with someone—especially when that person has treated you badly. This Bible story helps us see that David knew that rewarding and punishing is up to God. Instead of hurting Saul, he forgave him. And, for a short time, Saul left David alone.

What Digby Dug Up

SAUL KEPT TRYING TO KILL DAVID, AND DAVID KEPT ON FORGIVING. YOU CAN READ ABOUT THE SECOND TIME DAVID CHOSE NOT TO GET EVEN IN 1 SAMUEL 26.

Herbie's Hideaway

GET LIST:
25 BEADS OR STONES
TWO SMALL BOWLS

Put all the beads or stones in one basket and label
it, "God rewards and punishes." Label the other basket,
"I forgive without getting even." Whenever a member of the
family gets involved in a quarrel or something that seems unfair, use the
bowls as a reminder of how God wants you to respond. If you're able to forgive
the wrong, move a bead from the first bowl to the second one. See how
quickly your family can fill up the forgiveness basket. Then celebrate with a
special treat and start all over again.

Forgiveness never ends!

God Talk
On a Sunday evening,
make a super forgiveness sundae
in a mixing bowl.
Use every kind of ice cream
and topping you have in the house!
Give everyone a spoon. Take turns saying sentence prayers that begin:
"God, help me to forgive when _____." After each prayer, enjoy a bite together.
Pray until the treat is gone. Make sure no "unforgiveness" drags over into the new week.

A Soldier's Diary

DEAR DIARY,
Just arrived in the Paran wilderness. David wants some time away after the funeral of the great prophet Samuel. He and Samuel must have been pretty close. Samuel did anoint David to be king, after all. I wonder how long we'll stay here?

DEAR DIARY,
We delivered David's greeting to Nabal this afternoon. Peace be to you, Nabal, we told him. Peace be to all of your household, too. That's the standard friendly greeting. It covers men, women, children, servants—even sheep. We wished 'em all well. But Nabal didn't seem to get it. He was rude and refused to give us anything to eat. What a creep! Like he didn't have more than enough to go around. David isn't going to like this. Not one bit.

DEAR DIARY,
Got my assignment this morning. I'm going to Carmel with nine other guys to take greetings to Nabal. a rich landowner with thousands of goats and sheep. It's sheep shearing time, so there's a big celebration. David is hoping they'll hand out food as they usually do at these things. We're running short on rations, so we're all hoping Nabal will be generous.

DEAR DIARY,
Yep. David is mad all right. I might even say he's hopping mad. I don't blame him. While we've been camped near Nabal's place, we've guarded all his people and flocks. It's only right that we should be rewarded with a share of the food! David says 400 of us will go and attack Nabal. The other 200 will stay here to look after the camp. I wonder which assignment I'll get?

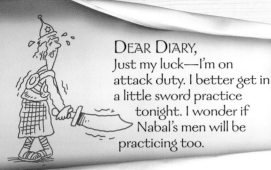

DEAR DIARY,
Just my luck—I'm on attack duty. I better get in a little sword practice tonight. I wonder if Nabal's men will be practicing too.

DEAR DIARY,
Abigail is terrific! When she talked to David, he actually listened. She apologized for Nabal's rudeness, then managed to talk David out of going after him. She used just the right words to remind David that he was about to be king, and that he'd probably regret avenging himself with a big huge fight. She was right, of course.

DEAR DIARY,
Unbelievable! Creepy Nabal's men ratted on him. I guess they're not too crazy about him either, because they went straight to his wife, Abigail. They told her what happened—how he wouldn't share any food. Abigail didn't lose any time. She loaded up her donkeys with all kinds of good stuff and brought it out to our camp. Bread, meat, raisins, figs...it was a huge feast. I'd forgotten how good it feels to lie back and relax after a good meal.

DEAR DIARY,
God has been watching over us! Not only did we get our fair share of the food, but we avoided a bloody battle. Good thing Abigail came along when she did, because we were about to wipe out Nabal's whole place. David would have been sorry afterward, and things would have been a big mess. But that's all behind us now.

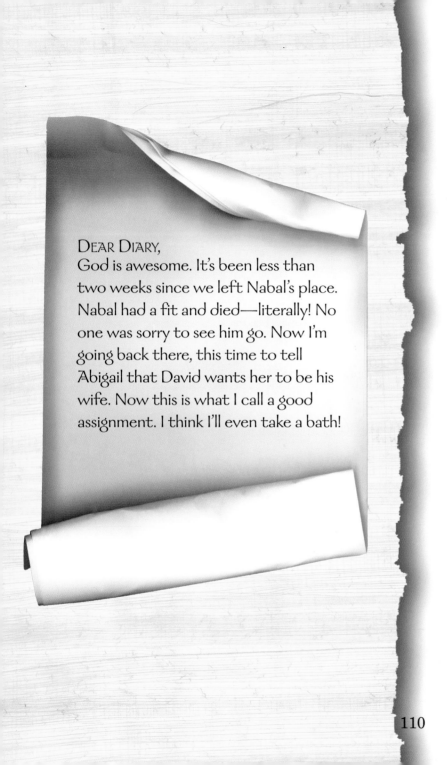

DEAR DIARY,
God is awesome. It's been less than two weeks since we left Nabal's place. Nabal had a fit and died—literally! No one was sorry to see him go. Now I'm going back there, this time to tell Abigail that David wants her to be his wife. Now this is what I call a good assignment. I think I'll even take a bath!

Go for the Godprint

Fairness: "Hey! That's not fair!" Have you ever said that? When we're treated fairly, we're more likely to treat others fairly in return. Sometimes people get confused about what's fair. And there are even people—like Nabal—who don't care what's fair and what's not. But God is always fair. Because God gives us what we need, we can be more than fair—we can be generous. Be an Abigail, not a Nabal!

What Digby Dug Up

In Hebrew, the name "Nabal" means fool. In 1 Samuel 25:25 Abigail tells David that Nabal is just like his name—a fool. How was Nabal foolish?

Jake's Mirth Quake

Just for fun, play a favorite board game with your family. Give one person an "unfair advantage" like spinning the spinner twice on each turn or drawing two cards instead of one. See who wins the game. Then talk about:

- **How did the person with the unfair advantage feel?**

- **How did other family members feel?**

- **What would happen if that person always had the advantage?**

Play the game again. After the game, shake hands and agree to treat each other fairly this week.

God Talk

Have each person in your family
draw something that happened
this week that didn't seem fair.
Talk about how you handled it.
Would you do the same thing again?
Brainstorm ways you could trust God if something like that happened again.
Then make big Xs over your drawings.
Pray and ask God to help you be generous and fair, no matter how others treat you.

Wrong Time, Right Time

Time to get up. Time to go to bed. Time to eat dinner. Time to clean up. Time to go to school. The Bible says there's an appointed time for everything. Sometimes it's easy to know when it's the right time for something.

When is it a bad time to shout and make noise? When is it a good time?

When is it the wrong time to cross the street? When is it the right time?

The prophet Samuel knew just the right time to anoint David to be king. How did he know? God told him. Guess which time was the right time for David to be anointed.

(Check your guess in 1 Samuel 16:11–13.)

Did you guess right?

Even though David was anointed as a young man, it would be many years before it was time for him to be crowned king. First, it was time for David to serve King Saul by playing his harp. Next it was time for David to fight in King Saul's army against Goliath and many other enemies. Then it was time for David to hide when King Saul got angry and jealous.

Time to serve. Time to fight. Time to hide. When would it be time for David to be king?

The Bible says that there's a time for crying and sadness and a time for laughing and celebrating.

When is it the wrong time to celebrate? When is it the right time?

David waited many years, and finally King Saul died in battle. The throne of Israel was waiting for David. Was it a time for sadness or a time for celebration?

When King Saul died, it was a time of great sadness in Israel. Saul was Israel's first king, and he had ruled for many years. The people would miss him. It wasn't the right time to throw a big celebration and crown a new king.

Even if we're not sure when it's the right time, God's timing is always right. So even though David knew he'd be the next king, he waited for God to show him the right time to be crowned. Guess when that time came.

David didn't have to wait much longer. After the people had finished grieving over Saul's death, David asked God to tell him where to go. God sent David to the city of Hebron, and the men from the tribes of Judah anointed David as their king right away. Then David went up to Jerusalem and became king of the tribes of Israel, too. Finally, it was the right time—in God's time—for David to be king.

Go for the Godprint

Purposefulness: At first, no one thought David would be chosen to be king. But God had a special plan for David. The skills David learned as a shepherd—playing music and fighting off wild animals—came in handy later on. What talents has God given you? How can you use them in God's service?

What Digby Dug Up

David was anointed by Samuel when he was about 15 years old. He didn't become king until he was 30. David waited 15 years for God to show him the right time to take the throne. How old will you be 15 years from now? What do you think you'll be doing to serve God then?

Izzy's Art Cart

1 Samuel 16:18 mentions five talents David used for God's service. It says that David was:

- **a skilled musician**
- brave
- **a warrior**
- **a good speaker**
- handsome

You may not be a king like David was, but God has big plans for your life. When the time is right, God will show you how to use your talents for his service just as he showed David.

Make a crown out of poster board. First measure your head with a measuring tape. Make your crown one inch larger than your measurement so you can tape the ends together. Draw your crown with several points. On each point of the crown, write one talent God has given you. (Extra crown points can be reserved for talents God might show you in the future.)

Decorate your crown with plastic gems, glitter glue or hard candy. Then crown yourself king or queen for a day. Hang your crown where it will remind you of the ways God can use you.

God Talk

In Psalm 31:14–15, David wrote:
"But I trust in you, O LORD;
I say, 'You are my God.' My times are in your hands."
Put your family's times in God's hands this week.
Choose a certain time each day to pray for each person in your family.
For example, you might all pray for your mom at 2:00
or pray for your dad at 4:30. (If you have a big family,
you might need to set an alarm to help you remember.)
At the end of the day, talk about how God answered your prayers.

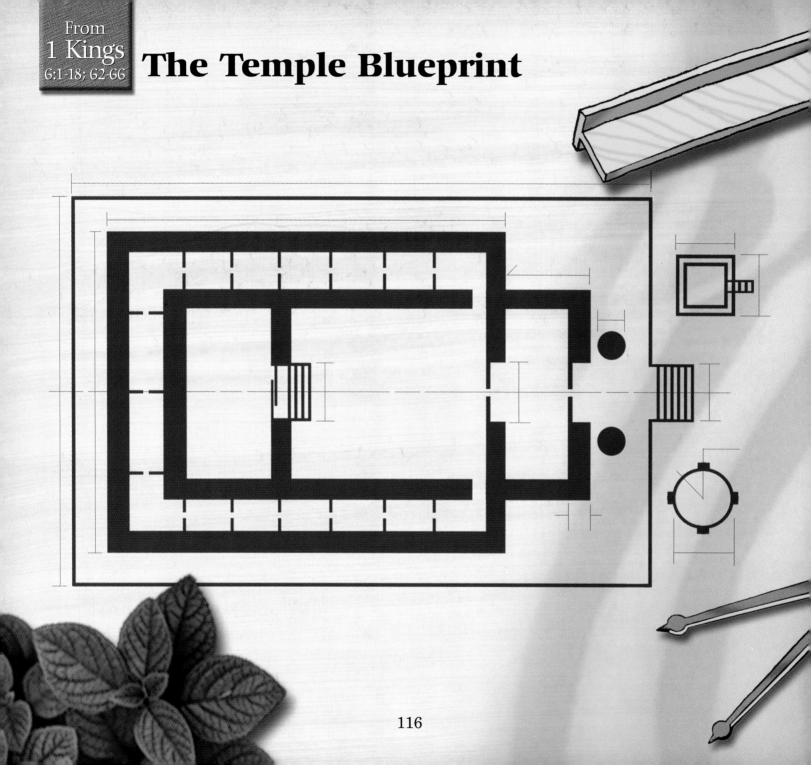

The Temple Blueprint

David's son Solomon led the land of Israel wisely and made it a greater nation than ever before. When he had been king for four years, he began building a temple where everyone in the kingdom could come worship God. Skilled craftspeople worked together to make the temple one of the most beautiful buildings in the world. This blueprint shows how Solomon's workers constructed the temple.

- The temple was divided into different sections. The two main sections were the Holy Place and the Most Holy Place. These rooms were 45 feet high and used for special ceremonies.

- Along the sides of the temple were three stories of side rooms. The side rooms were small on the first floor, bigger on the second floor, and biggest on the third floor. Hallways and staircases connected the side rooms.

- The temple faced east.

- It was built of limestone. The walls were covered with boards of cedar and the floor was covered with boards of pine. Pictures of flowers and plants were creatively carved into the cedar, then all of these boards were covered with gold!

- The stones were cut at a quarry far from the temple, so there wouldn't be any noise of hammers, axes, or other iron tools.

- It took seven years to complete God's temple.

- The holy places inside the temple were covered with pure gold to show the glory of God.

As Solomon directed the construction, God spoke to him. "As for this temple you are building, if you follow my decrees, carry out my regulations and keep all my commands and obey them, I will fulfill through you the promise I gave to David your father. And I will live among the Israelites and will not abandon my people Israel" (1 Kings 6:12–13).

When the temple was finished, King Solomon gathered all the people to worship God. The priests carried the ark of the covenant into the Most Holy Place–it still held the stones with the Ten Commandments that God gave Moses on Mount Sinai! Then God's glory filled the temple and the priests couldn't even carry on the service!

The king and priests and people gave God thousands of offerings of cows, sheep and grain in a great celebration of worship. They celebrated for fourteen days! King Solomon spread his hands toward heaven and prayed, "O LORD, God of Israel, there is no God like you in heaven above or on earth below." Everyone rejoiced and praised God.

Then Solomon sent everyone home. As the people left they were full of joy because God had done so many good things for them and their king. God deserved their praise then, and God still deserves our praise today!

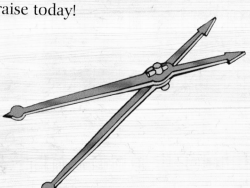

Go for the Godprint

Creativity: The people who built the temple used their imaginations and gifts to worship God. God still gives people new ideas for how to do things. We can use the creativity that comes from God to solve problems and honor God. Can you think of a problem that needs a creative solution?

What Digby Dug Up

The cedar logs used in the temple were from the far-away country of Lebanon. Can you find Lebanon on a map? The people might have made the logs into rafts and floated them along rivers until they were near the place where the temple was being built.

Wally's Walkabout

GET LIST:
MEASURING TAPE
STRING OR YARN

Go to a park or other open area and use a measuring tape and a ball of yarn or string to mark off a space 30 feet by 90 feet. Use the blueprint to mark the other areas of the temple. Sit inside the space you've marked and talk about:

• **If you were building a temple for God today, what materials would you use and what would it look like? How would your design help people worship God?**

• **What are some creative abilities God gave you? Do you have a clever imagination? Are you skilled at making things with your hands? Do you have ideas that help people? What else?**

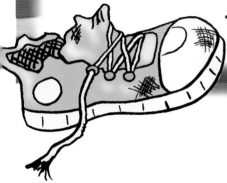

• **How are you already using the creative abilities God's given you? How can you use them to worship God?**

God Talk
You'll need
pencils and a pad of "sticky notes."
Take turns sitting in a chair of honor
that you've draped with a quilt or bedspread.
Other family members can write on sticky notes
all the creative gifts of the person in the chair of honor,
then stick them to the person.
As God's people dedicated the temple, dedicate that person's gifts to God.

450 to 1

Good afternoon, prophet watchers, and welcome to KSRL sports. Thanks for coming to witness this exciting challenge.

As you know, Elijah, the prophet of the Lord, has challenged the prophets of Baal. The prophets of Baal have been calling people away from the Lord, and Elijah wants them back. Today the Lord and Baal go head to head for the faith of the people. Earlier today we spoke with Elijah.

KSRL: Elijah, what are your chances of claiming a victory for the Lord today?

Elijah: I believe the Lord will answer when I call.

KSRL: But will he even hear you? Baal's prophets have you outnumbered 450 to 1.

Elijah: The Lord will listen when I call. Excuse me. I must prepare my sacrifice.

The odds aren't good, but Elijah remains in good spirits as he prepares to battle the prophets of Baal. Let's review the rules. Each side will receive one bull. They'll prepare to sacrifice their bulls by cutting them into pieces and laying the pieces on a stack of wood. Then the excitement begins. Both groups will call their gods by name. The god who answers by lighting the sacrifice on fire will be declared the winner here today.

The crowds are gathering. The sacrifices are ready. Let's go up to Mount Carmel and check in with the prophets of Baal. Elijah has agreed to give them the first call.

KSRL: You're ready to sacrifice. How are you feeling right now?

Prophets of Baal: Fantastic. With so many prophets, Baal is going to hear us. We'll shout out his name. He'll send the fire.

KSRL: So you don't give Elijah much of a chance?

Prophets of Baal: No way. See you at the sacrifice.

The prophets of Baal are confident. With their superior numbers they should have no trouble wrapping up this title for their god today.

The bulls are ready and the prophets are gathered. They're beginning to call on the name of their god. Their call is brief and to the point: "O Baal, answer us!" They're shouting together. They're shouting out loud. No answer from Baal yet, but they're keeping it going.

"O Baal, answer us! O Baal, answer us! O Baal, answer us!"

It's growing into a chant now, and the prophets are taking positions around the sacrifice. They're dancing around the altar, and they'll keep right on dancing their way to victory. It's noon now, and the prophets of Baal still have no answer. Baal has not sent fire to light their sacrifice. Elijah is standing by, waiting to enter the game.

Now Elijah is taunting the prophets. He wants them to shout louder in case Baal is sleeping! Oh, the prophets of Baal don't like to hear that. They're shouting louder. They're dancing faster. They're slashing themselves with their swords! Yes, folks, blood is flowing, but they won't give up.

Now Elijah will step up to the altar. Notice that Elijah's stone altar is surrounded by a trench. Elijah is laying his wood on the altar, and he's asked someone in the crowd to bring him something. What could it be? Wait a minute...it's...it's water! Elijah has asked members of the crowd to pour water on the wood. One jar, two, three, four jars of water have been poured on his altar, and he's sending out for more. The water is flowing down the altar and into the trench. It's filling the trench. How will Elijah's god light this wet, soggy mess?

Elijah is stepping forward. He's starting to speak. Let's listen in.

Elijah: "O Lord, God of Abraham, Isaac and Israel, let it be known today that you are God in Israel and that I am your servant. Answer me so these people will know that you, O Lord, are God."

Very well spoken, but will it be enough to light the sacrifice? Yes! It's burning. The wood, the stones, the soil—even the water is on fire now. The crowd is going wild. They're up on their feet cheering Elijah. Now they're down on their knees, worshiping Elijah's God. Elijah has won. The Lord is victorious!

What an exciting day! The Lord is the one true God. Baal is a fake! Elijah and the Lord have won back the faith of the people.

Go for the Godprint

Faith: Elijah knew that God can do anything—even light water on fire. No phony god could do that. When the people saw that God had heard Elijah's prayer, they responded by kneeling and saying, "The Lord, he is God." The same God who answered Elijah's prayer answers our prayers today.

What Digby Dug Up

Why was Elijah the only prophet of the Lord? When Queen Jezebel married King Ahab, she wanted him to worship Baal (1 Kings 16:31–32). Later, Jezebel had many of the Lord's prophets killed (1 Kings 18:4). Any prophets who survived probably went into hiding. Elijah was the only one brave enough to stand up to Ahab and Jezebel.

Café de Click

Instead of celebrating the anniversary of your birth (otherwise known as your birthday), celebrate the anniversary of answered prayer. Bake a prayer cake and put candles on it. Have family members share prayers that God has answered, then light one candle for each answered prayer. As you look at the burning candles, let the flames remind you that God hears and answers your prayers. Sing this song, to the tune of "Happy Birthday," then blow out the candles and celebrate God's power to answer prayer.

We thank you, dear God
For hearing our prayer.
We're glad that you keep us
In your love and care.

God Talk
Pray a prayer like the one Elijah prayed:
Lord, Let it be known that
you are God in_____(fill in the name of your city)
and I am your servant.
Help me stand up for you by_____.

What Elijah Heard

Elijah heard what Jezebel said. And he ran for his life!

Wicked queen Jezebel was furious with Elijah. A wicked queen who is also mad is a very bad thing. Jezebel wanted to kill Elijah because he proved that his God was the true God and that her god, Baal, was no god at all.

Elijah was afraid and ran. He ran a long way, miles into the desert. There he collapsed under a broom tree. "I've had enough, Lord," he said. "Take my life." Elijah didn't want to do anything except die. He rested in the shade of the tree until he fell asleep.

Elijah didn't hear the angel at first. But when the angel touched him, he woke up fast. The angel said, "Get up and eat." So Elijah got up and ate. The angel gave him a cake of bread and a jar of water. Eating made Elijah sleepy and he went back to sleep.

The angel woke him up again. "Get up and eat," he said again. So Elijah ate. Then he felt stronger and was ready to keep going. He traveled for 40 days and 40 nights, until he reached Horeb, the mountain of God. He went into a cave to spend the night.

What do you suppose Elijah heard in that cave? God spoke to him! "What are you doing here, Elijah?"

Now Elijah heard a lot of moaning and groaning and complaining. And it was coming from him. He told God, "I've done everything you wanted me to do, and I've been enthusiastic about it. But nobody cares, the work is too hard, and I'm tired. Now Jezebel wants to kill me."

God told Elijah to stand out on the mountain and wait for the Lord to pass by.

Elijah heard the wind. It howled and ripped and roared and crashed. The mountain shuddered. Rocks split open. But the Lord was not in the wind.

Elijah heard an earthquake. The mountain heaved and rolled and rumbled. But God was not in the earthquake.

Elijah heard the snapping flames of a great fire. Flames leaped up all around him. But the Lord was not in the fire.

How could Elijah hear anything else after all that noise and commotion? But he did. He heard a gentle whisper. The voice said to him, "What are you doing here, Elijah?"

It was God, whispering to Elijah. God still had some work for Elijah to do—with no moaning and groaning and complaining.

"Go back the way you came," God told Elijah. When you get there, anoint Hazael king over Aram and Jehu king of Israel. And choose Elisha to be the next prophet. You're not alone. I have lots of people who still believe in me."

Elijah heard what God said. And he did just what God told him to do. He didn't feel so alone any more. It wasn't true that nobody cared what happened to him. God cared. Elijah was ready to get back to work.

Go for the Godprint

Enthusiasm: Elijah got discouraged, even though he knew he was doing God's work. But when God reminded Elijah that he was not alone, Elijah was able to do God's work with a glad spirit once again. God has work for all of us to do. It might even be cleaning your room or mowing the lawn without complaining. Attitude counts!

What Digby Dug Up

Mount Horeb was more than 200 miles from Mount Carmel, where Elijah battled the priests of Baal. (See the story on page 120.) To get there, Elijah crossed miles of wilderness all by himself.

GP Theater Company

Retell the story of Elijah and God's gentle whisper with sound effects. Scout around the house for ordinary items you can use to make these sounds:

ELIJAH RUNNING

ANGEL ARRIVING

ELIJAH WHINING

WIND STORM

EARTHQUAKE

FIRE

GOD'S WHISPER

ELIJAH GETTING BACK TO WORK

Talk about:

- **What's the most important thing to remember from this story?**

God Talk

Light a candle and gather around the flame.
Pass the candle around and take turns praying.
Thank God for being with you with all his power
and ask him to help you with the hard jobs
you need to do in the next few days.

Seven Dips

Have you ever played a game of "Pass It On"? One person starts a message and passes it on to another person, who passes the message on to someone else. This story from the Bible is like that game, and it all began with a man called Naaman.

My name is Naaman. I'm the commander of the king's army in my country of Aram. I'm strong and brave and have been honored by the king. You probably think my life is great. But I have a serious skin disease. Everyone in my home knows how sad and miserable I am. I pass my sadness to my wife and to others in our house.

I'm only a young girl, but a lot has happened in my life. One day Naaman led an army of men through our city. They took some of us away as captives. Naaman brought me here to be a servant for his wife. Even though I'm far from my family, I remember how much they loved God and how they obeyed God. I know God is powerful enough to heal people. I also remember a man named Elisha. God uses Elisha to do his work, even healing people. I told Naaman's wife, "If only my master would see the prophet who is in Samaria! He would cure him."

You must bow in my presence because I am the king of Aram! I have great power, but even I can't heal anyone. Perhaps this man called Elisha can help Naaman. But he might be expensive. I'm going to send 750 pounds of silver to the king of Israel, where Elisha lives. I'll also send ten changes of clothes. And I'll send a note that says, "I'm sending my servant Naaman to you so you can heal him of his skin disease."

I'm the king of Israel. I was very upset when I got this message. I tore my clothes to show how upset I was! I told everyone, "I'm not God! Why are they sending this man here for me to heal?" No amount of silver or new clothes will give me the power to heal this skin disease! Is the king of Aram looking for an excuse to start a war with me? Is he tricking me?

I'm Elisha, a man of God. When I heard that the king of Israel had torn his clothes, I sent a message to him. The message said, "Why have you torn your clothes? Let Naaman come to me."

When I got to Elisha's house his messenger told me, "Go and wash in the Jordan River seven times. Then your skin will be healed, and you will be clean." I was angry at this message! Elisha should come out of his house and wave his hands over me to heal me. I don't want to get myself dirty in that Jordan River. I know other rivers that are better. Elisha's crazy if he thinks I'm going to obey him and his God. I told my servants to pack up and take me home.

129

We're Naaman's servants. We thought this cure was at least worth a try. We told Naaman, "If Elisha had asked you to do something hard or that cost a lot of money you would have done it. Why not obey this easy thing? It's not hard to wash in the river."

I decided to listen to the message of Elisha. I went to the Jordan River and dipped in and out seven times, just like Elisha said. And do you know what happened? My skin became just like new—right before my eyes! I was healed! This time I didn't bother with passing messages around. I went right to Elisha myself to thank him. I told him, "Now I know that there is no God in all the world except in Israel. Please accept a gift from your servant." But Elisha wouldn't take it. He told me that he serves God, and doesn't need a gift for obeying God. I decided I wanted to learn to obey God just like Elisha.

Go for the Godprint

Obedience: "Why should I?" Have you ever said that? Or wanted to say it? We sometimes think there are too many rules to obey. Have you ever thought about what could go wrong if we didn't have rules to keep us safe and healthy? Naaman was glad he decided to obey God. We obey God because we know that he plans what's best for us.

What Digby Dug Up

THE BIBLE SAYS NAAMAN'S SKIN DISEASE WAS LEPROSY. PEOPLE WITH LEPROSY CAN'T FEEL BURNS OR CUTS OR OTHER PAIN IN THE PARTS OF THEIR BODIES WITH THE DISEASE. IT CAN TAKE 10 TO 20 YEARS TO BE CURED.

Herbie's Hideaway

Tell a made-up story. After a few minutes, come to a point where the main character must decide whether or not to obey. For example, "Jenny had to decide: would she stop for the traffic light or would she keep on walking?" Say, "Pass," and let someone else in the family continue the story, deciding if the character will obey or not, and what happens as a result of the decision. Continue the story until the character faces another decision about obedience. Say, "Pass," and have another family member continue the story. Keep the story going until everyone has contributed three or four times. Then talk about:

• **What color do you feel like on the inside when you obey? Why?**
• **Name three good things that happen when we obey God.**

God Talk

Line up the family players at one end of the room.
Anyone who can complete one of these sentences
advances three long steps.
Lord, help me obey when I don't want to _____.
Lord, help me obey when I feel _____.
Lord, help me obey when it's hard to _____.
Lord, help me obey when I would rather _____.
Add starter sentences of your own until everyone gets across the room.
Then share high fives and say, "Way to obey!"

The Case of the Lost Treasure

There was a boy in Judah,
Who at the age of eight
Became a king who followed God—
A king both wise and great!

Josiah was the young king's name;
He reigned for many years.
But his people's evil ways
Brought him grief and tears.

When he'd reigned for eighteen years
(That made him twenty-six)
Josiah said, "The house of God
Is needing to be fixed.

My people have done evil things
And worshiped idols there.
I will bring a stop to that
And order its repair."

The temple was God's special place
For prayer and sacrifice
The king would make it beautiful
No matter what the price.

"Shaphan, Hilkiah, you're in charge.
Begin the work today.
Gather skillful workers
And give them their fair pay.

Get carpenters and masons,
And men who supervise
Let them use the money
In ways they think are wise.

They must get fine materials—
Stone and cedar wood—
And see to it this job's well done.
We've got to make it good!"

As workers dug into the walls
They found a wondrous treasure
An old book of the law was there—
Priceless beyond measure!

It outlined for God's people
The way that they should live
It told of feasts and festivals
And offerings they should give.

Shaphan read, then shook his head
And hurried to the king,
Knowing he held in his hand
A most important thing.

"O King, we found the Book of Law;
I came quick as I could.
It seems to me our fathers
Have not acted as they should."

Josiah listened carefully,
His kingly face grew sad.
He tore his robes and then replied,
"Things are very bad."

"What was written in this book
And mislaid long ago
Are things God wants us to obey—
But we didn't know!"

132

Now go and talk to Huldah
Who is a prophetess.
She'll pray and find out what to do
Then tell us what is best.

Here's what God told Huldah:
"Israel did not obey.
And so I'll send disaster,
But not in this king's day."

Josiah gathered everyone
To listen to him read.
"We'll do what God commands," he said.
And they all agreed.

When the work was finished
The temple stood in beauty.
Then Josiah held a feast
Which was his kingly duty.

People came to Passover
From all across the nation.
Not for years had Israel seen
Such a celebration.

The priests led all the people—
They prayed and sang and praised.
And on God's holy altars,
The sacrifices blazed.

And that's how King Josiah
Made sure his people heard
How he wanted them to live:
According to God's Word!

Go for the Godprint

Responsibility: Josiah accepted responsibility to clean the run-down temple. And once he found the Law, he held himself accountable in his attitude, too. Josiah's responsible action to clean the temple—and his people's hearts!—was a way to show God's holiness. Look at things in your life that you are responsible for. What happens when you forget to feed the cat? Or walk the dog? Being responsible not only means doing the job but doing it with a super attitude.

What Digby Dug Up

Did you know that many ancient books were not books at all? The Book of the Law was written on sheets of woven papyrus stems which were then pressed into a long paper-like roll called a scroll.

Café de Click

Pour some alphabet cereal on a clean table top. Discover God's words for yourself! Spell out: God's Law shows us how to live. After you've finished your "construction project," celebrate like Josiah did in the Bible story. Invite your family and friends and make a delicious party mix to share. Toss the cereal sentence into a large bowl, then take turns adding these ingredients:

1 cup of additional cereal
6 ounces chocolate chips
6 ounces butterscotch chips
6 ounces peanut butter chips
2 handfuls golden raisins
2 cups salted pretzel sticks
2 cups popcorn
nuts (optional)

God Talk

Cleaning a temple takes supplies!
Put clean, damp sponges in a pie pan.
Pass around the pan.
Let family members take turns
telling how they'll live by God's Word,
then sprinkle a little grass seed on the sponges.
Pray around the "seeds of obedience" you've planted.
Everyone is responsible to keep the sponges moist so the seeds will sprout.

GOD'S PEOPLE WERE IN RUIN, WITH FALLEN WALLS AND FALLEN LIVES. OVER THE YEARS THEY TURNED AWAY FROM GOD, THEN HAD TO FACE THE CONSEQUENCES. THE BABYLONIANS CONQUERED THEM, TOOK THEM CAPTIVE AND MARCHED THEM OFF TO A FARAWAY LAND. HOWEVER, GOD PROMISED

EZRA AND NEHEMIAH:
God's Super Heroes

THIS IS EZRA. What made him a superhero for God? Ezra helped the people rebuild their lives on the foundation of God's Word.

✳ LIGHTNING SPEED: Ezra dedicated himself to studying God's Word every day. He soaked up God's Word with lightning speed. Understanding God's Word gave Ezra what he needed to rebuild a nation of wayward people.

✳ EXECUTES ORDERS WITH PRECISION: Ezra obeyed God's Word and showed that he understood it by the way he lived every day. He listened to God and never hesitated to do what God told him. Ezra's success was not because of his own abilities, but because he obeyed God.

✳ X-RAY VISION: Ezra was a teacher who saw right through to the hearts of God's people. He knew what was deep inside them. He taught the people to love God and follow his Word, and so he helped heal the heart of the nation.

✳ HEART OF GOLD: Ezra focused his heart on the pure things of God. He was totally committed to God. He set an example for others to follow.

136

THAT ONE DAY HE WOULD ALLOW THEM TO GO BACK TO THEIR OWN LAND. THE FIRST GROUP OF PEOPLE RELEASED FROM CAPTIVITY RETURNED AND REBUILT THE TEMPLE IN JERUSALEM. LATER, GOD ALLOWED THE REST OF THE PEOPLE TO RETURN. EZRA AND NEHEMIAH GUIDED GOD'S PEOPLE DURING THIS TIME OF REBUILDING.

NEHEMIAH

THIS IS NEHEMIAH. What made him a superhero for God? He helped rebuild the fortress walls around God's city of Jerusalem.

✱ BIONIC KNEES: Nehemiah never did anything unless he spent time on his knees asking God for help. No matter what situation he found himself in, his bionic praying knees got a workout.

✱ LEAPS TALL WALLS IN A SINGLE BOUND: Rebuilding the wall was no easy task. Nehemiah was a cupbearer, not a construction worker. Yet God used Nehemiah's talents to get the job done. He was the one in charge of the huge construction project to rebuild the walls of God's city.

✱ DODGES BULLETS WITH EASE: Troublemakers bothered Nehemiah all the time. They got in his way as much as they could and made it hard for him to finish building the wall. But he never even thought of giving up. He overcame tough challenges and persevered to the very end.

✱ ATTITUDE OF STEEL: Nehemiah didn't let things get to him. He kept up a great attitude through discouraging situations. He focused on God's plan and never gave up.

Ezra and Nehemiah were two superheroes for God. God used them to restore his people and rebuild the wall around the city of Jerusalem. Together they built a nation dedicated to serving God. The people came together to celebrate. Ezra stood on a high wooden platform built especially for the celebration. He read God's Word to the people, so everyone could learn about being a superhero for God. It was the best party in many, many years!

Go for the Godprint

Perseverance: Have you ever felt frustrated because everything seemed to be going wrong? Did you feel like quitting because doing the job was too hard? Ezra and Nehemiah could have given up because of all the problems they faced. But the didn't give up—they relied on God. Through prayer and living out God's Word, they persevered and finished the job.

Before he traveled to Jerusalem to rebuild the walls, Nehemiah was a cupbearer to the king. A cupbearer guarded against anyone poisoning the cup that the king drank from. Nehemiah took the first sip to make sure there was no poison in the cup. The life of the king was in the hands of Nehemiah. Nehemiah was also a high-ranking, trusted advisor to the king.

Mo's Fab Lab

GET LIST:
TWO TRAYS OF ICE CUBES
SALT

Build a wall of ice! This will take perseverance, but it's tons of fun. You will need two trays of small ice cubes, salt and paper towels. On a table top, build a wall by stacking the ice cubes and sprinkling lots of salt all over the cubes. Can you get the structure to stand up like a wall? What happened to the ice when you put the salt on it? Talk about:

• *How did you feel when you were building the wall and ran into problems?*

• *How did you feel when you got the job done?*

God Talk
Be a superhero for God!
Fill in the blanks.
Dear God, if I were a superhero for you, I would…
Listen to you as if I had super sonic _____.
Tell others about you by _____.
Read and soak up the Bible like a huge _____.
I would pray to you on my _____.
Love you with my heart of solid _____.

Just-in-Time Courage

Esther

King Xerxes

Haman

Mordecai

 was a beautiful young Jewish woman. The king, , chose to be his queen, put a royal crown on her head, threw a big party and even had a holiday in her honor. was a mean man who worked for . He didn't like God's people, the Jews, and wanted to kill them all. was sneaky and got to sign a law saying that on a certain date all the Jews would be killed. didn't know that was a Jew, and didn't know that had signed this law.

 had a cousin named . When found out that had signed that law, he tore his clothes put ashes on his head to show how sad he was and cried loudly. Other Jews did the same thing. saw how sad the people were and sent a messenger to to find out what was going on.

sent a message to back to . He told her what had done.

 reminded that she would be killed too. He wanted her to go to and ask him to change the law.

Going to talk to 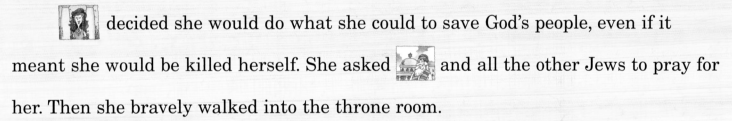 would be risky for . The law said no one was allowed to go in and see the king without an invitation. hadn't sent for for 30 days. If she dared to walk into his room, he could have her killed.

 decided she would do what she could to save God's people, even if it meant she would be killed herself. She asked and all the other Jews to pray for her. Then she bravely walked into the throne room.

was glad to see her and welcomed her. Whew! Then asked and to join her for a special dinner. At that special dinner asked , "What do you want? I will give you whatever you want, even up to half of the kingdom."

 said, "If you are pleased with me, let me live. And let my people live too. We are going to be killed."

asked, "Who is going to kill you? Who would dare to do this?"

 pointed to and said, "He is the enemy of me and my people."

was so angry that he got up and left the room. was afraid and begged to save him from the king. But when came back, he ordered to be killed for what he had done.

The law had signed couldn't be changed, so asked about writing a new law. agreed. He signed a new law that said the Jews could protect themselves from anyone who tried to kill them. took a big risk, but found a way to save her people!

142

Go for the Godprint

Resourcefulness: Being resourceful means doing the best you can with what you have. Esther didn't have the power to save the Jews by herself, so she used the resources she did have instead. These included her position as queen, her intelligence, and her faith in God. What resources do you have to help you solve problems?

What Digby Dug Up

ESTHER ALSO HAD A HEBREW NAME: HADASSAH. "ESTHER" WAS HER PERSIAN NAME. IT MEANT "STAR," PERHAPS BECAUSE SHE WAS BEAUTIFUL.

PJ's Good to Go

Esther used the abilities God gave her to solve a big problem. Here is a list of problems that happen around us every day. Brainstorm together about resources you and your family have that could help solve these problems:

• **People in your town who can't afford to buy the medicine they need.**

• Children in other countries don't have food, homes, or parents.

• **Places near your home such as schools, churches, nursing homes, and food banks, that need volunteers.**

• Children in your state who don't have any toys.

• Homeless shelters that need food and other supplies.

• **Older people who need help with simple chores.**

After you've thought of ways you can use what God has given you, choose just one of your solutions and put it into action!

God Talk
Trace your hands onto pieces of paper.
On each finger of each hand
write one way God can use you.
Then pray, offering these hands of service
and resourcefulness to God.

Never Give Up!

"Things are so good, in fact they seem great! I have a big family and quite an estate!"

"This is so bad, I hope it won't get worse, Thank you for telling me. Now go get a nurse!"

Job was a wealthy man. He had seven sons, three daughters, 7,000 sheep, 3,000 camels, 500 teams of oxen, 500 donkeys and many servants.

Job was also an honest man who honored God. Job even asked God to forgive the sins of his children, just in case they'd done anything wrong.

One day all the angels came before God. Satan was with them.

"Where have you been?" God asked.

"I've been wandering around the earth," Satan answered.

"While you were wandering around," God said, "Did you notice Job? There isn't anyone else on the earth like him. He's honest, he honors me and doesn't get into trouble."

Satan had noticed Job, and told God what he thought. "Job honors you for a good reason. You've made his life good. If you destroy everything he has, then Job will think you don't love him. He'll curse you instead of honoring you."

God agreed. Satan got busy making life hard for Job.

Soon after that, a messenger rushed into Job's home. "Your oxen were plowing," he said, "and the donkeys were nearby eating grass. Suddenly the Sabeans attacked us! They stole all the oxen and donkeys, then they killed all the servants who were around. I'm the

"Things are so bad and they're getting much worse! This sad situation is getting perverse!"

"Things are so bad and they're getting much worse! Each of you has such sad news to disperse!"

only one who escaped!"

Another messenger rushed in. He gasped, "A lightning storm hit out in the fields. It burned up all your sheep and the servants taking care of them. I'm the only one who escaped!"

Just at that moment a third messenger arrived. "The Chaldeans sent three groups of attackers!" he cried. "They stole all the camels and killed the servants. I'm the only one who escaped!"

"Things are quite bad and they're getting much worse! I'm so full of sadness. Now please call for a hearse."

At that moment another messenger burst through the door. "Your sons and daughters were all over at your oldest son's house for dinner," he said, gulping for air.

"Things are quite bad and they're getting much worse, But God still loves me and his name I'll not curse."

"Suddenly the wind started blowing like never before and the house collapsed! Everyone inside was killed. I'm the only one who escaped."

Job tore his robe and shaved his head to show how sad he was. He bowed down to the ground and worshiped God. Job didn't blame God for what had happened. Then Satan put itchy, painful sores all over Job's body. Job used a broken piece of pot to scrape the sores. His wife was angry. She said, "Curse God and die!"

Job's friends tried to give Job advice. But Job knew that God could give both

"Things are quite bad and they're getting much worse. I think that it's time now for us to converse."

good things and bad things. So he never said anything bad about God and he didn't sin. Instead, he talked to God.

Finally Satan gave up. He knew Job wasn't going to sin. Then God gave Job twice as much as he'd had before. His family and friends came over to celebrate. The rest of Job's life was better than ever. He had more sheep, camels, oxen and donkeys than before, and he had seven more sons and three more daughters.

"Things are so good, in fact they seem great! God's love is forever— there is no debate!"

Go for the Godprint

Hope: When one bad thing after another happened, Job could have thought that God had given up on him. But he had hope because he knew that God was in control, not Satan. God can make good things happen from bad things. Can you think of a time when something bad turned into something good?

What Digby Dug Up

AT THE TIME OF JOB, FLOCKS OF SHEEP, GOATS, CAMELS AND DONKEYS WERE EVEN MORE IMPORTANT THAN GOLD AND SILVER. THE NUMBER OF ANIMALS A PERSON OWNED SHOWED HOW RICH THE PERSON WAS.

Café de Click

Choose a recipe for cookies or brownies that you can make together. As you work in the kitchen, take a small taste of each ingredient before it's mixed in (except for the raw eggs). Which ones taste good and which ones taste bad? Then put the dough or batter into the hot oven. What will happen when all these things, both good and bad, are mixed together and baked? Of course the answer is "Something good to eat!"

While you enjoy eating your treat together, talk about how good and bad things in life can work together. For example, moving to a new house might seem bad at first, but it could lead to making a new friend or having your own room. Or, eating lots of candy might seem good, but it can lead to cavities or poor health. How can knowing that God loves us in both good and bad times give us a hopeful attitude?

God Talk

Build a tower of hope with index cards.
On each card write how God brought good
from something bad that happened.
Then tape the cards together to form a tower.
Keep your tower in a special place,
and add to it each time you see God bring good from a bad situation.

The Shepherd's Psalm • *Psalm 23*

What makes a good poem? Fancy words? Rhyming words? Rhythm?

The Bible is full of wonderful poetry. In fact, the Book of Psalms contains 150 poems. One of the most famous is Psalm 23. It was written by David—king of Israel, war hero, musician and shepherd. The greatest thing about David is how much he loved God. He captured that love in words that we can read to express our own thoughts and prayers to God centuries and centuries later.

Use this Psalm of David to worship God with your family. It tells about the wonderful trust we can put in our shepherd-king, Jesus Christ. Decide who will read the lines of the Psalm and who will read the responses.

The Lord is my shepherd, I shall not be in want.
God takes care of me and provides everything I need.

He makes me lie down in green pastures,
God takes care of me and gives me rest when I'm tired.

He leads me beside quiet waters, he restores my soul.
God takes care of me and quiets my soul when I'm worried and frazzled.

He guides me in paths of righteousness for his name's sake.
God takes care of me and helps me make good choices that honor him.

Even though I walk through the valley of the shadow of death,
God takes care of me when I'm in scary places.

I will fear no evil, for you are with me;
God takes care of me and stays close beside me.

your rod and your staff, they comfort me.
God takes care of me and helps me through difficult places in life.

You prepare a table before me in the presence of my enemies.
God takes care of me even when people are against me.

You anoint my head with oil; my cup overflows.
God takes care of me and chooses me to be his special child.

Surely goodness and love will follow me all the days of my life,
God takes care of me every Monday, Tuesday, Wednesday, Thursday, Friday, Saturday and Sunday!

And I will dwell in the house of the LORD forever.
God takes care of me now on earth and forever in heaven.

Go for the Godprint

Thankfulness: The Lord gives us what we need. He is like a shepherd taking care of great big field full of sheep. Shepherds make sure their sheep have plenty of grass and a good supply of clean water. They protect their sheep from predators and thieves. Sheep are pretty helpless without their shepherd. Talk to your shepherd every day, especially when you feel alone. Simply say, "Thank you, Lord, for watching over me and for giving me everything I need. Amen!"

What Digby Dug Up
David, who wrote this psalm, once killed a lion who was threatening his sheep. This poet knew exactly what he was writing about. David was a fine musician. He probably played his lute and sang to sheep at night to calm them.

Izzy's Art Cart

GET LIST:
TISSUE PAPER
CLEAR ADHESIVE SHELF PAPER

Think of what you are thankful for in your life. Make a list. Now choose one and cling to it! Use a small plate to trace two circles on clear adhesive shelf paper. Cut out the circles. Tear colored tissue paper into one-inch pieces. Peel the backing off the shelf paper and lay it out sticky side up. Stick on your tissue scraps in whatever design you like. Leave some room around the edge. Choose one thing you are thankful for and print it on a small strip of paper. Place this in the center of your window cling. Peel and then press the second piece of shelf paper over the colored tissue. Make sure both sticky sides are pressed against each other. Trim to a shape you like. Wet a window with a small amount of water and press your window cling into place.

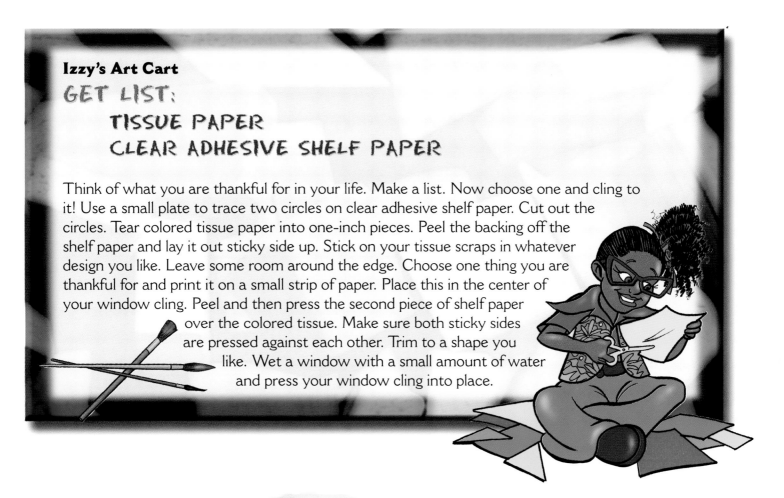

God Talk
Open up a brown paper grocery bag.
On the blank side draw an outline
of a pet animal you have in your home.
Take turns drawing on the outline things
each family member does to care for your pet.
Thank God for taking care of you in similar ways.
End by saying together: "Because the Lord is my shepherd, I have everything I need!"

Eli and Samuel are cousins as well as best friends. They're both eleven. Together since birth, both boys attended the "house of study" until Samuel moved away with his family a year ago. The cousins now see each other only at feast times.

April 26, 28 A.D.

Dear Eli,

Hi, cuz! Remember when we saw each other at Passover last year and I promised to write you? I'm finally doing it!

God made a promise, too—to King David. Remember how we learned about King David when we studied together with the rabbi? When David was just a young boy tending his father's sheep, God promised David that he would be a mighty king, mightier than any other king in the world! And not only that, God promised that David's children and their children would be kings, too. Imagine! David's descendants would rule forever. Who could promise such a thing but God?

Remember, Eli, when you and I first went to school in the synagogue? We memorized so many of King David's psalms. We sat at our teacher's feet so we wouldn't miss a single word. "Amazing" is what you said! David was a king and a warrior, but he wrote such wonderful songs to God. We repeated our favorite, Psalm 23, many times and then took turns writing the words on our slates. The teacher even sprinkled honey on the words so that God's words would always be sweet on our tongues.

And God promised David all the power he needed to accomplish God's will. What a wonderful thing—don't you think?—to be filled with the Spirit of God and to feel his power! But even though God promised David good things, our people didn't always obey God's commandments. There were bad kings who divided our country and even worshiped other gods. But do you know what, Eli? Even though we are weak and sinful, God promises never to break faith with us. What he promises, he will deliver. He helps us just like a loving father. He picks us up when we do wrong, dusts us off and sends us on our way again.

Eli, I have saved the best part of my story for last. There's a new king from David's family. His name is Jesus. And I will see him this very hour. He's not a king like Herod or any other king who ever lived. He's the Son of God. He tells us how much God loves us. He tells us not to worry about things—that God will bless us and take care of us. Talk about kingly promises! No one has ever spoken like this before.

Mother and I are just about ready to leave for the Temple to hear him again. Maybe Jesus will heal someone today. You should see him, Eli. I can't wait 'til you come to Jerusalem again.

When I'm near Jesus, I feel close to God—like I'm part of a kingdom even greater than King David had. In fact, I'm sure Jesus is the one King David was writing about. And I believe that Jesus will rule forever, just like the psalm said.

Well, I need to go before the crowd gathers. Write me soon.

Your friend and cousin,

Samuel

Go for the Godprint

Integrity: Standing firm in what you believe is a good quality. But what do you do when the people you care about keep making poor choices and act badly—like God's people did? You keep on keeping on! God keeps his promise to remain faithful to us no matter what. And his promise is true for today, tomorrow and for all time. We live as God's children when we make choices that please him.

What Digby Dug Up

The psalms are songs and prayers in which people express their honest and true feelings to God. In the psalms believers cry and sing, confess and talk to God much like we do today.

Izzy's Art Cart

GET LIST:
 EMPTY 15-OZ VEGETABLE OR FRUIT CAN
 WATER
 HAMMER
 NAIL
 VOTIVE CANDLE

Make a little candle lantern to remind you that you are a child of the king and that God is with you always.

Clean an empty vegetable or fruit can and peel off the label. Fill the can with water and freeze. Place the ice-filled can on a padded surface. Mark a design—like a crown or a star—with dots and a permanent marker on the can. Ask Mom or Dad to hold the can as you punch through the dots with a hammer and nail. Make the holes at least 1/2 inch apart. When your design is finished, run warm water over the can so the ice block melts and falls out. Dry the can and place a votive candle inside. Look at the beautiful pattern the light creates!

Caution: Lanterns may get hot when the candles are lit.

God Talk

Have each family member make a little candle lantern.
In the evening, when everyone is settling in,
gather everyone and place your lanterns on a shiny metal tray.
Take turns lighting candles as each person prays.
Thank God for keeping his word and for allowing you and your family
to be part of his mighty and wonderful kingdom.

ISAIAH'S MESSAGE

My name is Isaiah. Do you know what that means? It means, "The Lord saves." And that was exactly the message God gave me.

I was God's prophet during the reigns of King Jotham, King Ahaz and King Hezekiah in Judah. God called me to be a prophet the same year King Uzziah died. I said what God told me to say, but not everyone liked to hear it.

King Ahaz was evil. He would not listen to God's message. While he was king, God's people started worshiping idols. I watched in sorrow as the people of Judah turned away from the one true God. I wondered how God would save his people. But I always believed "The Lord saves." Then God gave me a special message of hope. You can read it in Isaiah chapter 7, verse 14.

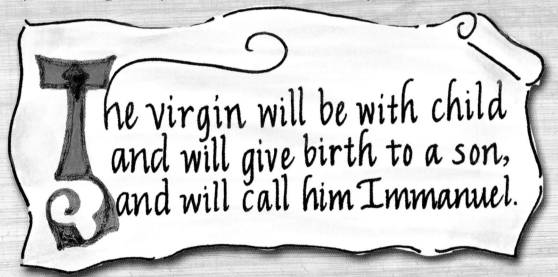

The virgin will be with child and will give birth to a son, and will call him Immanuel.

Immanuel means "God with us."

Hundreds of years passed before this came true. But it did, when Jesus was born. God was with his people, in the flesh, living right along with them!

God told me about the birth of Jesus more than once. I wrote about it again in Isaiah chapter 9, verses 6 and 7.

For unto us a child is born, to us a son is given, and the government will be on his shoulders. And he will be called Wonderful Counselor, Mighty God, Everlasting Father, Prince of Peace. Of the increase of his government and peace there will be no end. He will reign on David's throne and over his kingdom from that time on and forever. The zeal of the Lord Almighty will accomplish this.

When God decides to do something, he really does it. That's what "zeal" means. I had no doubt these words would come true. And they did! Jesus was no ordinary baby. He changed the world!

God gave me yet another message about the coming Savior. I wrote it in chapter 11, verses 1 through 9. God told me that the Savior would come from the family of Jesse. The Spirit of the Lord would rest on him. He would be wise and understanding. He would make wise plans and carry them out. He would have respect for the Lord. This branch of Jesse would be fair and do what's right. God said that the earth would be full of the knowledge of the Lord the way the oceans are full of water.

Not all of this has happened yet. But I know it will someday. God made a way for people to know him through his Son, Jesus Christ. He is Immanuel, God with us. When his heavenly kingdom finally comes, everything God promised will come true.

We can trust God to do what he said he would. God can do anything. He promised that he would send a Savior for us—and he did! He's promised that our Savior's kingdom will be full of righteousness, peace and justice. And it will be. It's not a what-if kind of hope. It's a sure thing!

Go for the Godprint

Hope: Can good things happen from bad things? Absolutely! God can bring good from anything. Believing that God is in control of what happens is what true hope is all about. God sent Jesus into the world because he cares about what happens to us. Can you think of some ways that the world is better because Jesus came?

What Digby Dug Up

God used many people to be his spokespersons. You can read about these prophets and what God told them to say in the Old Testament books named after them. They are: Joel, Obadiah, Amos, Hosea, Isaiah, Micah, Nahum, Zephaniah, Jeremiah, Habakkuk, Daniel, Ezekiel, Haggai and Malachi.

Izzy's Art Cart

GET LIST:
    ONE APPLE PER PERSON
    APPLE PEELER
    SMALL SHARP KNIFE

When you think of prophets in the Bible, you might picture older men who were wise. You can make your own prophet with an apple. Carefully take the peel off the entire apple. Then carve features into your apple—create ears, eyes, a nose and a mouth. Then put your apple up on shelf or where it can be in the sunshine. In a few weeks, your apple will be dried. Your prophet will look very old and wise! Let it remind you that God planned for your salvation long, long ago!

God Talk

We can trust God that he sent a Savior for us—Jesus.
What are some other things you can trust God for or in?
After a brief discussion, pray together.
Thank God for all the things you can trust him for.
Also pray that he will help your trust in him grow even stronger

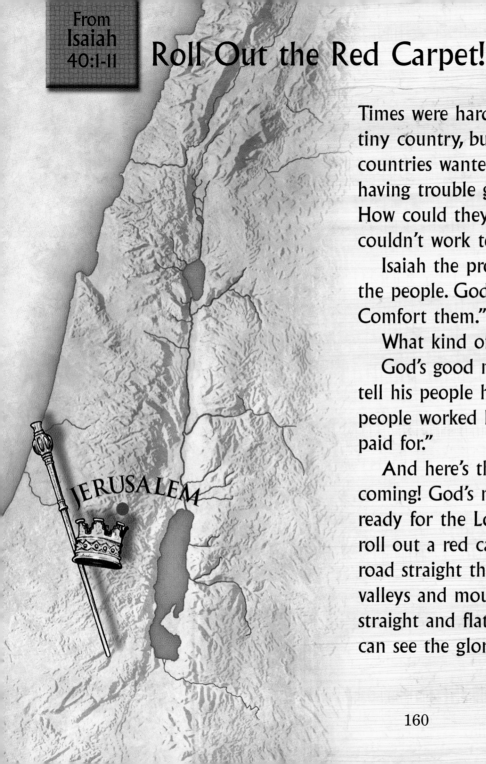

Roll Out the Red Carpet!

Times were hard for God's people. Israel was a tiny country, but they had land that the big countries wanted. And people in Israel were having trouble getting along with each other. How could they fight off the enemy if they couldn't work together?

Isaiah the prophet gave God's good news to the people. God said, "Comfort my people. Comfort them."

What kind of news comforts you?

God's good news was full of tender words to tell his people he cared for them. He knew the people worked hard. He said, "Their sin has been paid for."

And here's the best news of all: The Lord is coming! God's message told the people to get ready for the Lord. What we might do today is roll out a red carpet! Isaiah told them to make a road straight through the desert. No more valleys and mountains. The Lord's road should be straight and flat and smooth. That way everyone can see the glory of the Lord when he comes.

JERUSALEM

The people thought that Isaiah meant God would give them their land back and make them a powerful nation. But Isaiah was talking about the kind of good news that makes people free on the inside, not just the outside.

God's good news lasts forever. When a hot, fierce wind blows over a field of flowers, the flowers wilt and the grass dries up. The words that people say blow away like the wind—in one ear and out the other. But what God says lasts forever. God's words never dry up. The wind can't blow down God's plans.

Tell God's good news!
Tell it to all the people.
Tell it from the high mountain.
Tell it in the cities.
Tell the people everywhere.
Don't be afraid to shout it out.
What's the good news? The king is coming, and the king is God! God is coming with power to set his people free. He will win any battle. Nothing is too hard for God.

But God the king is also a tender shepherd who takes cares of the sheep he loves. The tender shepherd picks up the littlest sheep and carries it in his arms, close to his heart.

God is coming to rule the earth. He cheers up his people with joy that sets them free on the inside. God's joy lasts forever.

Go for the Godprint

Community: When God's people hear his good news, they worship him and look for ways to serve the king together. God's people work together because they're on the same team—God's team. Can you think of a way to serve God the king with other people?

What Digby Dug Up:

IN BIBLE TIMES, THE KING SENT AN ANNOUNCER DOWN THE ROAD AHEAD OF HIM. THE ANNOUNCER TOLD EVERYONE THE KING WAS COMING. THEN THE PEOPLE COULD GET READY TO GREET THE KING.

Wally's Walkabout

Imagine that the king is coming to your house! What can you do to be ready? Invite a friend or another family to celebrate and welcome the king. Pick up clutter and get everything shiny clean. Rearrange furniture to make a straight, flat path for the king to walk. Lay towels or blankets end to end to make a royal path. At the end of the path, enjoy a feast fit for a king. Plan a special snack or a meal with all your favorite foods. Use index cards or folded paper to make place cards with special messages like, "Spread the joy of Jesus," and "The King is coming for you!" Decorate a special chair for Jesus. Tell all the ways Jesus the King makes a difference in your life.

God Talk

Go around the house looking for ways
that people communicate with each other,
such as a telephone, mail box or newspaper.
Talk about how you could use each item to
spread the joy of God's comfort to other people.
Then thank God for the comfort he gives you.

Jumpin' Jeremiah

To play *Jumpin' Jeremiah*, you'll need a Bible, buttons, beads or other markers and a coin. To move around the board, flip the coin. If it's heads, move one space. If it's tails, move two spaces. Let the youngest player go first. Play until everyone reaches the new scroll.

START

Jeremiah was a prophet. God gave him messages to give to the people. One day God told Jeremiah: "Take a scroll and write on it all the words I have spoken to you concerning Israel and Judah. Perhaps when the people hear about the disasters that will come, they'll turn away from their sin and I will forgive them."

The servant couldn't find Jeremiah and Baruch. God kept them safely hidden. And even though the king had burned the scroll, God helped Jeremiah and Baruch write a new one. Because of Jeremiah's commitment to the Lord, God's Word survived!

Read Jeremiah 36:20–26

You have to clean the ashes out of the king's fireplace. Lose one turn.

Read Jeremiah 36:1–3.

FINISH!

Read Jeremiah 36:27–32

Say "Jehoiakim, son of Josiah, king of Judah" 5 times fast.

Read Psalm 119:9–11. Tell one way you'll obey God's Word this week.

Go visit Jeremiah in "jail" (under the table). Lose one turn.

Jeremiah told God's words to Baruch (bah-RUKE). Baruch was a scribe. It was his job to write things down. He wrote God's words on a scroll. Since the wicked king had put Jeremiah in prison, he couldn't go to the temple to read the scroll to the people. Jeremiah sent Baruch to read the scroll in his place.

Baruch knocks over the ink. Go back to the beginning.

Read Jeremiah 36:4–7.

Baruch finishes the scroll. Move ahead to Picture 3.

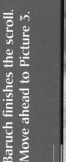

Read Psalm 32:7. Tell about a time God protected you from trouble.

You helped Jeremiah find a hiding place. Move forward one space.

Read Jeremiah 36:16–19.

When the king heard about the scroll, he asked his servant to bring it to the palace and read it to him. As the servant read the scroll, the king cut it into pieces and burned it in the fire. The king's officials begged him not to burn the scroll, but the king wouldn't listen. He ordered another servant to go arrest Jeremiah and Baruch.

The king's officials told Baruch, "We must report all these words to the king. You and Jeremiah, go and hide. Don't tell anyone where you are."

Read your favorite Bible verse. Take another turn if you can say it from memory.

Read Jeremiah 36:11–15

Baruch did everything Jeremiah told him to do. He went to the temple and read the scroll. The people listened.

Read Jeremiah 36:8–10.

Name another Bible book (not Jeremiah) that's named after a prophet.

You feel a little weak from fasting. Skip a turn to rest.

When the king's officials heard Baruch read the scroll, they couldn't believe their ears. They asked Baruch to come read it again. Then they asked Baruch, "Did Jeremiah dictate these words to you?" "Yes," Baruch answered, "he did."

Jumpin' Jeremiah wasn't playing a game. His job was not a fun one. It got him in a lot of trouble. But it was the job God gave him to do. Jeremiah spoke God's word for over 40 years. God's people were having hard times. Jeremiah wanted them to jump right back into listening to what God wanted them to do. He let them know that no matter what happened, God would never stop caring about them.

Go for the Godprint

Commitment: Many of the kings in Jeremiah's time chose to worship other gods. They didn't like it when Jeremiah read God's word to the people. But Jeremiah was committed to sharing God's word, even when it wasn't popular. Thanks to brave prophets like Jeremiah, we have a written record of God's word in the Bible. How is the Bible your guidebook?

What Digby Dug Up

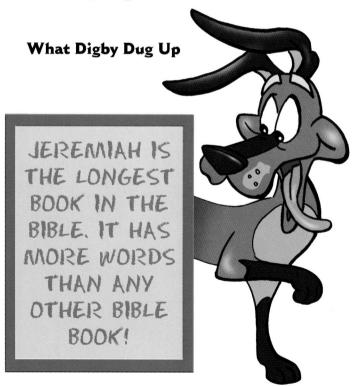

JEREMIAH IS THE LONGEST BOOK IN THE BIBLE. IT HAS MORE WORDS THAN ANY OTHER BIBLE BOOK!

Jake's Mirth Quake

GET LIST:
INDEX CARDS, PENCILS,
SHEET OR BLANKET

Have each family member write a favorite Bible verse on an index card. Lay one of the verses in the center of a sheet or blanket on the floor. Have one family member lie on each end of the sheet or blanket. When you say, "go," have the two players create a human scroll by holding the edges of the sheet or blanket and rolling toward the verse card in the center. The family member who gets to the verse first gets to read it (after you've unrolled the human scroll!). Repeat until you've read all the verses.

God Talk
In Psalm 119:103,
the Bible says that God's Word is sweeter than honey.
Fill a squeeze bottle with honey and "write"
your favorite Bible verse on a tortilla.
Before you eat, ask God to hide his Word in your heart as well as your stomach.
Roll up the tortilla like a scroll, then gobble up God's Word!

167

Four Wise Men

Ashpenaz was in a pickle. King Nebuchadnezzar of Babylon had captured the Israelites. Now he wanted some of them to work for him. Ashpenaz was in charge of everyone who worked in the king's palace, so he had to find the four best men. Ashpenaz wasn't sure about this. The Israelites had strange laws and a strange God. But the king ordered it, so Ashpenaz did it.

Ashpenaz chose Daniel, Shadrach, Meshach and Abednego. King Nebuchadnezzar told Ashpenaz, "Teach these men our language and way of life. Give them the best food from my own kitchen. I want them to be strong and smart like me!" Ashpenaz wasn't sure about this. Babylonian food was very different from food in Israel. But the king ordered it, so Ashpenaz did it.

He told the cooks to make the very best! He brought the four wise men:

Juicy steaks and the very best wine
Fit for a king—the food was so fine.

Daniel, Shadrach, Meshach and Abednego looked at the food. Daniel, Shadrach, Meshach and Abednego sniffed the food. Then Daniel, Shadrach, Meshach and Abednego said, "I'm sorry. We can't eat this food."

Ashpenaz jumped. Ashpenaz gaped. This was the best food the cooks could make. Ashpenaz said, "Don't you like our food?"

Daniel, Shadrach, Meshach and Abednego said, "God has given us special laws about the food we eat. We won't disobey him."

Well, thought Ashpenaz, *I will bring them different food.* He told the cooks to prepare the best food in Babylon. He brought the four wise men:

Roasted pork just swimming in gravy.
It was the best, and I don't mean maybe!

Daniel, Shadrach, Meshach and Abednego looked at the food. Daniel, Shadrach, Meshach and Abednego sniffed the food. Then Daniel, Shadrach, Meshach and Abednego said, "I'm sorry. We can't eat this food."

Ashpenaz turned. Ashpenaz blinked. He had never seen such great food. Ashpenaz said, "What's wrong with our food?"

Daniel, Shadrach, Meshach and Abednego said, "We won't disobey God."

Well, thought Ashpenaz, I will just have to try harder. He went to the cooks and told them to prepare a feast fit for a king. He brought the four wise men:

Pork chops simmered in tasty stew.
Nothing but the very best would do.

There, thought Ashpenaz, *they will love that!* Daniel, Shadrach, Meshach and Abednego looked at the food. Daniel, Shadrach, Meshach and Abednego sniffed the food. Then Daniel Shadrach, Meshach and Abednego said, "I'm sorry. We can't eat this food."

Ashpenaz flipped. Ashpenaz fumed. No one had ever seen food this good. Ashpenaz hollered, "What's wrong now?"

Daniel, Shadrach, Meshach and Abednego said, "We won't disobey God."

Ashpenaz cried, "What food *will* you eat?"

Daniel said, "Bring us vegetables and water. We will eat those."

Ashpenaz stared. Ashpenaz stuttered. "That's all? Just vegetables and water? But what if you get weak and sick? The king will be angry with me."

But Daniel said, "Why don't we try it for ten days? Then compare us to the other men who eat the king's food. We'll see who looks better."

That sounded fair to Ashpenaz. "All right," he said, "what should I bring you?"

Daniel, Shadrach, Meshach and Abednego grinned. They said, "Bring us

Carrots and zucchini, lettuce and tomatoes,
Fresh, green spinach with peppers and
potatoes."

So that's what Ashpenaz did. He brought the four wise men all the vegetables they could eat. Daniel, Shadrach, Meshach and Abednego looked at the food. Daniel, Shadrach, Meshach and Abednego sniffed the food. Then Daniel, Shadrach, Meshach and Abednego ate the food.

Ashpenaz smiled. Ashpenaz laughed. After ten days, Ashpenaz looked at Daniel, Shadrach, Meshach and Abednego, and he said, "You look better than any of the men in the king's palace!"

Ashpenaz took the four friends to King Nebuchadnezzar. The king talked to them for a long time and asked them hard questions. Then King Nebuchadnezzar said, "These men are wiser than any man in my kingdom. I want them to be in charge of everything important." Ashpenaz wasn't sure about this. But the king ordered it, so Ashpenaz did it.

Daniel, Shadrach, Meshach and Abednego were put in charge of everything important. And no one in Babylon was as healthy or as wise as the four friends who made wise choices.

Go for the Godprint

Discernment: Have you ever had trouble making the right choice, especially when your friends tell you to do something that you know isn't right? Making the right choice takes a lot of wisdom. The Bible says God will give us wisdom whenever we need it—no matter what the problem is! What a deal! Next time you have a problem, you know who to ask.

What Digby Dug Up
God gave the Israelites special laws about what they could eat and drink. That may seem strange to us today. But God wanted to make sure his people were different from the other people around them who believed in other gods. Those rules were God's way of telling them, "You are my special people."

"YOU ARE MY SPECIAL PEOPLE."

Café de Click

Read Leviticus 11:1-31 to find the rules Daniel and his friends followed. Some animals were all right to eat and some were not. The Israelites ate beef, chicken and fish. But not pork, ham and shellfish. The Israelites could even eat grasshoppers if they wanted to! But other bugs were not on the menu. Here are some of the animals God talked about:

Okay: beef, chicken, white fish, lamb, grasshopper, trout, quail, duck

No Way: pork, vulture, shrimp, crab, beetle, lobster, raven, eagle

Go into your kitchen and see if you can find foods Daniel and his friends would eat. Remember, any fruits and vegetables are okay to eat. Here are some examples: Roast lamb, fish, carrots, spinach, apples, flatbread, olives, with figs and dates for dessert. While you eat, talk about:

• **Tell about a time when it was hard to choose God's way.**

• **What helped you be faithful to God when you made that choice?**

God Talk

Take turns reading the light and dark print:
God, you give us wisdom
to choose the right thing to do.
Help us when we need wisdom from you.
When I am at school or at my job,
I will choose God's way.
When I am playing with my friends,
I will choose God's way.
When I am far away from home,
I will choose God's way.
When I am all by myself,
I will choose God's way.
All the time, every day,
I will choose God's way.

From Daniel 3

Three Guys Who Stuck Out

Nebuchadnezzar. Now that's a hard name to say. Can you say it? We can just call him Neb.

Neb was a proud guy. He was king of one of the most powerful nations in the world—Babylon. Babylon took over Israel and captured God's people.

Neb was proud of that. And he was proud of his own gods. So he built an enormous gold statue to honor his gods. If 12,000 kids all piled together, the pile might be as big as that statue. That's a lot of kids. That's a lot of gold statue.

Neb wanted to show off his statue. So he called all his satraps, prefects, governors, advisers, treasurers, judges, magistrates and provincial officials together. Now those words are long to say. We can just call them the referees. They were the guys who helped the king run the country and make sure everyone followed the rules.

When all the referees were there, the king made an announcement. The people were supposed to listen for the sound of the horn, flute, zither, lyre, harp and pipes. That's a lot of sounds to say. We can just call them the band. When the band played, all the people were supposed to bow down and worship the statue Neb made.

The band played, and the people bowed. But not everyone did. The referees noticed three guys sticking out of the crowd. When the band played, they ignored it. They didn't bow. They didn't worship the statue. Shadrach, Meshach and Abednego were their names. Those are interesting names to say. So we'll just call them by their names. They didn't believe that statue was a god, even if it was made out of gold. They believed in the true God.

Now the referees were afraid to disobey Neb. And they were jealous that Shadrach, Meshach and Abednego were brave enough to do what they thought was right. So when the band played again and Shadrach, Meshach and Abednego didn't bow, the referees tattled on them to Neb.

That made Neb mad! He called for the three guys who stuck out. "Is it true," he shouted, "that you do not serve my gods? When the band plays, you'd better bow or I'll throw you in a blazing furnace!"

Shadrach, Meshach and Abednego said, "Even if you throw us in a furnace, God will save us. And even if he doesn't, we still won't serve your gods."

The band played again. Shadrach, Meshach and Abednego stood up straight and tall while everyone else bowed to the statue. Neb was furious. He told the referees to heat the furnace hotter than it had ever been before. Then Neb ordered the referees to throw Shadrach, Meshach and Abednego into the furnace. So the referees tied up the three guys and threw them in, clothes and all. Neb sat back to watch them burn!

Suddenly he leaped to his feet. "Weren't there three men we tied up and threw into the fire?"

Of course there were three. Neb knew that. But he saw four! And they weren't tied up, either. They were walking around in the flames like they were out for a nice afternoon stroll.

Neb went to the edge of the furnace. "Shadrach, Meshach and Abednego, servants of the Most High God, come out!"

So they came out. Wouldn't you? All the referees tried to get close enough to see them. They weren't burned. Not even scorched. Not even a little bit hot. They didn't even smell like they'd been near a fire. And there were only three. An angel had come to save them, and now the angel was gone. Neb was amazed. Wouldn't you be?

Neb changed his attitude. He saw that Shadrach, Meshach and Abednego trusted God and God saved them. He gave a new command to the referees and all the people. No one was allowed to say anything bad about the magnificent God of Shadrach, Meshach and Abednego.

Go for the Godprint

Wonder: How do you feel when you see something amazing? Maybe your eyes get big. Maybe you can't think of words to describe what you see. That's probably how King Nebuchadnezzar felt when God saved Shadrach, Meshach and Abednego. God still helps people in amazing ways—including you!

What Digby Dug Up

The furnace in this story might have been a giant oven used to make mud bricks for building projects. King Nebuchadnezzar might have talked to Shadrach, Meshach and Abednego through an opening in one side.

Izzy's Art Cart

GET LIST: CORNSTARCH, WATER, COLD CREAM, FOOD COLORING, SPOONS, PAINTBRUSHES

Make your own face and body paint. For each color you want, mix 1 teaspoon cornstarch, 1/2 teaspoon water, 1/2 teaspoon cold cream and 2 drops of food coloring. Choose fiery colors. Mix them in muffin tins or small bowls. Use the paintbrushes to paint fiery flames on each other and imagine what it was like to be in the middle of the fiery furnace but not get burned. Be careful not to eat the paint. Before you clean up with soap and water, talk about:

• **Have the oldest person in the family share about a time God helped in time of danger.**

• **What does it feel like to be afraid? How does it feel when you get the help you need?**

God Talk
Take turns thanking God
for helping you in amazing ways.
After each way that someone tells about,
say together "Wow!" or "Whoa!" or "Yeah, God!"

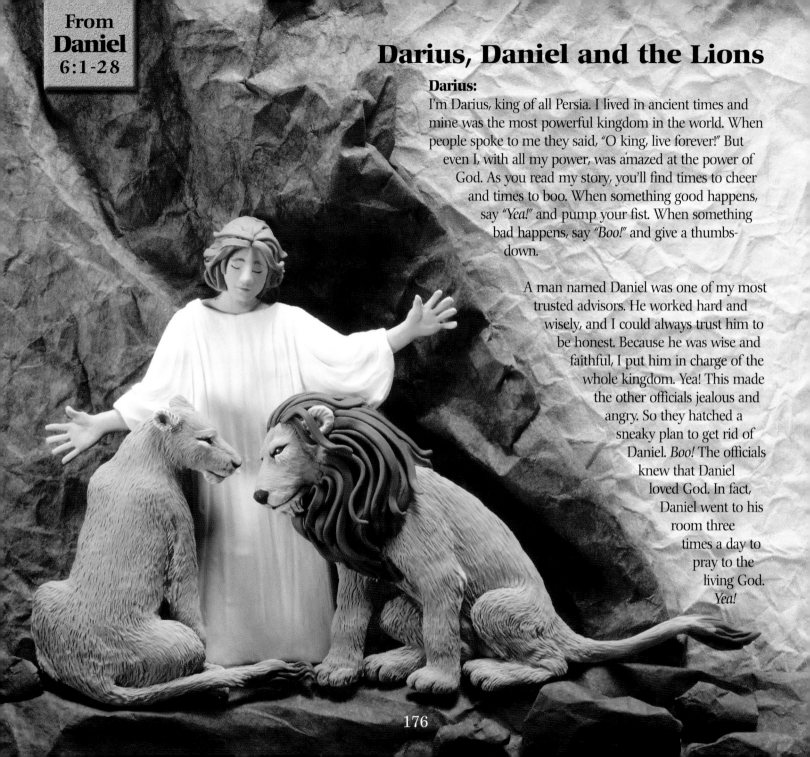

Darius, Daniel and the Lions

Darius:

I'm Darius, king of all Persia. I lived in ancient times and mine was the most powerful kingdom in the world. When people spoke to me they said, "O king, live forever!" But even I, with all my power, was amazed at the power of God. As you read my story, you'll find times to cheer and times to boo. When something good happens, say *"Yea!"* and pump your fist. When something bad happens, say *"Boo!"* and give a thumbs-down.

A man named Daniel was one of my most trusted advisors. He worked hard and wisely, and I could always trust him to be honest. Because he was wise and faithful, I put him in charge of the whole kingdom. Yea! This made the other officials jealous and angry. So they hatched a sneaky plan to get rid of Daniel. *Boo!* The officials knew that Daniel loved God. In fact, Daniel went to his room three times a day to pray to the living God. *Yea!*

Daniel:

O God of heaven, keep me safe, keep me strong,
And help me serve you faithfully all day long.

Darius:

The officials came to me and said, "O king, live forever! We all agree
that you should make a new rule. Anyone who prays to a god other
than you should be thrown into the lions' den. Put it into writing so it
becomes law." Now, I should have asked them, "Why do you want
this new rule?" But I didn't think about anything but my own pride. I
forgot all about Daniel. *Boo!* When Daniel heard about the new law,
he went to his room to pray.

Daniel:

O God of heaven, keep me safe, keep me strong,
And help me keep obeying you all day long.

Darius:

Soon after that, the officials came to me. They said, "O king,
live forever! We happened to see Daniel in his room,
praying to his God. Doesn't your law say that if a
person prays to anyone but you, he must be thrown
into the lions' den?" I realized my mistake. These
men had set a trap and I'd walked right into it.
There was nothing I could do. Once I'd signed a
law, it couldn't be changed. So I said, to Daniel,
"May the God whom you serve continually
rescue you." I was very sad to give the order
for him to be thrown into the lions' den.
Boo! What would happen to my trusted
friend?

Daniel:

O God in heaven, keep me safe, keep me strong,
And close these hungry lions' mouths all night long.

Darius:

That night I couldn't think about anything but Daniel. I couldn't eat. I couldn't sleep. The moment the sun came up, I ran to the lions' den. "Daniel," I shouted, "has your God been able to rescue you from the lions?"

Daniel:

My God in heaven kept me safe and kept me strong
And closed the hungry lions' mouths all night long.

Darius:

I was so happy! I gave the order to pull Daniel up. He wasn't hurt. He wasn't even scratched. *Yea!* Then I remembered the jealous officials. They had done a wicked thing. I ordered them to be thrown into the lions' den. *Boo!*

That day I was so happy that I sent a new message throughout my kingdom: "Everyone must respect the God of Daniel. He is the living God because he rescued Daniel from the power of lions." *Yea!*

Go for the Godprint

Prayerfulness: Think about a time when you were afraid. Did you remember to pray to God? Daniel prayed and asked for God's help. God was faithful and sent an angel to shut the lions' mouths. The next time you are afraid, pray to God. You can trust that he will be faithful to you just as he was to Daniel.

What Digby Dug Up

All the books in the Bible except for five mention angels. Angels worship God and help take care of people. Two special angels in the Bible are Gabriel, a messenger angel and Michael, a warrior angel.

Izzy's Art Cart

GET LIST: MANILA FOLDER OR POSTER BOARD, BLACK MARKER, SCISSORS, PEN

If you use poster board, fold it in half the long way. With your fingers straight and held tightly together, place the edge of your hand along the fold. Trace all around your hand on both sides and about three inches down your wrist. Cut around your hand shape, except for the part that's right on the fold. Fold the wrist pieces so your "praying hands" stand up. Write the following Bible verse on the hands in fancy writing: *"The Lord will hear when I call to him"* (Psalm 4:3). Keep your prayer pop-up card in a place that reminds you to pray.

God Talk
You can use the words of Psalm 4:3 as a prayer:
The Lord will hear when I call.
Make up a motion for each word,
then practice using the words and motions
together until everyone in your family can do it.

179

Jonah Takes A Dive

Jonah: But I don't want to go to Nineveh and tell the people to repent.

Narrator: God spoke to Jonah again.

Jonah: I don't want to go. I know they will listen to me. I think they deserve to be punished. If they listen to me, you will forgive them and then they won't be punished.

Narrator: God spoke to Jonah once again and told him to go to Nineveh.

Jonah: No, I don't want to!

Enjoy this drama as a family. For special effects, use spray bottles of water, sheets, and a fish belly made from a sleeping bag.

Narrator: God saw that the people of Nineveh were doing wicked things that didn't please him. He needed someone to go to Nineveh and tell the people to repent or they would be punished. So God sent Jonah.

Narrator: Jonah decided to run away from God, so he got on a ship and went to Tarshish–the opposite direction from Nineveh. But God got Jonah's attention by sending a gigantic wind that caused a terrible storm. The sailors were terrified the ship would sink and they would all drown. But Jonah was sound asleep in the bottom of the boat.

Sailor: Get up, Jonah! Pray that we won't sink.

Jonah: I worship the true God who made the sea and the land.

Sailor: What have you done to bring this trouble on us?

Jonah: God wants me to preach to the people of Nineveh, but I'm running away.

Sailor: Tell us what we can do to stop this storm.

Jonah: Throw me into the sea. Then the storm will stop. I know it's my fault that we're having all this trouble.

Sailor: No, we'll try to row back to land.

Narrator: But the storm grew wilder than before, so the sailors tossed Jonah into the sea.

Jonah: Ahhhhh!

Narrator: Immediately the storm grew calm, and the sailors believed in God and worshiped him right there on the boat. But the Lord didn't forget about Jonah. He sent a big fish to come and swallow Jonah. Jonah was safe inside the fish for three days and three nights. Finally he decided to stop running from God and asked for God's help.

Jonah: Lord, you have listened to my cry and saved me from the depths of the sea. My prayers rise to you. I'll keep my vows to you.

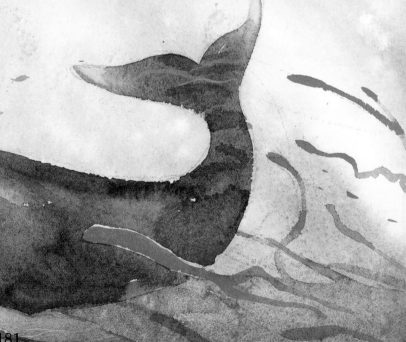

Narrator: God made the fish toss Jonah up onto the shore. Once again God told Jonah to go to Nineveh and preach. This time Jonah obeyed.

Jonah: You must turn from your evil ways and obey God.

Ninevites: We will do as you say! We're sorry for our sins!

Narrator: The people of Nineveh changed their ways. God forgave them. But Jonah was unhappy.

Jonah: I knew it! God is loving and gracious. He's forgiven the people of Nineveh. But they are Israel's enemies. I wanted God to destroy them.

Narrator: God was willing to forgive the people of Nineveh because he loved them. They said they were sorry and they changed the way they lived. God loved Jonah, too. God was patient and forgiving when Jonah tried to run away. God is loving and kind to everyone who turns away from their sins, asks forgiveness and obeys him.

182

Go for the Godprint

Repentance: Jonah and the people of Nineveh needed to repent for disobeying God. Repentance means to turn away from doing wrong—sin—and turn back to God. To repent all you need to do is to tell God you are sorry for things you have done wrong and ask him to help you to do what is right.

What Digby Dug Up
We don't know exactly what kind of "great fish" God prepared to swallow Jonah and keep him safe. We do know that some modern sailors have survived inside sperm whales. How slimy do you think a whale's belly would be?

Izzy's Art Cart

GET LIST: 2 WHITE PAPER PLATES, GLUE, COLORED CHALK, BLACK PERMANENT MARKER

Use two plates to make the fish that swallowed Jonah. One plate will be the body. The other will be the tail and fins. To make the tail and fins, fold a plate in half. Cut out a tail and fins as shown. Glue the two tail pieces together and glue the tail to the body. Glue one fin to the top of the body and one to the bottom. "Paint" scales on the fish with glue. Make a big eye with a drop of glue. Let the glue dry, then color in between and over the glue lines with colored chalk. Blend the colors with your fingers or a paper towel. On the back of the body, draw a simple picture of Jonah with a black permanent marker. Hang your Jonah fish in a window and you can see Jonah inside the belly of the fish!

God Talk

As a family, make yummy fish snacks by cutting fish shapes from bread. Spread on peanut butter or cheese spread, then add "scales" made of thin apple slices. You may want to sprinkle a little lemon juice on the apple slices to keep them from turning brown. As you prepare the treats, talk about times when you've been stubborn and resisted obeying God. Pray together and ask God to help you serve him with a willing heart.

Mary's Tale

Mary had an amazing tale to tell after she was visited by an angel. Some of the facts in this story are confused! To straighten them out, open your Bible to Luke 1:26-38.
How many mistakes can you find and correct? (Check your answers on page 186.)

In the sixth month, God sent the angel Gabriel to Nazareth, a town in Mississippi, to a virgin pledged to be buried to a man named Joseph, a descendant of David. The virgin's name was Mary. The angel went to her and said, "Greetings, you who are highly favored! The Lord is with you."

Mary was greatly bubbled at his words and wondered what kind of meeting this might be.

But the angel said to her, Do not be a maid, Mary, you have found favor with God. You will be with child and give birth to a son, and you are to give him the name Jesus.

He will be great and will be called the Son of the Most High. The Lord God will give him the bone of his father David.

And he will rain over the mouse of Jacob forever; his kingdom will never end.

"How will this be," Mary asked the angel, "since I am a virgin?"

The angel answered, "The Holy Spirit will come upon you, and the power of the Most High will overshadow you. So the holy one to be born will be called the Son of God.

185

Even Elizabeth, your relative, is going to have a child in her old cage, and she who was said to be barren is in her sixth month. For nothing is impossible with God.

"I am the Lord's servant," Mary answered. "May it be to me as you have said." Then the angel left her.

Mary's Tale
Corrections Collection

- Nazareth was a town in Galilee, not Mississippi.

  How would people react if an angel delivered a message to someone in your town?

- Mary was greatly troubled, not greatly bubbled.

  How would you feel if you saw an angel?

- The angel told Mary, "Do not be afraid," not "Do not be a maid."

  Why do you think Mary might have been afraid of the angel?

- God will give Jesus the throne of David, not the bone of David.

- Jesus will reign over the house of Jacob, not rain over the mouse of Jacob.

  How is Jesus like a king? How can you let King Jesus rule in your life?

- Elizabeth had a child in her old age, not her old cage.

  What amazing things has God done for your family?

Go for the Godprint

Purposefulness: When the angel first came to Mary, she must have felt like there had been some mistake. Not a silly mistake like the ones in this story, but a real mistake. How could an unmarried young woman be about to have a baby, and how could that baby be God's Son? But after the angel told Mary about God's plan, Mary chose to accept her part in it. God has plans for you, too. And if you think God's plans seem strange at first, remember: Nothing is impossible with God!

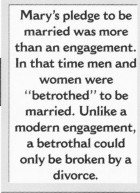

What Digby Dug Up

Mary's pledge to be married was more than an engagement. In that time men and women were "betrothed" to be married. Unlike a modern engagement, a betrothal could only be broken by a divorce.

Herbie's Hideaway

Make a pinecone angel to remind you that God has special plans for you just as he did for Mary. For the body of the angel, choose a long pinecone and place it with the point down. Ask an adult to help you hot glue the rest of the angel. For the head, use a walnut, acorn or tiny pinecone. For wings, glue small sticks or spreading branches to the back of the pinecone. You may want to add moss "hair" and a small halo of dried flowers or foil garland. Hot glue a paper clip hanger to the back of the angel.

God Talk

When Mary accepted her place in God's plan,
she praised God with a prayer of thankfulness.
Mary's prayer is known as "The Magnificat of Mary," and it's found in Luke 1:46–55.
(*Magnificat* means "glorifies" or "praises" in Latin.)
Using Mary's prayer for a model, write your own "magnificat" prayer of thanks to God
for the things he's done for you.

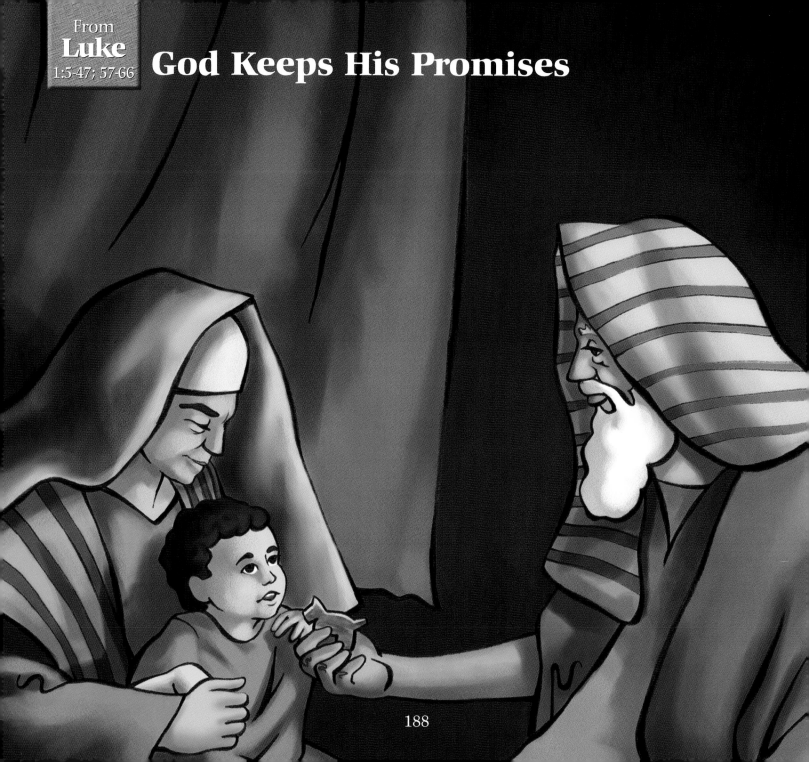

God Keeps His Promises

Whenever you come to the word "because," say: God keeps his promises to you and to me. God keeps his promises, just trust him and see.

Zechariah and his wife Elizabeth were good people who loved and served God. All their lives they hoped to have children. But they grew old and gray and still had no child. One day Zechariah was serving God in the temple. Suddenly an angel appeared. Zechariah froze in fear.

The angel said, "Don't be afraid. Your prayer has been heard. Your wife Elizabeth will have a son. You are to name him John. He will bring many of the people of Israel back to God and prepare them for the coming of the Lord."

"A son?" Zechariah asked in astonishment. "How can I be sure of this? My wife and I are old!" Zechariah shouldn't have doubted the angel's word, *because:* God keeps his promises to you and to me. God keeps his promises, just trust him and see.

The angel said, "I'm Gabriel. God sent me here to tell you this wonderful news. Since you didn't believe me, you're not going to be able to say a word until this promise comes true."

The people at the temple wondered why Zechariah was taking so long. When he finally came out, they were shocked to realize he couldn't speak. Zechariah made motions with his hands, and they knew he had seen a vision.

After he finished his service at the temple, Zechariah went home. Sure enough, it wasn't long before Elizabeth and Zechariah knew a baby was on the way. They knew their miracle baby was from God, *because:* God keeps his promises to you and to me. God keeps his promises, just trust him and see.

Meanwhile, the angel Gabriel appeared to Elizabeth's relative, Mary, who lived in Nazareth. "Greetings, you who are highly favored! The Lord is with you." Mary didn't know what to think!

Gabriel went on: "Don't be afraid. You have found favor with God. You'll give birth to a son. You're to name him Jesus. He will be great and will be called the Son of the Most High. The Lord God will give him the throne of his father David, and he will reign over the house of Jacob forever; his kingdom will never end."

Mary wondered how she could have a baby. Gabriel explained that the child would be God's own Son. Then he told her the good news about Elizabeth. "Even your relative Elizabeth is going to have a baby," Gabriel said. "You see, nothing is impossible with God."

Mary knew what the angel said was true, *because:* God keeps his promises to you and to me. God keeps his promises, just trust him and see.

Mary hurried to the town where Elizabeth and Zechariah lived. When she entered their house, Elizabeth felt her own baby leap for joy inside her.

Then the Holy Spirit filled Elizabeth and she exclaimed, "Blessed are you among women and blessed is the child you will bear! How wonderful that you believed the Lord would do what he said for you." Mary's heart was filled with joy and she praised God, *because:* God keeps his promises to you and to me. God keeps his promises, just trust him and see.

Friends and relatives celebrated when Elizabeth's son was born. They thought he would be named Zechariah after his father. "No!" Elizabeth said. "He is to be called John."

"But none of your relatives is named John," someone protested. Then Zechariah wrote on a tablet, "His name is John."

Suddenly Zechariah could speak again! The first words out of his mouth were praises to God. Everyone for miles around talked about the miracles God had done. They wondered what wonderful things God would do through this child *because:* God keeps his promises to you and to me. God keeps his promises, just trust him and see.

Go for the Godprint

Hope: Elizabeth hoped and prayed for a child for a long time. Her hope finally came true. We can be sure that God hears our prayers, even if we have to wait years and years for the answer. God doesn't think of time the same way we do. He wants us to keep trusting him and believing his promises.

What Digby Dug Up

GABRIEL, THE ANGEL IN THIS BIBLE STORY, IS ONE OF ONLY TWO ANGELS NAMED IN ALL OF THE BIBLE. GABRIEL MEANS "GOD IS MY HERO." THE OTHER ANGEL MENTIONED BY NAME IN THE BIBLE IS MICHAEL.

Izzy's Art Cart

Make a shimmering rainbow to remind you to trust God and never lose hope. First, write the word "HOPE" in white crayon on the center of a paper plate. Make the letters large and thick. Gently mist the plate with a spray bottle of water. The plate should be damp but there shouldn't be any puddles. With three different brushes, stir up red, yellow and blue watercolor or tempera paint until the paint is thin and watery. Drop the watery colors onto the damp plate and tip it so the colors run together and form all the colors of the rainbow! See how the word "HOPE" shines through? Decorate the edge of the plate with ribbon or glitter and hang it.

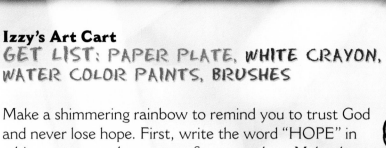

God Talk

Make a "baby" by rolling up a towel
and adding a neck with a rubber band.
Wrap the baby in a soft blanket.
Elizabeth trusted God and God sent her the son she prayed for.
Pass the baby around and tell what you're trusting God for.
Remind each other of God's promises and pray together
that you will keep trusting God to keep his promises.

In Your Dreams

"I will try to sleep. But how? With no wife to call my own, life will be hard now. I'll trust in God and try and get some rest."

"Joseph."

"ZZZZzzzzzzz."

"Joseph!"

"What? Who's there?"

"Joseph, son of David. Do not wake. Sleep and I'll talk while you dream."

"But…"

"I am an angel of the Lord, Joseph. I'm here to talk about Mary."

"No, not Mary. Please! I'm heartsick about Mary. We were engaged to be married, you know."

"Joseph, do not be afraid to take Mary as your wife."

"Haven't you heard? Mary is already with child, and the child is not mine."

"Joseph, do not be afraid to take Mary as your wife."

"Listen. I've made a plan. I will divorce Mary quietly and not bring her shame. I will do this because I love her."

"Joseph, do not be afraid to take Mary as your wife."

"This evening I watched her as she went to the well to gather water with the other women of Nazareth. Her kindness and gentleness almost broke my heart. But how can I forgive her? What she has done cannot be undone."

"Joseph, do not be afraid to take Mary as your wife."

"How many times will you say these words? I can hear what you're saying."

"You hear, Joseph, but you are not listening. What is conceived in Mary is of the Holy Spirit. Mary will have a son, and you are to give the baby the name Jesus."

"A son?"

"Yes."

"Jesus?"

"Yes, Jesus. Because he will save

people from their sins."

"You mean, Mary..."

"Yes, she has been faithful to you."

"Mary...my Mary, will give birth to the Son of God!"

"What you have spoken is true."

"Oh, my. I am amazed, and a little afraid. But I will do what the Lord commands me. I will not divorce Mary. She will be my wife and her baby will be my son. And I will protect him and raise him as if he were my own flesh and blood. Thank you, angel, for coming tonight with such wonderful news!

"Good night, Joseph. Sweet dreams."

194

Go for the Godprint

Perseverance: God gave Joseph a very special job. Joseph obeyed God and was willing to follow God's plan wherever the "dream" led. Have you ever tried and tried again to complete a task? Were you frustrated? Ready to give up? In God's eyes we persevere in holiness when he gives us a task and we rely on God's strength to accomplish it. Live a life of perseverance, and let God help you every step of the way.

What Digby Dug Up

The word "angel" occurs over 275 times in the Bible. The Bible never mentions messenger angels having wings, but often refers to them as men dressed in shining white robes.

Izzy's Art Cart

GET LIST:
CARDBOARD TUBES, TISSUE PAPER, TAPE, CURLING RIBBON, CANDIES, SCISSORS, MARKER

When we commit ourselves to following God's plan, he can change our difficult problems into sweet dreams. Make Sweet Dream Poppers to tuck as a surprise under family members' pillows. Cut a paper towel tube in half. Wrap the tube in colorful tissue paper and tape the tissue down. Leave about four inches of tissue paper on each end and then cut away the extra. With a piece of curling ribbon, tie off one end of your Sweet Dream Popper. Put small candies inside the open end of the cardboard tube, then tie off the end with ribbon. Cut fringes into the ends of the tissue paper. Write, "God is with you. Sweet dreams!" on the outside of the finished popper.

God Talk
Joseph thought the wrong thing
about Mary and his feelings were hurt.
But when he found out the truth from the angel,
he went ahead and married her.
Sometimes we get the wrong idea about people.
We get our feelings hurt and our friendships are damaged.
Talk together about friendships you need to mend.
Ask God to give you the strength to make things right.

The Twelve Clues of Christmas

Think you know the Christmas story? Let's find out. Cover this page with a sheet of paper. Uncover the clues one line at a time. How many clues will you need to discover the answer to each riddle?

1
I gave directions but never spoke,
I never touched the earth,
I knew exactly where to stop
To mark a royal birth.

Who am I?
Matthew 2:2, 7, 9-10

2
I've been outsmarted. Ruined! Tricked!
The Magi went away.
My soldiers must destroy this child.
There's no time to delay.

Who am I?
Matthew 2:1, 16-17

4
I'm just a small Judean town
In the countryside.
At census time my inns were full
When Joseph brought his bride.

What am I?
Luke 2:4-7

3
Some moms have a lot of kids;
Some may have a dozen.
I'll have just one child—a son.
He'll be Jesus' cousin.

Who am I?
Luke 1:57-58

5
The angel called my name and said
"Your child will be from God."
In Nazareth the folks may think
My situation's odd.

Who am I?
Luke 1:26-38

6
Animals within my walls
Made room for tired strangers.
A child was born and wrapped in cloths
And slept safe in my manger.

What am I?
Luke 2:6-7

7
I rested in a quiet field
With my sleeping flock.
When suddenly the sky lit up.
It was quite a shock!

Who am I?
Luke 2:8

8
I may visit in a dream
Or in a flash of light.
I brought messages from God
To shepherds one dark night.

Who am I?
Luke 2:9

9
We came searching for a king.
A star served as our guide.
We gave the child our treasures
When we worshiped at his side.

Who are we?
Matthew 2:2

197

10 Marry her or call things off?
I didn't have a clue.
An angel told me of God's plan,
Then I knew what to do.

Who am I?
Matthew 1:18-20

11 I gave a very precious gift—
My son became a man.
At Christmas you remember
When his life on earth began.

Who am I?
Matthew 1:20-22

12 I lived before my time on earth.
I loved you from the start.
I came to set you free from sin
And give you a loving heart.

Who am I?
John 1:10-14

Answers:

1) Star, 2) King Herod, 3) Elizabeth, 4) Bethlehem,
5) Mary, 6) Stable, 7) Shepherd, 8) Angel, 9) Magi,
10) Joseph, 11) God, 12) Jesus

198

Go for the Godprint

Worship: What's the most incredibly surprising gift you ever got? What did you say to the person who gave it to you? The gift God gave the world at Christmastime goes far beyond anything you could ever unwrap. Think of the all the power and knowledge and wisdom of our creator wrapped up in baby blankets. In your mind, kneel on the cold dirt floor of the stable by the manger. Will you worship the tiny savior-king?

What Digby Dug Up

BETHLEHEM MEANS "HOUSE OF BREAD" IN HEBREW. THE VILLAGE IS LOCATED FIVE MILES SOUTH OF THE CAPITAL CITY OF JERUSALEM.

Café de Click

GET LIST: A MICROWAVE SAFE BOWL, PEANUT BUTTER, A JAR OF MARSHMALLOW CREME, A PACKAGE CHOW MEIN NOODLES, WAXED PAPER, AND PRETZELS.

Mix up some Manger Munchies to enjoy with your family.

1) Make hay! Mix: 1/2 cup peanut butter and 7-ounce jar of marshmallow crème. Microwave on low power for 30 seconds. Stir in 1 package chow mein noodles. Now you have nice sticky hay.

2) Lay out a sheet of waxed paper. Put pretzels together to make the base of a manger.

3) Drop some hay onto the pretzels. If you wish, add a circus peanut to represent the baby in the manger. Before you enjoy your treats, talk about:

• **What would it be like to leave heaven and be born in a cold stable?**

• **Why did Jesus do that?**

• How would you have worshiped Jesus if you had been at the stable?

God Talk
Use a container such as a wagon
or box as a manger.
Tear newspaper into narrow strips to form straw.
Roll up a soft blanket to represent baby Jesus.
Kneel with your family around the manger.
Take turns finishing these prayer starters.
Jesus, I love you because… I believe you're… I want to honor you by…

An Unforgettable Night

You'll never believe what happened tonight! I was out with my dad watching the sheep. Now that I'm ten years old, he lets me go with him. I'm learning all about being a shepherd. At first it seemed like any other night. The air was cool and the sheep were starting to settle down. I was sitting with all the big shepherds listening to their stories. I felt really grown up.

Suddenly, there was a bright light and an angel appeared right there in front of us. It was beautiful, but nothing has ever scared me more. I wanted to run and hide. Even my dad and the other shepherds were afraid. But the angel spoke in a voice like I had never heard before: "Do not be afraid. I bring you good news of great joy that will be for all the people. Today in the town of David a Savior has been born to you; he is Christ the Lord. This will be a sign to you: You will find a baby wrapped in cloths and lying in a manger."

Then the whole sky lit up, and it was full of angels. I've never seen anything like it. My heart was pounding, and I could hardly breathe. I grabbed my dad's hand and held on tight. The angels were all praising God.

> *"Glory to God in the highest,*
> *and on earth peace to men on*
> *whom his favor rests."*

Their voices filled the sky. Then, just like that, they were gone.

Everyone began to talk at once. We were all so excited. Someone said, "Let's go and find this special baby right now!" We hurried toward Bethlehem. The men were going so fast I had to run to keep up. We finally reached the city and were surprised to find that no one else seemed to know what was going on. The angels came to us, not to the important people in the city. Wow! I wondered why God chose us for this wonderful, unbelievable, incredible message. All my life I had heard about the Messiah that God promised. I remember hearing that he would come to the world as a baby. Could this baby really be the one?

We finally found him, just like the angel had said. His mother had wrapped him up and put him in the manger to sleep. We just worshiped him quietly. This baby was God's own Son! No one could think of anything to say. I mean, what could we say? The Messiah we had waited for all these years was sleeping right there in front of us. My whole body tingled, and I got goose bumps thinking about the incredible gift God had given us.

When we left, I wanted to jump and shout and tell the whole world what had happened! We told everyone we saw about the angel's message. "The Savior is born in Bethlehem this very night!" we shouted. Everyone we talked to was amazed. I don't know if they all believed us, but I know I'll never be the same. I saw him, and I know in my heart that all God's promises have come true tonight! The Lord has come. His name is Jesus.

Go for the Godprint

Worship: What is the most powerful thing you can think of? A storm? The ocean? That power is nothing compared to God's power. Do you know someone who is really smart? Even the smartest person doesn't know everything, but God does. Have you ever met a really creative person? God is the Great Creator. He made the whole world. Only God deserves our worship. Spend some time today telling God how wonderful he is!

What Digby Dug Up
Hundreds of years before Jesus came, God told the prophet Isaiah that this special baby would be born.

In Isaiah 9:6, the Bible says, "For to us a child is born, to us a son is given." Many verses in the Book of Isaiah tell of God's promise of the coming Christ. See if you can find some more (or look at the story that starts on page 156).

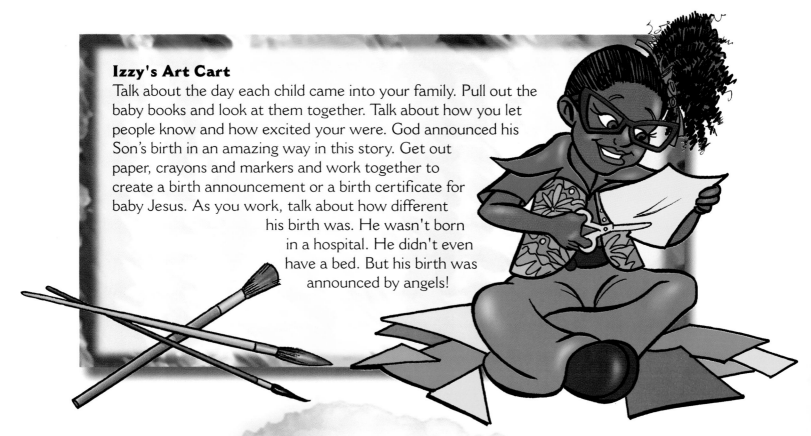

Izzy's Art Cart

Talk about the day each child came into your family. Pull out the baby books and look at them together. Talk about how you let people know and how excited your were. God announced his Son's birth in an amazing way in this story. Get out paper, crayons and markers and work together to create a birth announcement or a birth certificate for baby Jesus. As you work, talk about how different his birth was. He wasn't born in a hospital. He didn't even have a bed. But his birth was announced by angels!

God Talk

Let one person in your family
lead the following responsive prayer.
After each phrase, the rest of the family will say,
"I will worship you!"
Lord, your promises are true.
I will worship you!
Your mighty power is forever.
I will worship you!
Angels in heaven sing your praises.
I will worship you!
You loved us so much you sent your Son.
I will worship you! Forever!
Amen.

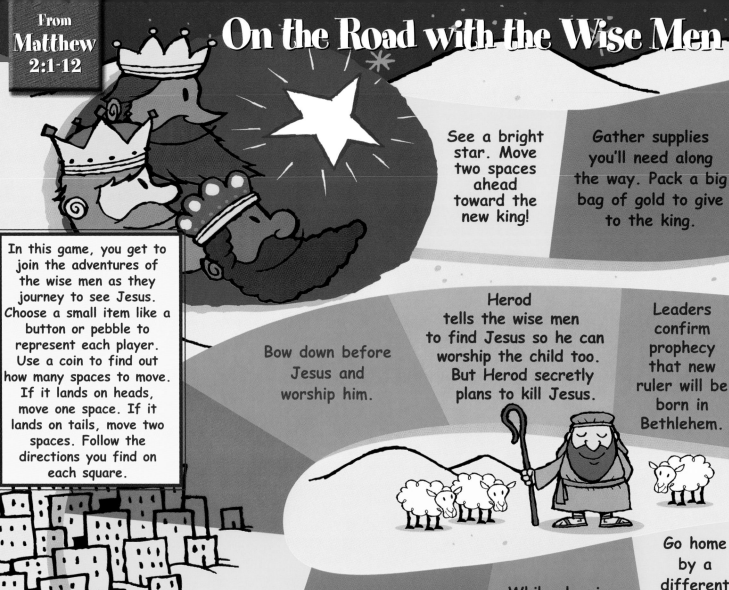

On the Road with the Wise Men

In this game, you get to join the adventures of the wise men as they journey to see Jesus. Choose a small item like a button or pebble to represent each player. Use a coin to find out how many spaces to move. If it lands on heads, move one space. If it lands on tails, move two spaces. Follow the directions you find on each square.

See a bright star. Move two spaces ahead toward the new king!

Gather supplies you'll need along the way. Pack a big bag of gold to give to the king.

Bow down before Jesus and worship him.

Herod tells the wise men to find Jesus so he can worship the child too. But Herod secretly plans to kill Jesus.

Leaders confirm prophecy that new ruler will be born in Bethlehem.

Give your gifts of gold, incense and myrrh to Jesus.

While sleeping, dream a message from God telling you not to report back to Herod.

Go home by a different route, so Herod won't find Jesus.

Begin traveling west.

Camels need to stop for water. Miss one turn.

Buy frankincense and myrrh from a passing caravan.

Arrive in Jerusalem. Give a cheer because you can stop for a rest!

King Herod is upset by the news of a new king.

Ask for directions to the home of the king of the Jews.

Keep following the star until you find the home where the child, Jesus, lives.

Jump with joy because you found the new king!

Do you think the wise men got discouraged on their journey to find Jesus? They journeyed a long time and didn't know exactly where they were going until they got there. They stayed faithful to their mission even when King Herod tried to trick them. God rewarded their faithfulness by sending the star again to light their way. Finally they found their way to Bethlehem and worshiped the king they had looked for so long. The wise men knew their goal and stuck to it. Imagine their joy as they worshiped God's Son!

Go for the Godprint

Faithfulness: Herod tried to make the kings forget what was really important. But they stayed true to God, even when it meant going against King Herod. That's faithfulness. God is always faithful to us. Can you think of a way that you can show faithfulness to God?

What Digby Dug Up

Most people think there were three wise men, because there were three gifts given to Jesus, but the Bible doesn't say exactly how many wise men there were. The holiday "Epiphany" comes 12 days after Christmas. It celebrates the wise men's visit to Jesus.

Café de Click

GET LIST: GRAHAM CRACKERS, CHOCOLATE BARS, MARSHMALLOWS, COOKIE SHEET, SPATULA

Make "Three Kings S'mores" together. Ask an adult to turn on the broiler in your oven. Lay whole graham crackers on a cookie sheet. Put pieces of a chocolate bar and three large marshmallows on each graham cracker. Let Mom or Dad put the treats under the broiler until the marshmallows start to turn toasty brown. Use a spatula to move the s'mores to a cool plate. As you enjoy them together, talk about:

• **Why is it important to follow directions in a recipe?**

• **What other directions are important to follow?**

• **The wise men followed the star and the words of God to find Jesus. What do you need to follow to find Jesus?**

• **How does God show us the way to follow today?**

God Talk
This is a "Follow-the-Leader" prayer.
The first person names a prayer request
and each person follows his or her lead by also praying for this request.
Then the second person names a request
and everyone else prays for this concern.
Continue until each person has been the prayer leader.

A Temple Visit

You can read this story as a play, or make puppets first (see next page) and use them to tell the story.

Narrator: Mary and Joseph were careful to follow the laws of Israel. So when Jesus was a few weeks old, they presented him at the temple in Jerusalem.

Mary: Sweet baby Jesus, today we travel to Jerusalem!

Joseph: Yes, young man, you are the firstborn, so we will take you to the great temple and present you to the Lord!

Narrator: The little family made their way along the well-worn paths to the great city.

Joseph: Look! I can see the temple on the hill. We're almost there.

Mary: See, Jesus? There is the place where God lives among his people. That is your Father's house.

Joseph: C'mon, let's hurry.

Narrator: Finally, they reached the temple. Almost as soon as they went in, an old man named Simeon came up to them. He was a good man who loved and served God. The Holy Spirit had told him that he wouldn't die until he had seen the Messiah with his own eyes. He had waited a long time.

Simeon: He's here at last! May I hold him? *(He takes the baby from Mary.)* I praise you, Lord, for you have kept your promise. Now I can die in peace. Right here in my arms, I see your salvation. This child is for all people, a light of truth for the Gentiles and the glory of your people Israel.

Narrator: Mary and Joseph were amazed at the things Simeon said about their baby.

Simeon: May God bless and keep you, Mary and Joseph. Mary, your son will cause many to rise and fall in Israel. People will speak against him. Even you will suffer. *(He hands the baby back to Mary.)*

Narrator: At that very moment an 84-year-old woman named Anna came up to them. She was a prophetess. She had been married only seven years before her husband died. Ever since then, she had stayed in the temple, fasting and praying night and day.

Anna: *(Raising her hands into the air and looking at the baby.)* Thank you, Lord! Oh, thank you! The Messiah is here at last! Everyone, look! The Lord has sent redemption to Jerusalem! He has come! Praise the Lord!

Joseph: Come, Mary, we must do what the law requires.

Mary: Have you remembered to bring the sacrifice—two young doves or two pigeons?

Joseph: Yes, I have them. Let's go present our son to his Father.

Narrator: And when they had done everything according to the Lord's law, they left Jerusalem and returned to their own city of Nazareth in Galilee. The child grew and became strong and wise. And he was full of God's grace.

Go for the Godprint

Community: Simeon and Anna came to the temple to show their love for God and worship him. Just imagine how their words must have encouraged Joseph and Mary. Other people who were close to God knew who Jesus was! The faith of other believers can boost your faith when you come together. Making time to be with God's people is important!

What Digby Dug Up

All of Israel's firstborn sons belonged to God and went to the temple for a special ceremony. This reminded God's people of Passover, when the firstborn sons of Egypt died, but God saved the firstborn sons of his own people. You can read about it in Exodus 13:1, 11-16.

GP Theater Company

GET LIST: FIBERFILL, RUBBER BANDS, MARKERS, TISSUES, SAFETY PINS, FIVE LIGHT-COLORED SOCKS (four adult and one baby-size)

Have fun making simple sock puppets to tell this story together!

• **Baby Jesus:** Fill the baby sock with fiberfill. Sew the ankle closed or wrap it with a rubber band. Place a rubber band about one-third of the way down from the toe of the sock to form a head. Draw the face and blanket.

• **Mary, Joseph, Simeon and Anna:** Stuff each sock's toe with fiberfill. Wrap a rubber band loosely around it to form a head. Then draw a face and robe. Pin pieces of tissue to Mary's and Anna's heads for veils.

To use the adult puppets, place the sock over your hand. Poke your index finger into the head and use your thumb and third finger for arms. Now the adult puppets can hold the baby puppet in their arms.

God Talk

The Bible tells us that Anna worshiped in the temple day and night.
Think of ways that you and your family can worship God all the time.
Here are a few ideas to get you started:
• When you say good morning to each other, say it to God, too.
• When you come into your house, praise God for giving you a place to live.
• When you get the mail, praise God for giving you his Word, the Bible.
• Throughout the day, when you see something to praise God for, say aloud, "Yea, God!"

Lost and Found in Jerusalem

Use this script to create a family drama.
Double up on some of the smaller roles.

- *Narrator*
- *Mary*
- *Joseph*
- *Jesus*
- *Naomi*
- *Man in temple*
- *Jesse*

Narrator: When Jesus was 12 years old, he went with his parents, Mary and Joseph, to the temple in Jerusalem for the feast. We join them now on the road as they approach the city.

Mary: Look, Jesus. What a beautiful sight Jerusalem is! I remember how I felt when I was your age. The sight of God's holy temple made me want to leap and run like a deer.

Narrator: When the family reached Jerusalem, their Passover feast was just like other years. They ate lamb, unleavened bread and other good foods. They worshiped at the temple and rejoiced with relatives and friends.

212

Joseph: We celebrate Passover to remember how God punished Egypt but protected the children of Israel. Then God brought the Israelites out of Egypt to the Promised Land.

Narrator: After an exciting week, the joyous feast was over and the people who had come from all over Israel left Jerusalem to go home. They traveled together in large groups. Mary and Joseph traveled with one of the large groups going back to Nazareth, their home town.

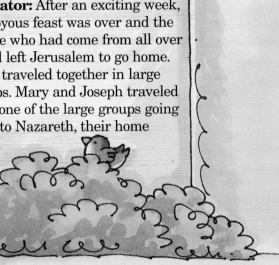

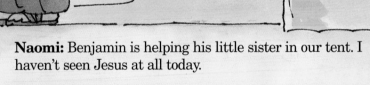

They stopped after a day of travel to rest.

Mary: Joseph, have you seen Jesus?

Joseph: I'm sure he's somewhere around here, playing with his cousins or talking to an uncle. Are you worried about him?

Mary: It seems strange that we haven't seen him all day.

Joseph: Okay, we'll ask around. (Shouting.) Jesse, have you seen our boy, Jesus?

Jesse: No, I haven't seen him.

Mary: Naomi, we're looking for our son. Is he with your Benjamin?

Naomi: Benjamin is helping his little sister in our tent. I haven't seen Jesus at all today.

Narrator: After searching all over, Mary and Joseph realized that Jesus was not with their family at all!

Joseph: We must return to Jerusalem at once. Don't be concerned, Mary. God will help us find him.

Mary: I know, Joseph, but he's so young to be in that big city alone!

Narrator: They hurried back to Jerusalem and searched for a full day. Night came.

Mary: Jesus is somewhere out there in the dark. Father in heaven, he's your Son. Please keep him safe.

Narrator: The next two days seemed endless as Mary and Joseph searched and searched. Finally, they came to the temple courts.

Mary: Joseph, I hear his voice!

Joseph: Look, there he is! Over there with the priests.

Narrator: They both hurried to where Jesus was talking with the priests.

Man in temple: Is he your son?

Joseph: Yes.

Man in temple: What intelligent questions he asks! And his answers! His understanding of God is amazing! How could such a young boy have this kind of wisdom?

Mary: Son, why have you treated us like this? Your father and I have been searching for you. You had us so worried!

Jesus: Why were you searching for me? Didn't you know I had to be here in my Father's house?

Narrator: All Mary and Joseph could think about was relief that Jesus was safe. They knew he was God's Son, but didn't understand everything God had planned for Jesus' life. Jesus went back to Nazareth with Mary and Joseph and obeyed them in everything. His mother held onto these memories as treasures in her heart. As he grew taller, Jesus also gained wisdom. And both God and the people around him were pleased to see the kind of man he was becoming.

214

Go for the Godprint

Confidence: Jesus wasn't afraid to be lost. He felt safe teaching his Father's words in his Father's house. With faith and trust in God, Jesus was confident doing the work God sent him to do. What do you love to do most in the world? This may be the gift God gave you to help accomplish tasks with confidence.

What Digby Dug Up

Jesus was 12 years old when he went to the Feast of the Passover with his family. In Jewish tradition Jesus was considered almost an adult and did not need to stay with his parents in Jerusalem.

Mo's Fab Lab

GET LIST:
INDEX CARD, DRINKING STRAW, STRING, BALLOON, TAPE,
SMALL OBJECT SUCH AS WRAPPED CANDY

Pick partners and play this lively "Lost and Found" game. Tape a "lost" item such as a small piece of wrapped candy to an index card. Tape the card to the side of a drinking straw. Cut a string about eight feet long and slip the string through the straw. Blow up a balloon. While you hold the mouth of the balloon shut (don't tie it!), ask your partner to tape the straw to the side of the balloon using two pieces of tape. Now it should look like your index card is standing on the balloon. Keep holding the balloon shut and slide the straw and balloon to one end of the string. Have your partner hold the other end taut. Yell, "Lost!" and let the balloon go. Your partner yells, "Found!" when the balloon reaches the other end. Blow up the balloon and start again!

Talk about:

- **Were you confident the balloon would move down the string? Why?**

- **Why is it important to feel confident that God has a purpose for you?**

God Talk
Use an inflated balloon
to help your family prayer time.
Toss the balloon and take turns tapping it to keep it afloat.
With each tap, say a short prayer that finishes this sentence:
"Lord, help me be confident when _____."

216

John the "Wild Man" Baptist

*"Go tell it on the mountain
Over the hills and everywhere..."*

Have you ever sung this song? Have you ever felt like shouting from the mountaintops about something wonderful in your life? Maybe it was the winning goal in the second half of the championship soccer game or the A you received for that really tough math assignment. Whatever it was, it was so great you just had to tell someone!

John the "Wild Man" Baptist had something to shout about. It was so important and so wonderful that he lived in the desert so he could be alone—alone with God. Sounds funny, doesn't it? Here was a man who needed to talk to the people about Jesus' coming, yet he needed to be alone to listen to God. And when John was done listening, he had some important telling to do. In fact, the prophet Isaiah talked about John the Baptist long before his birth:

"A voice of one calling in the desert,
Prepare the way for the Lord,
Make straight paths for him.
Every valley shall be filled in
Every mountain and hill made low.
The crooked roads shall become straight,
The rough ways smooth.
And all mankind will see God's salvation."

John the "Wild Man" Baptist was indeed the "voice of one calling in the desert." And in the desert where John lived was a river called Jordan. God told John to go to the river and talk to the people. People came to hear the "wild man" who ate locusts and dressed in camel skins. But John didn't live this way to get attention. All of his energy went to preaching obedience to God. John told the people to be sorry for their sins. Not head sorry, but heart sorry. He told them it didn't matter how important they were or even how important their fathers or grandfathers were.

Sometimes John's words were harsh. He didn't pull any punches. He wanted people to understand that they needed to repent of their sins, to tell God they were sorry for the wrongs they had done and to turn their hearts toward God.

217

Crowds of people came to John to be baptized. He dipped them in the waters of the Jordan as a sign that they had turned from their sins, received God's forgiveness and wanted to honor and obey God.

People were astonished by this man called John. He preached and talked about God as if he knew God personally. Could he be the Savior, God's chosen one spoken of by the prophets long ago?

John told them no. "I baptize you with water. But one more powerful than I will come, the thongs of whose sandals I am not worthy to untie."

John did not know who this great man was. But God knew. Jesus would one day come to the water and be baptized, not for sins, but so that the Holy Spirit would come and rest on him.

John carried the good news of salvation to everyone. You might not live in a desert or near a river, but you can tell the good news too—at the playground, in the park, or even on your own front steps.

Go for the Godprint

Evangelism: John the Baptist had a lot of telling to do! God wants everyone to hear the Gospel. How can you spread the Gospel? You don't need fancy equipment or the latest electronic gadgets. Use your voice and let God speak to people's hearts. People need to hear that God loves them and sent Jesus to earth to live and die and rise again so their sins can be forgiven. Spread the good news!

What Digby Dug Up

IN THE DESERT JOHN THE BAPTIST ATE LOCUSTS AND WILD HONEY. HE MAY ALSO HAVE EATEN LOCUST BEANS WHICH GREW IN PODS AND HUNG FROM TREES. THESE BEANS ARE STICKY AND SWEET AND TASTE LIKE CANDY.

GET LIST:
TWO PLASTIC CUPS
A SHARP PENCIL
60-INCH PIECE OF STRING.

Make your own good news lifeline to practice sharing the good news about Jesus. Use the pencil to put a small hole in the center of the bottom of each cup. Insert one end of the string into each cup and knot it. Hold the cup to your ear and listen. Hot tip: This activity works well only if the string between the cups is taut. What happens if our string loses its shape? You may be the "lifeline" to bring the good news about Jesus into someone's life!

God Talk
Make folded paper airplanes together.
On one wing of each plane, write:
"Because God wants everyone to know about him, I can tell others about Jesus."
On the other wing, write the name of somebody who needs to know about Jesus.
Pray and ask God to give you a chance to tell the good news of Jesus.
Then let the good news fly!

GALILEE GAZETTE

JESUS BAPTIZED

JORDAN RIVER—Crowds gathered at the Jordan River today witnessed an amazing event and heard a voice from heaven which many claimed was the voice of God.

220

This remarkable occurrence centers around the teachings and practices of a man locals call "John the Baptist." John the Baptist has been sighted in recent months preaching in the desert area of Judea. Bart the Bricklayer, a follower of John the Baptist, says, "John's a little different, that's for sure. He wears clothes made from camel hair and eats locusts and honey. Not exactly what I'd choose for myself, but it's not what he eats or wears that makes John so special. It's the way he preaches. He tells it like it is."

As Bart suggests, the message of John the Baptist has been one of repentance and change. His most common statement is "Change your hearts and lives because the kingdom of heaven is near." Many of those who hear John admit doing wrong things, then ask John to baptize them in the river to show their determination to change.

Reporters spoke with Claudia the Candlemaker about the changes in her life. "John told me straight out I wasn't doing the right things and I knew he was telling the truth. I decided to stop cheating people. I want to obey God now. John baptized me. I've been trying my best to do what's right ever since."

This religious movement gained even greater momentum when a local man, Jesus of Nazareth, appeared yesterday at John's preaching site. Insiders say Jesus and John are cousins, and that John's preaching has something to do with ancient prophecies being fulfilled through the life of Jesus.

According to witnesses, when Jesus asked John to baptize him, John replied,

"I need to be baptized by you, and do you come to me?" This comment refers to the ancient writings John often speaks of. Onlookers heard Jesus reply, "Let it be so now; it is proper for us to do this to fulfill all righteousness." Then John agreed to baptize Jesus.

The two men entered the water as crowds pressed around. When Jesus came out of the water, the skies seemed to open up. What looked like a dove came down from the sky. Many said it was God's Spirit taking the shape of a dove. A voice from heaven said, "This is my Son, whom I love; with him I am well pleased."

Reporters will continue to follow both Jesus and John the Baptist to discover more about their teachings and to determine just what this dove and voice from heaven really mean.

Go for the Godprint

Obedience: We would all like to think we don't have to obey the rules while everyone else does. Jesus had never sinned and didn't need to change his heart. But when he was baptized, he showed us how to please God by doing what God wants us to do.

What Digby Dug Up
The Jordan River is mentioned more times in the Bible than any other river—about 200 times. This is the same river the Israelites had to cross in order to enter the Promised Land.

Mo's Fab Lab

GET LIST:

- TABLE SALT
- FINELY GROUND PEPPER
- SAUCER
- METAL SPOON
- WOOL CLOTHING

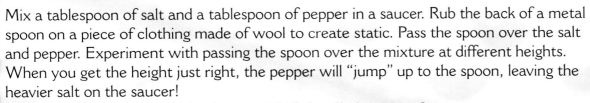

Mix a tablespoon of salt and a tablespoon of pepper in a saucer. Rub the back of a metal spoon on a piece of clothing made of wool to create static. Pass the spoon over the salt and pepper. Experiment with passing the spoon over the mixture at different heights. When you get the height just right, the pepper will "jump" up to the spoon, leaving the heavier salt on the saucer!

- **What power made the pepper "obey" the spoon?**
- **What power helps you obey God?**

God Talk
Have a family "listening prayer."
Give everyone paper and a pencil.
Pray aloud,
"Lord, we love you and want to obey you.
Speak to our hearts and teach us how to please you."
Set your kitchen timer for three minutes,
go to separate quiet places and listen to God.
Write down thoughts that come to you.
When the timer goes off,
come back together and share your "God-pleasing" ideas.

Jesus Is Tempted

224

A lone figure stumbled across the fiery sand, his robes torn and dirty. He guarded his sun-leathered face from the dust-filled wind that never stopped. He had wandered the desert for 40 days and 40 nights. Not a bite of food passed his lips all that time. Imagine the desert heat. Imagine how hungry and tired he felt.

Jesus trudged on. His mind was made up. The harshness of the desert would not defeat him. All the while, he spoke with his Heavenly Father. His lonely venture would help him do what God wanted him to do.

Satan came to Jesus, knowing the Lord was tired and weak with hunger. "If you are the Son of God, tell these stones to become bread!" Satan suggested.

Jesus hadn't eaten for more than a month. Imagine how he must have wanted food. Even just a crust of bread was tempting. But Jesus knew the Word of God. He told Satan, "It is written: 'Man does not live on bread alone.'"

Satan didn't let up. He took Jesus to a high mountain. The prince of darkness showed Jesus all the kingdoms of the world.

"I will give you all their authority and splendor, for it has been given to me," Satan whispered. "I can give it to anyone I want to. Sooo," he hissed, "if you worship me, it will all be yours!"

Surely the earthly kingdoms Jesus saw were tempting. Imagine the magnificent kingdoms below. Imagine what it would feel like to rule them all. But Jesus knew the Word of God. Jesus answered, "It is written: 'Worship the Lord your God and serve him only.'"

Suddenly Satan took Jesus to Jerusalem. They stood on the highest point of the temple. Jesus looked down upon the people scurrying through the streets—the very people he came to earth to save. They had been waiting hundreds of years for the Messiah. Now he was here, and they did not believe it.

"If you truly are the Son of God," Satan snarled, "throw yourself down from here. For it is written: 'He will command his angels concerning you to guard you carefully; they will lift you up in their hands, so that you will not strike your foot against a stone!'"

Imagine how good it would feel for Jesus to have the people below see the angels rescue him. Perhaps then they would believe he was the Messiah. But Jesus knew the Word of God. "It says: 'Do not put the Lord your God to the test!'" Jesus responded.

Furious that he could not tempt Jesus away from God's perfect plan, Satan fled. Angels immediately came to Jesus and cared for him.

Go for the Godprint

Discernment: Jesus depended on God to help him see the difference between good and evil. When we depend on God to help us, we can make wise choices. We make choices every day. Can you think of a wise choice that God can help you make?

What Digby Dug Up

WHILE JESUS WAS IN THE DESERT, HE FASTED. HE DIDN'T EAT ANYTHING. THIS WAS ONE WAY HE SHOWED GOD THAT HE WAS SERIOUS ABOUT DOING WHAT GOD WANTED HIM TO DO.

GET LIST:
20 INDEX CARDS
BIBLE
PENCILS

Separate the cards into two piles of ten. On each card in one pile, write a situation that a family member might face where he or she has to make choices, such as: when a friend wants to do something you know is wrong; when you're tempted to lie; when you find something that doesn't belong to you. On the remaining cards, write favorite Bible verses.

Turn the two piles upside down. Take turns drawing one card from each pile. Read the situation and the verse, and then explain how the verse from God's Word can help you make a wise choice. Shuffle the cards and play again.

God Talk

Pray this prayer together,
or take turns reading the lines.

Thank you, Lord, for helping me
Resist temptation to do wrong.
Help me spend more time with you.
Then, like Jesus, I'll grow strong. Amen

From Matthew 4:18-22; Luke 5:1-11; 6:12-16

Fishers of Men

This story needs one reader and one or more sound effects person. See how many sound effects you can create!

Jesus was at the Sea of Galilee, strolling along the water's edge. He listened to the waves swooshing along the shore. Water birds called out above. People crowded around Jesus. They pushed and shoved a little to get closer. The lake water lapped quietly against two boats near shore. Simon Peter and his brother Andrew stood in the water nearby washing their fishing nets. Jesus climbed into the boat that belonged to Simon Peter. His sandals made a hollow clunking sound on the bottom of the wooden boat. He asked Simon to push the boat out from shore a little. Jesus sat down and taught the people. Afterwards, Jesus told Simon to take the boat out to deep water to catch some fish.
Simon said, "We fished all night and didn't catch anything. But if you say so, we'll do it." The two brothers threw out their nets to catch some fish. It whooshed through the air and hit the water with a gentle slap.

Water gurgled under the boat as they pulled away from the shallows and made their way to the deep part of the lake. They threw their nets out over the water. Suddenly, the nets were brimming with flapping, flopping fish! The nets started to break as the men strained to pull them in. Simon and Andrew called their friends James and John to come help in another boat.

229

That's My Spot! A Crowded Hillside

One day a huge crowd listened to Jesus teach. He climbed up a hill so everyone could hear him. He wanted to teach them to love each other and get along better.

It was crowded on the hillside. Maybe people were getting crabby. Maybe people said things like,

"It's all your fault!"

"Ha, ha! You look weird!"

"Let me do it. You don't know how."

Oooh, nasty words! Have you ever said something like that?

If you think other people should never make a mistake, they'll expect you to be perfect, too. Worry about fixing your own mistakes instead of picking on someone else.

Jesus said, "Do not judge, or you too will be judged."

Do you think there was somebody on the hillside with Jesus who was lonely?

How would you like it if no one wanted to be your friend? How would you feel if no one ever said "Good job!" when you tried your best or "Thank you!" when you did something extra special nice?

Jesus said, "Do to others what you would have them do to you." That's a good way to live your life every day.

Maybe somebody on the hillside only pretended to like Jesus. Nobody fools Jesus. He had something to say to those people, too.

Can you pick fat, red grapes from a thorn bush? Of course not.

Can you pick soft, sweet figs from a weed patch? Of course not.

Grapes come from grapevines, and if the vine is rotten, the grapes will be, too. Figs come from fig trees, and if the tree is healthy, the figs will be scrumptious, too.

Imagine a beautiful tree with smelly rotten fruit. What a silly picture!

Imagine a dried up dead tree with simply delicious fruit. Now that's impossible.

A bad tree only grows bad fruit. And a good tree grows good fruit. You can tell what the whole tree is like by tasting one piece of fruit.

People are like fruit trees. Jesus wants us to show what we're like on the inside by what we do on the outside.

Jesus said, "Everyone who hears these words of mine and puts them into practice is like a wise man."

The wise man doesn't build his house in just any ol' spot. He doesn't grab his hammer and start pounding away. He thinks long and hard. He wants to build this house right. He wants it to stand up long enough for his children and grandchildren to grow up in it. So he looks for the best place to build a house—on solid ground. The wise man builds his house on the rock.

The rain comes. It seems like it's never going to quit. The drops become puddles, and the puddles become a pond. Pretty soon the house is in the middle of a raging river. But the wise man's house is high and dry on the rock.

And the wind comes, a twisting tornado, a howling hurricane. The wind bangs and blows and beats on the house. The windows rattle. The walls shake. But the house stands firm.

233

Anyone who ignores what Jesus says is like a foolish man. The foolish man wants to build his house as fast as he can. He finds some empty ground, grabs a hammer and starts building. Whack! Thwack! Thud! The house goes up quick as a lick. So what if the ground underneath is soft sand?

The rain comes. It seems like it's never going to quit. The drops become puddles, and the puddles become a pond. Pretty soon the house is in the middle of a raging river. And then the walls start to sink.

And the wind comes, a twisting tornado, a howling hurricane. The wind bangs and blows and beats on the house. The windows rattle. The walls shake. Whack! Thwack! Thud! Crash! The whole house caves in and the foolish man has nothing.

"Wow! He knows what he's talking about!" the people on the hillside said. Because Jesus teaches us how to treat other people, we can love them the way Jesus does.

Go for the Godprint

Love: It's not easy to think about what someone else needs, especially if it means giving up something that you want for yourself. But that's what love is. God loves us and gives us the example of how to love each other.

What Digby Dug Up
The story of the wise and foolish builders comes from the Sermon on the Mount. It's called this because Jesus was on the side of a mountain while he talked. It's one of the most famous parts of the Bible.

Café de Click

GET LIST: VARIETY OF FRUIT, THAWED NON-DAIRY WHIPPED TOPPING, GRAHAM CRACKERS

Gather fruit with a variety of textures and colors. Slice the fruit into various shapes and sizes. Use the fruit as bricks or boards and use the whipped topping as mortar. Build a house out of the fruit. Some ideas: use grapes as bricks, stand apple slices on end, stack strawberries, slice bananas lengthwise for a roof. If you need more firm reinforcements for a foundation or walls, use graham crackers. While you build (and eat!), talk about these questions:

- **Tell about a time when someone did something for you that made you feel loved.**
- **Choose a person that you want to show your love to. What's something you can do to make that person feel loved?**

Parents, share something from your own experience first. Then encourage others to answer the questions.

God Talk

Choose one family member to be the "prayer leader"
and lead the family in this prayer.
Everyone else repeats the line,
"Make us wise. Be our rock."

Lord, remind us to pay attention to you. **Make us wise. Be our rock.**
Help us love one another. **Make us wise. Be our rock.**
Help us treat others the way we want them to treat us. **Make us wise. Be our rock.**
Remind us that we can love others because you love us. **Make us wise. Be our rock.**
Amen.

A Centurion's Plea

My servant's sick. What shall I do?
I'm not a healer—I have no clue.
It doesn't help to sit and stew.
Who can I call to help me?

I've heard of someone new in town—
A teacher and prophet of great renown.
He preaches and heals folks all around.
I wonder if he'll help me.

A hundred men do what I say.
I give orders—they obey.
But I can't make men well—no way!
I need someone to help me.

I'll go look for Jesus now.
I'll seek his help—I'll plead and bow.
I believe he'll help somehow.
I pray that he will help me.

"Jesus," I said, "My servant lies
At home—and he is paralyzed!
The pain is bad—he cries and cries.
Help me, Jesus! Help me!

236

"His suffering is terrible,
But you could make it bearable
If you did a miracle.
Please, Lord, will you help me?"

Jesus answered, "I will go
And heal this man who suffers so."
Then I answered, "No, Lord, no—
Just your word will help me.

"You don't need to come with me.
You're too busy—I can see.
I don't deserve your company.
But still, Lord, you can help me.

"All you need to do is say
The word and he'll be healed today.
Then I'll just be on my way.
Please, Lord, won't you help me?

"A hundred soldiers wait at hand
To do whatever I command.
That's something I can understand.
Just say the word to help me.

"If I say, 'Go!' my soldiers go.
If I say, 'Slow,' they go so slow.
I march them high, I march them low.
Your command can help me."

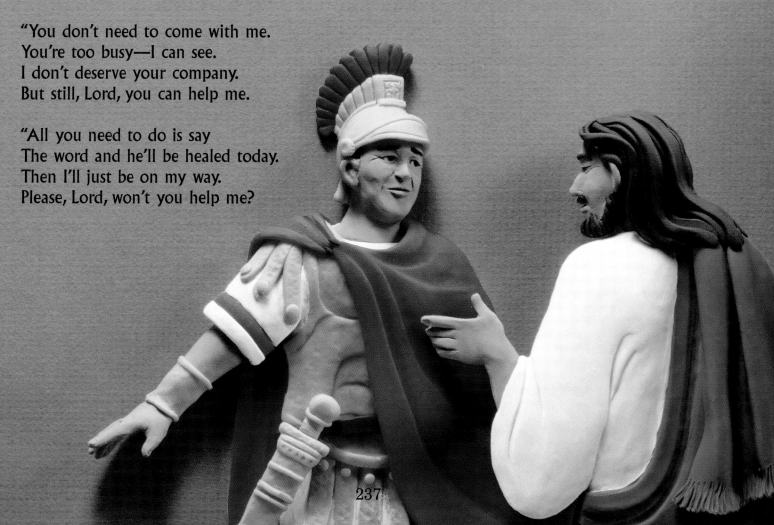

Jesus looked into my eyes.
He saw my faith; he was surprised.
His answer came, so kind and wise:
He said that he would help me.

"As you've believed, it will be done."
And then he said to everyone,
"His faith is greater than Israel's sons."
Yes! The Lord would help me.

I felt so thankful. It was great!
My servant healed...I couldn't wait
To hurry home and celebrate
Because the Lord had helped me.

I went straight home. I got there quick.
My servant was no longer sick!
He could walk without a stick!
He helped me. Jesus helped me!

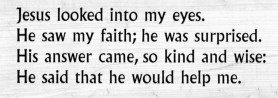

Go for the Godprint

Prayerfulness: Jesus could have healed the servant from another town or another country. Jesus can do anything. And if we trust Jesus' loving power as the centurion did, he can help us in any situation—no matter where we are or what we're doing. How will you trust in Jesus' power this week?

What Digby Dug Up

The Greek word "cent-" means 100. The man with the sick servant was a centurion in the Roman army. A cent-urion was a Roman military officer in charge of 100 soldiers. In today's language: A cent-ury is 100 years. A cent-enarian is someone who lives for 100 years. It takes 100 cents (pennies) to make a dollar. What other "cent-" words can you come up with?

Herbie's Hideaway

You can ask Jesus to use his power to help the people you love.
Have each family member choose a friend or relative to pray for this week.
Then design a prayer page for each
person you'll pray for. On the page,
include a photo (or drawing if you don't
have a photo) of the person, pictures
or words that describe the person, and any
specific things you'd like to pray about. Keep
the pages in a notebook or folder. Have your whole family
pray for one person each day!

God Talk

Play Musical Prayers with your family,
or invite friends to join you.
You'll need a chair for each person,
a music CD or cassette, and a CD or cassette player.
Line up the chairs back-to-back.
Under the seat of one chair, tape a sign that says "Prayer Chair."
When you're ready to play, have people walk around the chairs as the music plays.
Stop the music and have everyone scramble into the chairs.
Check to see who's sitting in the Prayer Chair.
Then take turns praying (out loud or silently) for that person.
Play (and pray!) as many times as you want.

A Hiker's Guide to Israel:
Jesus' Instructions to the Twelve

Hiking in Israel is not for the weak. The trails are rugged and dusty and full of unexpected problems. If you plan to hit the trails, make sure you're prepared. Read these instructions carefully and take only the right equipment with you.

Historical Trails

Q: How did hiking in Israel begin?

A: When Jesus lived, people didn't have cars or trains or airplanes. People had to walk from place to place. Most hikers walked about 20 miles every day. Superhikers, working as messengers, sometimes went as far as 75 miles.

Q: Who are the some of the most famous hikers in Israel's history?

A: Jesus chose twelve disciples from among all the people who followed him. These special friends would tell everyone about him. Their names were:

Simon Peter and his brother, Andrew
The brothers, James and John
Philip and Bartholomew
Thomas and Matthew
Another James and Thaddeus
Simon and Judas Iscariot.

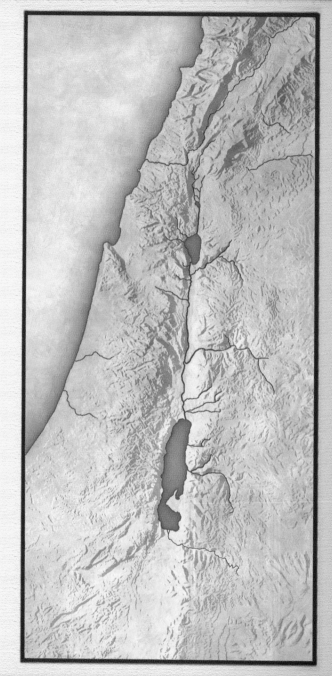

Q: Where are the best trails?
A: Trails don't have to take you to faraway places or people you don't know. Check out the ones where you live first. Look for people you know. If you do, you'll be doing what Jesus told the disciples to do.

Q: Are there many hikers on the trail?
A: You might run into some lost sheep. That's what Jesus called the people his disciples met on the trails. People who are lost and confused need to hear that God's kingdom is near. The disciples made sure people heard the message.

Q: Did Jesus' famous hikers do other things besides walking and talking?
A: They healed people who were sick, cured people with diseases, and helped those with problems to be happy again. Jesus' disciples did all these things.

Hiking Equipment— Not What You Expect

Q: What should a hiker take on the hike?
A: Nothing. Many hikers hope to take gold, silver or copper in their money belts. But Jesus says not to. God provides what his hikers need.

Q: Can hikers take a bag to carry things?
A: No. Travel light. Don't get attached to things that keep you comfortable.

Q: Are walking sticks allowed to help with tired feet?
A: No. God will give you strength.

Q: What if clothes or shoes wear out? Do hikers take extras?
A: No. God makes sure hikers have everything they need.

Warning! Hiking is Hard Work

Q: Is it safe to hike overnight?
A: Yes, if you find the right place. When you come to a town, find someone friendly. Stay at that person's house and be friends with the family who lives there. If someone doesn't want to welcome you in, go away peacefully and look for another place.

Q: Are the trails dangerous?
A: If you're hiking to tell people about God's kingdom, not everyone will like what you have to say. People might be mean. Some officials might even want to arrest you. Be courteous, and don't get in any fights. Make wise choices. But don't worry; God knows everything about you, even how many hairs are on your head. And he'll take care of you.

Q: Hiking for Jesus sounds hard. Is there a prize?

A: The people who pay attention will listen because Jesus sends the hikers. Anyone who listens to you is really listening to Jesus. And anyone who is the friend of a hiker is also a friend of Jesus. The smallest act of giving to someone you meet on the trail, even just a cup of water for a child, means you're one of Jesus' hikers. That's the best reward of all.

Modern Day Hiking

Jesus' disciples didn't have a booklet to help them hike around Israel spreading the news about God's kingdom. But they did have Jesus' words. They told lots of people about Jesus, and you can too. You don't have to have special clothes or lots of money. Just do what Jesus said. Tell the people you know well first and be a good friend to them. If you care for the people you meet, they'll know that God cares, too.

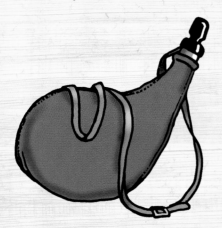

Go for the Godprint

Responsibility: Do you keep your promises? If you tell someone you're going to do something, then do it. Jesus asked his disciples to tell people about God. He also asks us to tell people about him. Because we love God, it is our responsibility to do what he wants us to do, including telling friends about Jesus.

What Digby Dug Up

Jesus' disciples were ordinary people, like fishermen and tax collectors. They all had different personalities. They had one thing in common: they all loved Jesus and wanted to spread his message about the kingdom of God.

Herbie's Hideaway

The names of Jesus' disciples are hidden in the puzzle below. As you find each one, imagine how that disciple might have told someone about Jesus.

```
B I W U J A M E S R N
J A S E D A R D M S E
A V R T T S B O P I B
M Y P T C I L N I M I
E U H H H M H P Y O J
S E I A W O S M T N A
W J L D J N L A H P N
C N I D R U J O O E D
T W P E R S D N M T R
H I A U Y C E A A E E
J V L S M O N D S R W
```

God Talk
Jesus told his disciples
that the Holy Spirit would help them
know what to say when they told people about him.
Think of a time when you need God's help
knowing what to say and pray about that.

243

Jesus Walks on Water

Do you know how your mom or dad says, "Keep your eye on the ball!" before pitching one to you? That's to help you hit it better. Well, I had to learn to keep my eyes on Jesus because when I looked away, I started sinking fast. My name is Peter and I was a disciple of Jesus. Let me tell you what happened.

I was a fisherman, big and strong.
I fished in the sea every day at dawn.
My oars went "splash" and the waves went "splish"
And my nets went "swish" 'til I had a load of fish.

My brother, Andrew, was also a fisherman. We used nets instead of fishing poles on our boat to catch lots of fish. Then Jesus came and told us to follow him—that he'd "make us fishers of men." So we left our boat and nets and followed him.

One night Jesus was especially tired. He had fed 5,000 people by blessing five loaves of bread and two fish. He wanted to go to a mountainside by himself to pray. Jesus told us to cross the Sea of Galilee in a boat. He said he would join us later.

Andrew and I got in the boat with James and John and the other disciples. We started for the opposite shore.

In the middle of the night, a nasty storm came up really fast. We were pulling hard on the oars of our rowboat.

The winds started blowing;
The waves started growing,
And I knew we were going…
Nowhere.

All of a sudden, we saw someone walking on top of the water towards us. One of the disciples yelled, "It's a ghost!" We were shaking in our sandals.

Then I realized it was Jesus. He called to us, "Don't be afraid. It is I." "Lord," I said, "If it is you, tell me to come to you on the water." "Come," he said.
So I thought:

> "The wind is still blowing,
> And the waves are still growing
> But I am going…
> To Jesus!"

I pulled off my sandals, hitched up my cloak, and got out of the boat. I went toward Jesus walking on top of the water. But then:

> The winds kept on blowing,
> The waves kept on growing,
> And suddenly I was going…
> Down!

I looked away from Jesus and began to sink down into the water. "O Lord, save me!" I cried out.

Immediately, Jesus reached out his hand and grabbed my hand. "You of little faith," he said, "why did you doubt?" We climbed into the boat and the winds and waves became quiet. Andrew, James, John and the others bowed down and worshipped Jesus saying, "Truly, you are the Son of God."

When we reached the opposite shore, people recognized Jesus. They brought to him all their relatives and friends who were sick , to touch his clothes and be blessed by him. And all the people who touched Jesus were healed.

I'll tell you what I learned that night:

When the winds start to blow,
And the waves start to grow,
I will always know…
To trust Jesus!

Truly Jesus is the Son of God. And I can trust him because he cares for me.

Go for the Godprint

Trust: Have you ever jumped off the diving board into Mom or Dad's arms? You knew they would catch you, didn't you? Now think about jumping into Jesus' arms. He loves you so very much—he will catch you every time. When you get worried or afraid, think about Jesus with his arms open wide, just waiting to hold you.

What Digby Dug Up

STORMS COME UP QUICKLY ON THE SEA OF GALILEE. THE DISCIPLES KNEW THAT THEY AND THEIR BOAT WERE IN DANGER FROM THE GROWING WINDS AND WAVES. LOOK AT A MAP OF ISRAEL IN THE BACK OF A BIBLE TO FIND THE SEA OF GALILEE.

Wally's Walkabout

GET LIST:
BLINDFOLD
SHORT PIECE OF ROPE

Want to take a trust walk? Blindfold one family member with a bandanna or strip of fabric. Make sure not to cover the nose! The leader and the follower should each hold one end of a short rope. Walk around the house or the backyard. Take turns being the careful leader and the trusting follower. Make sure everyone gets a turn being both leader and follower. Then talk about:

• **What made you nervous when you were the follower?**

  • **What did you do to be a good leader?**

    • How is trusting someone to lead you around the house like trusting Jesus?

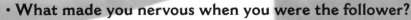

God Talk
Learn to say this Bible verse as a prayer:
"When I am afraid, I will trust in you." Psalm 56:3
Hold up two fists.
Say the verse and put up a finger for each syllable.
(There are ten syllables.)
Now practice saying the verse as you put up your fingers.
Use it as a prayer:
Dear Lord,
When I am afraid, I will trust in you.
Amen.

247

White, Whiter, Whitest

How many different words can you think of that mean the same as "bright." Did you think of

Blazing

Brilliant

Flaming

Beaming

Dazzling

Gleaming

Glowing

Sparkling

Shiny

Radiant

Glittering

Shimmering?

Peter, James and John went with Jesus to a mountain to pray. While they were there, the most incredible thing happened. Even if you could think of a hundred words that mean "bright," or even a thousand, that wouldn't be enough to describe what they saw.

When they went up the mountain, Jesus had an ordinary face and ordinary clothes. But at the top of the mountain, Jesus' face started to shine like the sun. And his clothes were as white as light. All the bleach in the world couldn't make his clothes any whiter or brighter than they were at that moment. The disciples were a little sleepy, but they woke up fast! Imagine standing next to someone who was shining like the sun.

Suddenly, there were two more people on that mountaintop—Moses and Elijah. Both of them had lived a long time before Jesus, but there they were, standing next to him. Peter, James and John didn't know what to think.

And there's more! All of a sudden, a bright cloud surrounded all of them. A voice from inside the cloud said, "This is my Son, whom I love; with him I am well pleased. Listen to him!"

Now the disciples were scared. They had never seen anything so terrifying in their whole lives. Was it real? Were they imagining it? That voice must have been God speaking! Was the glory of God really there on that mountaintop?

Yes, it was the voice of God. The disciples saw the glory of God, not just the human body of Jesus. God wanted them to know that he was about to finish what he had promised a long time ago. When Moses was alive, God made promises to save his people.

And Elijah's job was to help the people get ready for God's coming. Moses, Elijah and Jesus talked about how Jesus would go to Jerusalem very soon. He would finish God's work once and for all and save the people from their sins.

When God changed the way Jesus looked into blazing light and spoke from the cloud, he told the disciples that it was time. He was going to do what he had promised so long ago.

Jesus didn't want the disciples to be scared. He reached out and touched them. "Get up," he said. "Don't be afraid." Peter, James and John got up and opened their eyes. Moses and Elijah were gone. Jesus was by himself. And he looked just the same as he always had. Everything was back to normal.

But the disciples would never forget what they saw that day. Now they were sure that Jesus was going to do something incredible for the world.

Go for the Godprint

Wonder: Have you ever read a story or seen a movie that seemed so amazing that it couldn't be real? Maybe what you saw wasn't real. But what the disciples saw really happened. When we see the incredible power of God, we can't help but be amazed. Think of something that God does that amazes you.

What Digby Dug Up

Transfiguration—wow! What a big word. It means simply that Jesus' appearance was completely changed. Matthew, Mark and Luke all tell the story of the Transfiguration. Only Luke says that Jesus went up on the mountain to pray.

Izzy's Art Cart

GET LIST:
 PLAIN PAPER
 YELLOW FLUORESCENT MARKER
 VEGETABLE OIL
 COTTON BALL
 PLASTIC WRAP

Use a fluorescent yellow marker to draw the outline of a human figure. Fill in the outline completely. This will remind you how Jesus's appearance changed. Turn the page over and lay it face down on a smooth piece of plastic wrap that is twice as big as the paper. Dip the cotton ball in vegetable oil and rub it all over the back of your paper. Cover the paper thoroughly from edge to edge. As the oil soaks in, the paper will become translucent. Fold the rest of the plastic wrap around the back of your drawing, keeping the plastic wrap as smooth as you can. Tape your project to a window or door with bright sunlight coming in. You'll see the light come right through your drawing, even where it's colored. Talk about:
  • What do you think it would be like to see God's glory, bright as light?
  • How does God's incredible power make you feel?

God Talk
Take turns completing the sentence,
"Thank you, God,
for showing your amazing power when you _____."

Mercy! Mercy!

Once Peter came to Jesus and asked him, "When someone keeps treating me badly, how many times should I forgive him? Seven times?" Jesus told Peter, "Not seven times, but seventy-seven times." Then Jesus told a story to help Peter understand why we should forgive others.

Once there was a king who was known as being good and fair. The king had many servants, and they often asked to borrow money. Maybe they needed new donkeys, or a new barn, or were having company for dinner and wanted to serve a fancy feast. Being a kind man, the king usually loaned them the money. "I'll pay you back as soon as I can!" the servants always said, and the king was patient and waited for them to pay. After a while it seemed like a lot of people owed the king a lot of money. Finally he decided it was time to collect the money the servants owed him.

One of the servants who borrowed from the king was Zeke. Zeke liked to spend, spend, spend. Over the years he borrowed more money from the king than anyone else. Not fifty dollars. Not one hundred dollars. Not even a thousand dollars. Zeke borrowed millions and millions of dollars!

"It's time to pay me back," said the king.

Zeke gulped. "I don't have the money right now," he stammered.

The king turned to a nearby servant. "In that case," the king said, "sell all of Zeke's property—every single thing he has. Sell his wife and his children, too. Use that money to pay what he owes me."

The king wasn't being mean. It was Zeke's fault that he hadn't repaid the king. But he didn't want to lose everything—especially his family. Zeke fell to his knees and begged the king to change his mind.

"Please give me a chance. Be patient. I'll pay back everything—just don't sell my family!"

The king listened to Zeke and thought about this for a few minutes.

"Zeke, I've decided to do something even better," the king said. "I won't sell your family. I won't make you work harder. In fact, I've decided to forget the whole thing. You can go home without having to worry about ever paying me even one penny."

Zeke was so relieved he started to cry and laugh at the same time. He thanked the king over and over, then ran home to share the great news with his family. On his way

home, Zeke bumped into another servant named Zeb. Zeb had
borrowed three dollars from Zeke so he could buy vegetables for
his children to have for dinner. When Zeke saw Zeb he
forgot how happy he was. Instead he grabbed
Zeb around the throat and began to
choke him!

"Pay me back that three dollars!" Zeke demanded.

"Wait! Give me another day! I'll give you the money tomorrow!" Zeb managed to sputter.

But Zeke wasn't satisfied. He had Zeb thrown in jail until he could pay the three dollars back. Then he brushed off his clothes and started toward home again.

Zeke didn't know it, but other servants saw everything that happened. They went back and told the king what Zeke had done to Zeb. This made the king *really* angry! He had Zeke brought back and sternly said, "Even though you owed a huge amount, I told you that you didn't have to pay anything to me. You should have treated Zeb the same way. What you did was evil."

The king had Zeke put in prison to be punished until he could repay all the millions he had owed before.

Jesus ended the story by explaining that this is how God thinks of forgiveness. We can't expect God to forgive us if we aren't forgiving toward others. God forgives us when we ask him, and God expects us to forgive others too.

Go for the Godprint

Forgiveness: We all like to be forgiven when we do something wrong. But how easy is it to turn around and forgive a friend who breaks a toy, a brother who makes a mean face, or a sister who teases? Because God forgives us, we can forgive others. Who can you forgive right now?

What Digby Dug Up

In Jesus' time, "77" was a way of saying "no limit." Jesus was telling Peter never to stop forgiving.

Jake's Mirth Quake

Play a board game that involves play money, such as Monopoly®. Instead of playing to win, have the person who gets the most money share it with those who are running out.

• **How is playing this way like what happened in the Bible story?**

• **How is forgiving in real life different from giving away play money in a game?**

• **When is it hard to forgive?**

• **How can remembering this story help you?**

God Talk

Count out 77 coins or other small object,
such as buttons, beads or toothpicks.
Take turns trying to name 77 things that God can help you forgive.
For each one you name, say,
"God, help me forgive _____."

256

Come to the Party!

Jesus loved to tell stories. But his stories had hidden meanings. Can you figure out the hidden meaning of this story?

"It's time, it's time! Is everything ready?"

The king hustled and bustled around the palace. His son was getting married! The party was ready. The food was heaped on the tables. The band was standing by. The king had thought of everything. He had sent out the invitations long ago telling everyone about the party so they could prepare. Now he just had to let the guests know the party was ready. So he sent his servants out to the fancy guests, the rich guests, the important guests. The servants told everyone that it was time for the wedding banquet.

And no one came. Absolutely no one. They knew all about the party. They just didn't want to come.

The king didn't give up. "Tell them I've prepared my finest dinner," he told his servants. "I fattened my ox and cow for months. The meal will be one they won't want to miss!"

So the servants went out again, to the fancy guests, the rich guests, the important guests.

And no one came. Absolutely no one. The guests paid no attention to the king's invitation. One guest went off to look at his field. Another went on a business trip. The rest jumped on the king's servants and beat them up— almost killing them.

This made the king angry. Really angry. He sent his army out to destroy the city where those guests lived.

But the king still wanted to have a party for his son. So he told his servants, "The wedding banquet is ready. But the people I invited don't deserve to come. Go out to the street corners and invite anyone you can find."

So the servants went out again and invited people to the party. And they came. Lots of them. It didn't matter if they were good or bad, rich or poor. Everyone was welcome. The wedding hall was full of guests.

Now the king came in to see the guests. He was happy with what he saw. People were eating his fattened ox and cow. People were celebrating with his son. This was just the party he wanted.

And then he saw it—a man was wearing ordinary street clothes. Now the king knew the rules for a wedding banquet. He knew you were supposed to make sure all the guests had clean, fresh wedding clothes, even if you had to give them clothes yourself. Yet this man was wearing ordinary clothes, and they were dirty at that. What an insult! How could that be? The king marched right up to that man to find out.

"How did you get in here without any wedding clothes?" the king asked.

The man only stared at him and didn't answer the question.

The king called his servants once more. "Tie him hand and foot and throw him outside," the king said. "Throw him into the darkness, where there will be weeping and gnashing of teeth."

When Jesus finished the story, he said, "For many are invited, but few are chosen." Does that help you figure out the hidden meaning?

Many people were invited to the king's wedding banquet. But not everyone wanted to come. And not everyone who came really cared about the party. The man without wedding clothes didn't bother to get ready.

The king in this story is like God. God invites everyone to be part of his kingdom, but only the people who are truly sorry for their sins and change their ways will be able to go to heaven.

Go for the Godprint

Commitment: What do you do to get ready for a party? What if it were a party that never ends? When you make a commitment to follow Jesus, you go to a party that starts now and never ends. Jesus even gives you the right clothes for the party—a robe of righteousness that comes with believing in Jesus. Are you ready to wear it?

What Digby Dug Up

In Bible times, people received two invitations: one to say there was going to be a party, and a second one to announce that it was time to come. The king in this story gave his guests a third invitation and an extra chance to come to the party.

Jake's Mirth Quake

Throw a party with "Celebrate Jesus!" as your theme. What food, music and decorations can you use? Will you wear special clothes? What games can you play? Who will you invite? Make fancy invitations on your computer or draw them by hand. What message will you write? Make sure to invite someone who needs to know how good it is to be part of God's family.

God Talk

Have you accepted God's invitation
to be part of his family?
If you're ready now, you can pray this prayer:
Dear Lord, thank you for loving me
and wanting me in your family.
I love you, too.
I'm sorry that I don't always please you,
and I want to live the way you want me to live.
I know that Jesus will help me do that. In Jesus' name, amen.

Leaping Legs!

I had four friends who did something nice for me. But I have an even more wonderful friend named Jesus who cares for me. He can be your friend too, if you ask him.

I was a paralytic. Do you know what a paralytic is? It is someone who can't move his legs. I couldn't run or walk or even sit up. I lay on my mat day after day unable to move. Can you imagine lying on your bed without even rolling over? I was very sad.

One day four of my friends heard that Jesus was nearby. But they weren't the only ones who heard that news. Many people had heard about Jesus—he healed a man with leprosy and a lady who had a fever. All those people gathered in a home in Capernaum to listen to him talk.

My friends wanted to take me there. How do you think they did that?

Did they push me on a hospital bed with wheels?

Did they send me in a limousine?

Or did they carry me on a mat to see Jesus?

That's right, they each took one corner of the mat and carried me to see Jesus.

When we got there, the house was completely full of people. People stood outside and looked in the windows and blocked the doorway. My friends wanted to get me inside the house. How do you think they did that?

Did they make a parade go by so everyone would run outside to watch, and they could carry me in the back door?

Did they try to stuff me in through a window?

forgiven,' or to heal a paralytic?" (That was me.) Then what do you think Jesus did?

Did he give me a twenty-dollar bill to see a doctor?

Did he tell me that he was busy and to come back later after he finished talking?

Or did he say, "So that you know that the Son of Man has the authority to forgive sins... I tell you, get up, take your mat and go home." (Sometimes Jesus called himself the "Son of Man." We also know that he is the Son of God.)

Or did they carry me up to the roof and dig a hole through the ceiling?

My four friends dug through a layer of clay and branches, making a hole big enough for me. They lowered me on my mat through the roof in front of Jesus. He stopped talking and saw the love my friends had for me, and the faith they had in him. Jesus said to me, "Son, your sins are forgiven."

There were teachers of the law sitting there who thought, "Hey, no one can forgive sins except God. Who does Jesus think he is—God?" Jesus knew they had these thoughts and he asked them a question: "Which is easier, to say 'Your sins are

261

Jesus forgave my sins and he healed me. I picked up my mat and walked out. I wasn't a paralytic anymore. What do you think the people who saw this did?

Did they give Jesus a standing ovation?

Did they say, "Oh, wow! That's so totally awesome."

Or were they amazed and praised God saying, "We have never seen anything like this!"

As for me, I was thrilled. My four friends were thrilled, and we praised God.

My friends cared for me by bringing me to Jesus. Now I tell others about Jesus. Will you tell your friends that Jesus cares for them? He can be their friend too.

Go for the Godprint

Compassion: Do you have a pet? Or maybe you have a friend with a pet. Did the pet ever get sick and have to go to the veterinarian? You showed compassion by taking the pet to the vet so he could help it feel better. We also show compassion for other people who are sad or sick by praying for them and telling them that Jesus wants to be their friend.

What Digby Dug Up

WHEN JESUS LIVED IN ISRAEL, THE HOUSES HAD FLAT ROOFS. IF IT WAS HOT INSIDE THE HOUSE, A FAMILY COULD SLEEP ON THEIR ROOF IN THE COOL NIGHT AIR. WOULD YOU WANT TO SLEEP ON TOP OF YOUR ROOF?

Jake's Mirth Quake

CELEBRATE YOUR LEGS!

Standing Jump—Place a one-foot piece of masking tape on the floor. Stand with your toes on the masking tape. Take three turns jumping as far as you can. Measure each jump to see which one was the longest.

Frog Hop—Crouch like a frog with your toes on the masking tape. Make three frog hops. (It's okay for your hands to touch the floor.) Measure the distance to see how far you went. Was it as far as the Standing Jump?

One Leg Balance—Stand on your right foot with arms out and eyes closed. Time how long you can stand on one leg. Then stand on the other leg. Which leg can you balance on longer? Who is the family champion in each event? Talk about:

WHAT'S GREAT ABOUT LEGS?

WHAT'S GREAT ABOUT HOW GOD CARES FOR US?

CAN YOU THINK OF A WAY TO PRAISE GOD WITH YOUR LEGS?

God Talk

Psalm 145:9 says,
"The Lord is good to all;
he has compassion on all he has made."
God cares about everything and everybody he made.
Do you know someone who needs God's compassion today?
Fill in the blanks in this prayer.
Dear Lord,
I am thinking about _____. I know that you care for _____ because you care for everything you have made. Please help _____ to feel better. Thank you.
Amen.

From Wind and Waves to Breeze and Ripples

Wherever Jesus went, there were people. People to his left. People to his right. People with questions. People who were sick. They brought their children to him. They brought their friends to him. And he loved everyone. But sometimes even Jesus needed to rest. So many people, so many problems, so many questions. He needed to get away.

One day Jesus had been teaching all day by a lake. The crowds surrounded him, wanting to hear every word he said. At the end of the day he knew he needed to find a quiet place to go. He went to his closest followers, his disciples, and said,

"Let's go over to the other side of the lake."

So they all got into the boat and left that big crowd of people behind. Jesus was tired, so he went to the back of the boat, found a pillow and was asleep in no time. The lake was calm and quiet, and the boat gently rocked back and forth. Every once in a while a fish would jump out of the water or a seagull would fly overhead. A soft breeze blew, and the apostles sat together on the boat and talked about the day.

Suddenly the biggest storm you can imagine surrounded them. Huge waves crashed over the sides of the boat. It rocked wildly back and forth, and the disciples held on with all their might. Giant, rolling, black clouds filled the sky. Lightning flashed and thunder roared. It seemed the boat might be swallowed up by the angry waves. Jesus' friends were terrified. With every wave that hit, they feared the boat would turn over and toss them into the raging waters. How could they make it to land? There seemed to be no hope. And do you know where Jesus was this whole time? Still in the back of the boat, sleeping peacefully .

The disciples rushed to Jesus. They woke him up from his deep sleep and cried, "Lord, help us! Don't you even care if we drown?" Jesus calmly stood up and looked around him. He saw the waves and the lightning and the clouds, but he was not afraid. He spoke to the storm and said,

"Quiet! Be still!"

Then the most amazing thing happened. The storm stopped as quickly as it had started. The water was like glass. The wind calmed down and the sun reappeared. Then Jesus looked at his friends and said,

"Why are so afraid? Do you still have no faith?"

They looked at Jesus in wonder. They had seen him do miracles before—he made the lame walk and the blind see, but they had never seen anything like this. Even the wind and the waves obeyed him! Jesus had the magnificent power of God. Even though they knew him well, they asked themselves, "Who is this man?"

But we know who he is.
He is Jesus, the Son of God.

Go for the Godprint

Wonder: When the disciples saw Jesus calm the storm, they were amazed by his magnificent power. It was almost more than they could believe, but they had seen it, so they knew it was true. They had a deep sense of wonder. What things in God's world give you a sense of wonder and amazement?

What Digby Dug Up

The Sea of Galilee, where Jesus calmed the storm, is 680 feet below sea level and surrounded by hills. The winds blowing across the land cause furious storms on the water that come up very quickly and surprise even the most experienced fishermen.

Mo's Fab Lab

GET LIST:
EMPTY 2-LITER BOTTLE
WATER
FOOD COLORING
MINERAL OR BABY OIL

Make a "Storm in a Bottle." Fill a clear, two-liter bottle halfway with water colored with blue food coloring. Add mineral or baby oil, leaving about two inches at the top. Hold the bottle on its side and gently rock it back and forth to create waves. Watch the waves and talk about:

• **What's something that really scares you?**

• **How can remembering that Jesus has power over all creation help you feel safe?**

• **Tell how you can praise God for his amazing power.**

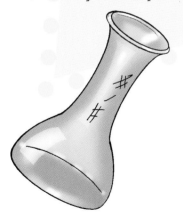

God Talk
Go outside together and look around.
Take turns praising God
for all the wonders of his creation that you see.
I praise you, God, for fluffy clouds!
I praise you, God, for _____!

The Feast of Fish and Bread

Grrrr. That's the sound of tummies rumbling.

Plop. Scrape. Plop. Scrape. That's the sound of tired feet dragging.

Jesus and his disciples were so busy they hadn't had a chance to feed their rumbling tummies. They were tired and wanted to get off their dragging feet. "Come with me to a quiet place and get some rest," Jesus told his disciples.

They got in a boat and pushed off from shore, hoping to find a quiet place on the other side of the Sea of Galilee to be alone. But the people on the shore saw them and figured out where they were going. Grown-ups and children raced around the lake and got there before Jesus. By the time Jesus arrived, a huge crowd was waiting for him.

"This crowd is like a flock of sheep without a shepherd," Jesus thought. So he started teaching them right there on that grassy hill.

More and more people came. No one wanted to go home. The rumbling tummies got louder.

A boy in the crowd tried to catch a glimpse of Jesus. He stood on his tiptoes to look for Jesus and used his hands to push past the cloaks and robes of everyone around him. There was something about Jesus that made the boy want to be near him. The boy kept squeezing his way closer to Jesus.

The sun moved over the hill. The people had been on the hill listening to Jesus for a long time. The tummies of Jesus and the disciples were still rumbling. And now the tummies of everyone in the crowd were rumbling too. It was time to go home and eat! But no one wanted to go home. The boy

didn't want to go home either. He kept getting closer to Jesus.

Jesus turned to Philip and the other disciples. "Where shall we buy bread for these people to eat?"

"It would take eight months to earn enough money to buy bread for everyone in this crowd," Philip said. "Even then, each person would only get a tiny piece. Besides, there's no place around here to buy food."

"Jesus," one of the disciples said, "I think we should just send this crowd away. Let them buy their own bread in a nearby village."

"You give them something to eat," Jesus answered. "Go and see how many loaves of bread you have."

Philip and the other disciples turned around and stared at the thousands of people on the hillside. There were more than 5,000 men, plus the women and children who were with them. How would the disciples ever find enough food for this crowd? But they began to search.

The boy saw the disciples searching and knew exactly what he wanted to do. His lunch wasn't very big. It wouldn't be enough food for all these people. But if Jesus wanted his food, then the boy would gladly give it. He lifted up his lunch with two hands.

"Here's my lunch," he said to the disciples. "Jesus can have my lunch."

"Come with us," Andrew said. And he led the boy to Jesus. Now the boy didn't have to stand on his tiptoes or push past the other people with his

hands. He just had to follow. Andrew took him straight to Jesus.

"Here is a boy with five small barley loaves and two small fish," Andrew said to Jesus. "But how far will they go with so many people to feed?"

Andrew and Peter thought it was impossible to feed the whole crowd with one boy's lunch. But Jesus wasn't worried.

"Have everyone sit down," Jesus said.

The crowd got comfortable on the grass. Jesus took the boy's bread in his fingers, looked up to heaven to give thanks, then broke the bread and passed it. He did the same thing with the fish. The boy's small lunch got bigger and bigger. Everybody ate as much as they wanted. No more rumbling tummies.

Then Jesus told the disciples to collect the leftovers. They gathered 12 baskets of broken pieces of bread and fish! The disciples couldn't believe their eyes. With just the small sack lunch, Jesus fed all those people, and there were 12 full baskets of food left over!

The little boy looked down at his toes, happy they had brought him up the hill. He looked at his fingers, glad they were willing to share. He gazed up at Jesus, thankful to be a sheep with a shepherd.

Go for the Godprint

Compassion: Jesus was human, just like we are. He knows our tummies rumble, our toes get sore and our fingers do all sorts of work. He knew the people on the hillside that day needed food, and he wanted to give it to them. How can you care for people around you the way Jesus did?

What Digby Dug Up

The bread Jesus broke and multiplied was most likely unleavened barley bread, similar to the pita bread we have today. Common "lunch" fish of the day were tilapia or sardines. Only the Son of God could miraculously make this small amount of food feed more than 5,000 people!

Café de Click

GET LIST:

GLASS BAKING PAN, FROZEN YEAST ROLL DOUGH, WAXED PAPER, FROZEN FISH STICKS, COOKIE SHEET, PICNIC BASKET

Serve your family a "loaves and fishes" picnic. At least an hour before you plan to eat, grease the glass baking pan and set balls of frozen roll dough in it. To get the dough started rising, microwave them for one minute. Then cover the pan loosely with waxed paper and put it in a warm place. After the rolls have doubled in size, bake them according to the directions on the package. As soon as the rolls have finished baking, place the fish sticks on a cookie sheet. Follow the directions on the package to bake them. Pack a picnic basket with the fish sticks and warm bread. Add other foods of your choice. Sit in the grass to enjoy loaves and fish, just as the people who listened to Jesus did! As you enjoy your meal, talk about:

- **What would it have been like to share something with Jesus?**
- **When have you shared something? How did that make you feel?**
- **When have friends shared with our family?**

God Talk

When you sit down for a family meal,
remember how Jesus took the bread
and shared it with those sitting on the hillside.
Pass a loaf of bread around the table. As you break off a piece,
pray for someone you know who needs special care.
That person could be an elderly woman at church, a single parent down the street,
a student at school or even someone in your family.

From Luke
8:4-8,- 11-15

Four Flying Seeds

Jesus often taught by telling stories—stories that had a deeper meaning. One day Jesus told a story about seeds that fell in different places. Can you figure out what deeper lesson Jesus might have been teaching?

Imagine you can shrink yourself to seed size and jump into a bag of seeds...

Seed 1

Hey! Move over. I'm squished. I'm sick of sitting in this bag packed together with all these other seeds. I mean, a guy needs room to grow, ya' know? Rrrrrip. What was that? The bag is open. Yippee!

Oooo—that warm, shimmering sunlight feels so good sliding all over me. Whoa! Here comes the farmer's hand. He scoops...he tosses...wheeee! I'm flying on the wind! I'm free!

Bonk! Ouch! That was not a soft landing. Well, no wonder. I'm right here on the path that donkeys and oxen and people walk on all the time. The earth is too hard for me to put down any roots. This is not what I thought life out side the bag would be like. Oh, no! Here come the birds. I'm a goner.

Aaaaaa!

Seed 2

Did you see what happened to Number 1 over there? That was scary. He landed on a hard path. There was no way he could put his roots down. A great big black bird swooped down and had him for breakfast. The poor little guy had no place to hide.

That won't happen to me—no, sirree! I'm tucked away in a nice patch of rocks. And I can feel soil underneath me. Well, there's a little soil anyway. My roots are going down and my stem is going up and life is just dandy.

Say, do think it's getting a little warm around here? The sun is awfully hot. I'd love to see a cloud about now. A rain cloud, to be specific. Or even a nice person with a watering can.

I'm so thirsty! I'm drooping. I'm wilting.

I'm gone.

Seed 3

Too bad about ole' Number 2 over there. He thought he had it made in the shade. Problem is, there was no shade. No water either. The hot sun finished him off in no time. Shucks. I thought he was going to be a good neighbor.

Oh, well. That won't happen to me. And I've got other neighbors. They're a different kind of seed than I am, but they're doing very well here. As a matter of fact, they're growing quite a bit faster than I am. And they're sprouting...THORNS!

They're wrapping around my stem. Now they've got my roots. They're squeezing, HEY, LET GO! I'm sure there's room for everyone here. Let's talk about...(choke!).

Seed 4

Ahhh! This mound of soil is so dark and warm and moist, I think I'll just snuggle in and take a nap. (Snore.)

(Yawn!) I can't believe it's morning all ready. Hey, I've got roots! I've got a nice, strong stem. And I've got leaves. I never knew that growing would feel so good.

I can't decide which I like better—my top half or my bottom half. My stem and leaves love to stretch toward the sun. But my strong, deep roots like to drink the fresh rain that trickles through the soil.

I'm growing so fast I hardly recognize myself. This is going to be a fruitful year; I can feel it in my stalk. At harvest time, the farmer will probably be able to gather 50 or a 100 seeds from me.

Good soil makes all the difference.

Jesus explained the story of the four seeds to his disciples. Jesus' words are like seeds and the different soils are like people's hearts.

Sometimes Jesus' words fall on hearts that are hard. A hard heart doesn't understand Jesus' message, and the seed can't sprout.

Sometimes Jesus' words fall on rocky hearts. A rocky heart seems to believe Jesus' words, but when tough times come, it gives up.

And sometimes Jesus' words fall on hearts filled with thorns and weeds that choke out his words. Thorny hearts are too full of worries and wishes to listen to Jesus and obey him.

When Jesus' words fall on a warm heart, they grow to spread good news to people all over the world!

Go for the Godprint

Commitment: Living things need a commitment to help them keep growing towards God's sunshine and light. What happens if you plant a garden and forget to water it? Choosing to follow Jesus means soaking up his Word like a plant soaks up water and sunshine—then obeying what he says. Soak up plenty of God's Word every day and your faith will grow deep and strong!

What Digby Dug Up

Grain farmers in Jesus' day did not plant seeds. Seeds of grain were carried into the fields in baskets or in the folds of clothing and then scattered with the sweep of an arm.

Mo's Fab Lab

GET LIST: COAT HANGER, WIRE CUTTERS, PLIERS, CLAY POT, SMALL ROCKS, IVY PLANT, SOIL

Seeds planted in good soil grow into plants that keep growing…and growing…and growing! Make a small topiary using a lightweight wire coat hanger, a small clay pot and an ivy plant. Use a wire cutter to cut off the left side of the coat hanger. Bend the hanger to form a circle and then use pliers to twist together the open ends. Place small rocks in the bottom of the clay pot to loosely cover the drainage hole. Place the coat wire (hook side down) into the pot and cover with good soil. You should now have a nice circular frame to gently wrap the vines around. As the plant grows, continue to wrap the vines.

- **How will you take good care of your topiary?**

- **How will you take good care of your growing faith in Jesus?**

- **How is shaping the vines like the way God shapes your heart?**

God Talk
Seed packets make good book marks.
Choose one at the store and use it
to mark your place in your Bible.
Each time you read your Bible,
ask God to make the words take root in your heart.
Think carefully about what you've read,
then make a commitment to obey it.

Is She Sleeping?

"My child, get up!"

When I heard those words, my eyes opened right up. For a moment I wasn't sure where I was, because I didn't recognize the man who was holding my hand. But then I saw that my parents were with him, and I knew that this man was Jesus.

But how did Jesus get in my room? I was still wondering about that when my father rushed toward me. Then I started remembering.

My father is Jairus, one of the rulers in the synagogue. That's where we go to pray, to give our offerings to God, and to learn about God. It's my father's job to schedule the services and make sure everything goes the way it's supposed to. It's a pretty important job! Some of the other leaders in the synagogue are against Jesus, but my father knows that Jesus is God's Son. I remembered that my father had gone to find Jesus.

A few weeks ago my head started to hurt. The sunlight made it pound so badly that I stayed inside all the time. Then it got hard to eat. I felt weaker every day, and I could tell my parents were worried. I spent more and more time sleeping. This morning I couldn't open my eyes. I remember my father saying, "I'm going to find Jesus." But I don't remember when he came back.

🐚   🐚   🐚

My beautiful 12-year-old daughter was dying. I had to see if I could get to Jesus. He had healed others—perhaps he could heal my daughter. I ran through town asking everyone where Jesus was. I found him in the middle of a crowd and threw myself at his feet.

"Please, Jesus, come to my house," I begged. "My only daughter is dying." Jesus just nodded his head and started to follow me. The crowd pushed against us. I was desperately afraid that we wouldn't get back in time.

Sure enough, a messenger came running toward me. "Your daughter is dead," he said. "Don't bother Jesus anymore."

My heart froze, but Jesus turned to me and said, "Don't be afraid. Just believe, and your daughter will be healed." We pushed on toward my house.

As we got closer I could hear my neighbors crying. Jesus told them, "Stop wailing! She's not dead. She's just sleeping." They knew she was dead, so they laughed at Jesus. But I kept trusting him.

Jesus sent all the neighbors away. He brought in three of his close friends and my wife and me. Then he took my dead daughter's hand and said, "My child, get up!"

🐦 🐦 🐦

I didn't remember when my father got home with Jesus, but there they were. Jesus was holding my hand. "My child, get up!" Jesus said. So I jumped out of bed. My head didn't hurt, and for the first time in a long time I felt hungry.

There were three strangers in the room along with Jesus and my mother and father. Everyone acted amazed. Jesus just smiled and told my parents to get me something to eat. I was just happy to be back alive and with my parents—and Jesus!

My father is right, you know. Jesus truly is the Son of God.

278

Go for the Godprint

Compassion: Compassion is feeling the hurts of others enough that you do something to help them. Jesus had compassion on Jairus's daughter and healed her. We can't heal others like Jesus can, but we can show them that we care with other actions. Can you think of a way?

What Digby Dug Up

THE WORD "SYNAGOGUE" MEANS "GATHERING TOGETHER PLACE." GOD'S PEOPLE MET THERE TO DISCUSS GOD'S WORD. SYNAGOGUES WERE EASY TO FIND BECAUSE PEOPLE BUILT THEM ON HIGH GROUND OR MADE THEM THE HIGHEST BUILDING AROUND.

GET LIST:
WAXED PAPER
SEVERAL FLAVORS OF CANNED PUDDING
SPOONS

Have a Bible story for dessert! (And have some finger-lickin' fun!) Read this story together after a meal, then give each person a piece of waxed paper. Decide who will draw each part of the story. Open different flavors of canned pudding and use them as your palette. Spoon pudding onto the paper, then use your fingers to create pictures to tell the story. After each artist tells his or her part of the story, dive in with your spoons and gobble that pudding picture together. Then talk about:

- **What did you learn about Jesus from this story?**
- **Can you think of a time when someone cared that you were hurt?**
- **What are some ways you can show you care for your friends when they're hurt?**

God Talk
Take a picture of someone you know
who might be feeling discouraged.
Put the picture near your bed
and pray each morning that God
will have compassion and bring hope and joy back into that person's life.

The Good Samaritan

Read this family drama together. You may want to have one person read while others act out the parts.

Characters: Narrator
George
Priest
Levite
Samaritan
1 or 2 robbers *(Optional)*

Narrator: One day an expert in the law came to Jesus to ask what God wanted him to do. Jesus said, "Love your God with all your heart, soul, mind and strength and love your neighbor as yourself." The man asked, "Who is my neighbor?" Jesus told him the story of the Good Samaritan. Let's imagine what the characters in Jesus' story were thinking. We will call the first man George.

George: This road looks very scary and dangerous. I know robbers attack travelers on this road, and it's getting dark.

Narrator: Suddenly robbers jump out from the bushes, attack George and take all of his money. They leave George hurt, bleeding and unconscious on the side of the road.

George: *(waking up)* What happened? Ooooh, my head! Oh, no, I'm bleeding! And I've been robbed! What am I going to do? Wait, wait, don't panic. I see a man coming down the road. Oh, look! He's a priest. A man of God will surely have mercy on me. He'll care that I'm hurt and have compassion on me. Now I am saved.

Priest: Oh, no! A man is hurt. I'll bet he was robbed. The poor man. I should stop and help him. I should. Yes, I definitely should.

Help him, that is. Definitely! But I am very late. What will the people think of me if I come in late to the service? I am also wearing my best robes. It would not do to get blood on the sacred robes. I'll just cross on the other side of the road and pretend I didn't see him.

George: He's walking around me! He sees me and he's ignoring me on purpose. Now what will I do? Wait, wait, don't panic. Here comes someone else. It's a Levite. Now I am saved.

Levite: That man is hurt! Surely he was robbed. They beat him and left him for dead. I wonder if the robbers are still around. Maybe this is a trick and the hurt man is just faking and others are hiding in the bushes to rob me. I'd better walk on the other side of the road.

George: Oh, no! He's walking around me, too. No one will help me. What will I do? Wait, wait, don't panic. Here comes someone else.

Never mind, go ahead, panic. It's a Samaritan. If a priest and a Levite wouldn't have compassion on me and help me, surely a Samaritan won't either. Now I'm doomed.

Narrator: The Jewish people did not like the Samaritan people in those days. When the Samaritan arrived, he stopped and thought to himself.

Samaritan: What is this? A man is hurt. The poor man is cold and frightened. I can use my cloak to stop the bleeding. He must have been robbed. I'd better be careful. This may take some time, but I know God wants me to care about him, the way God cares about me.

Narrator: The Samaritan didn't care about his clothes or being late or being robbed. He put medicine on the man. He carried him on his donkey to an inn. He used his own money to pay the innkeeper to take care of him and promised to come back and check on the man. That was the end of Jesus' story. Then Jesus asked the expert in the law, "Who was the good neighbor?" The expert said, "The man who had mercy on him." Jesus said, "Go and do likewise."

Go for the Godprint

Compassion: To have compassion is to be aware of another person's needs and want to do something to help, even if it is hard or at a bad time. The Good Samaritan didn't worry about what others thought of him or if it was a convenient time to help. He saw someone who needed help and gave it. Look for ways you can have compassion on others each day.

What Digby Dug Up
The Good Samaritan gave money to the innkeeper to help pay for the hurt man's care. The amount he gave equaled what he would have earned working for two whole days. That was a lot a money to give for a stranger's care!

PJ's Good to Go

Be a Good Samaritan! Many people in our world need someone to reach out and help them. Some countries don't have enough food to feed everyone; some people don't have homes and have to sleep under bridges; some people work as hard as they can, but don't earn enough money to take care of their families. As a family, go through all the bedrooms and closets in your house. Pick out the clothing, toys and household goods that you don't use any longer. Make sure everything is clean and in good condition. Take all those items to a local organization that helps the needy. Pray that the people who receive your items will be blessed.

God Talk

God can help us all be more compassionate.
Pray this together with your family.

Like the Samaritan who helped the man
Hurt and bleeding in the street,
Help me, Lord, to show compassion
To hurting people I may meet.

Jesus Visits Mary and Martha

"Mary! Mary! Hurry, dear! Jesus is coming—he's nearly here!" Martha scampered, clutching her skirt. She ran to the kitchen, avoiding some dirt.

"Aren't these lovely? Won't these be fine?" Mary collected ripe grapes from the vine. "I'm so excited that Jesus is coming! I'm so delighted, I just can't stop humming."

"The house must be cleaned! The floors must be scrubbed! The sleep-mats need airing, the metal things rubbed. The bread must be kneaded; the fire reheated. The figs should be drying. Oh, no! Time is flying!"

"Martha, dear sister, why do you scurry? You're moving so fast, you look rather blurry! Jesus is coming! Isn't that splendid? But why must the house become so up-ended? A cushion to sit on, a meal on the fire, is all that our Lord and his friends will require."

"How foolish! How simple! Of course that's not all! I'll make him a feast and we'll eat by nightfall! Now hurry, dear sister. We have much to do. We won't rest a moment until we're all through!"

When Jesus came walking with friends up the road, Mary stood waving. Her smiling face glowed! "Welcome, dear Master. We're glad you are here!" She was so joyful, she let out a cheer!

"Martha is cooking. Please, do come in! We're thrilled that you've come here to visit again. Please, dear Lord, what will you teach us today? I want to hear everything you have to say."

So Jesus sat down with his friends gathered 'round. Everyone listened—no one made a sound. Mary sat lovingly by Jesus' feet, not a bit worried about what they would eat.

But out in the kitchen, big trouble was brewing. Martha was fussing; Martha was stewing. Finally she burst in, whining and spewing, "Lord, do you see what our Mary is doing?"

"I've worked non-stop in the kitchen out there. Haven't you noticed? She doesn't care! Mary sits listening, and that's just not fair. Please say that she must help serve all this food. She's letting me do all the work, and that's rude!"

"Martha, dear Martha," said Jesus, her king. "You're worried—upset—about many things." Jesus felt sorry for Martha's distress, but said, "Mary's chosen the one thing that's best. And what she has chosen, I'll not take away." So Mary kept listening to Jesus that day.

Those must have been hard words for Martha to hear. I'd not be surprised if she shed a sad tear as she put down her apron and her cooking gear, then sat down by Jesus, her master so dear.

Everyone knows what it's like to get busy; when there's such stuff going on you feel dizzy. But don't be like Martha and get in a tizzy. Be like the listening Mary instead. Let Jesus' teaching be what fills your head!

Go for the Godprint

Purposefulness: What kind of person do you want to be? What kinds of things do you want to accomplish? You might not know all the answers right now. But God does, and he has something in mind just for you. Learning about the things Jesus said and did will help you discover God's plan for you. Will you pledge to read some of Jesus' words every day?

What Digby Dug Up

THE SMALL TOWN OF BETHANY, WHERE MARY AND MARTHA LIVED, STILL EXISTS TODAY. IT IS ABOUT TWO MILES EAST OF JERUSALEM IN ISRAEL. BETHANY WAS ONE OF JESUS' FAVORITE PLACES TO VISIT.

Café de Click

Choose items to eat from a list of foods that Jesus might have eaten. Dress as families would have dressed in Jesus' day, with long, loose clothing. Recline at a low table or on the floor, just as Jesus and his disciples would have done. Let everyone help cook, serve and clean up the meal. Make a marvelous menu from this list of Bible-time foods.

Bread—round loaves of barley or wheat

Fruit—olives, melons, figs, grapes, raisins, pomegranates, dates

Vegetables—beans and lentils, leeks, onions, garlic, cucumbers, almonds

Milk—yogurt, butter, cheese

Meat—fish, beef, mutton, game, fowl

While you eat, talk about things you've learned from Jesus.

God Talk

Mary got to sit at Jesus' feet.

How cool was that!

Ask family members to join you on the floor in front of a big, comfy chair.

Talk about what you would ask Jesus if he were sitting in the chair.

Look for answers to your questions in the books of Matthew, Mark, Luke and John.

Then close by talking to Jesus in prayer.

From Luke 11:1-4

The Lord's Prayer

FATHER

Hallowed be
your name,
Your kingdom come.
Give us this day
our daily bread.

Forgive us our sins,
for we also forgive
everyone who
sins against us.

And lead us not
into temptation.

One day Jesus was praying. His followers wanted to learn to pray the way Jesus prayed. So they said, "Teach us to pray." Jesus gave his followers a special prayer that let them know God cares about what they need. This is called the Lord's Prayer. For two thousand years, people who trust in Jesus have prayed these words.

Can you match up these words with what they mean?

Hallowed	What we really need
Daily bread	Feeling like doing something wrong
Forgive	What a king is in charge of
Temptation	Stop being angry
Kingdom	Honor

After Jesus told the disciples to say these words, he explained what they mean. God hears everything we say to him. He wants to give us the things that are good for us. He never turns away and says, "Don't bother me; I'm busy."

We can be sure God hears us every time we pray.

Go for the Godprint

Prayerfulness: Why are we often quiet and still when we pray? This helps us know that God is near and listening to us. It also helps open our hearts to hear what God has to say. Can you think of something that you need to talk about with God?

What Digby Dug Up

JESUS STARTED HIS PRAYER BY PRAISING GOD BEFORE HE ASKED GOD FOR ANYTHING. THIS GIVES US A PATTERN FOR THE WAY WE PRAY.

Herbie's Hideaway

Where is a good place to pray? We can pray anywhere and anytime, of course. But sometimes it helps to have a special place and time. Talk with family members about a place and time your family can pray together. Find a special "Prayer Place." Use these ideas to fix up your Prayer Place.

- **Make a special place to sit or kneel.**
- Light candles or turn on soft lights.
- **Hang a picture or poster that reminds you that God hears you.**
- **Play quiet music.**
- **Set out a Bible.**
- **Get a special journal for writing down prayer requests and answers.**

Choose a time once a week when the whole family can come to the Prayer Place to pray together.

God Talk

Write a family version of the Lord's Prayer. Work together to find words and phrases that everyone in the family can understand. Put your prayer on a poster or special paper where you can all see it and pray together.

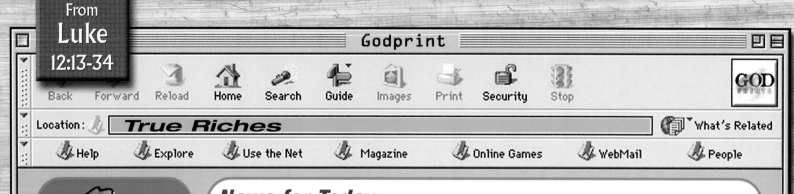

News for Today

Wealthy landowner I. M. Greedy passed away yesterday, leaving a huge estate. Mr. Greedy was known throughout his community as a man who had plenty and shared nothing. While neighbors went hungry, Mr. Greedy gathered all he had into huge storage areas. Last year his crop was so plentiful that he tore down his barns and built bigger ones. Mr. Greedy then announced that he had so much money and food stored up that he was going to retire and live off all he had gathered for himself. In a conversation with a neighbor, Mr. Greedy related his philosophy of life saying, "Take life easy; eat, drink and be merry!" That very night he died! Since he has no children or family, Mr. Greedy's property will be divided among his neighbors.

Dear Abba

Dear Abba: My mom gave my brother $20 and he won't share any of it with me. What should I tell my brother to make him give me half the money?

Signed,
Want My Share

Dear Want: Why do you want what was given to your brother? Money isn't the most important thing in life. Maybe you should think about what you already have and be thankful for that instead of becoming greedy for what others have.

Godprint

Back | Forward | Reload | Home | Search | Guide | Images | Print | Security | Stop

GOD

Location: True Riches

What's Related

Help | Explore | Use the Net | Magazine | Online Games | WebMail | People

Want to be rich? Instead of keeping everything you have for yourself, do things God's way and discover riches that last forever!

Simply follow these three easy steps.

One: Follow Jesus' example in everything.

Two: Ask God to fill your heart with his goodness.

Three: Obey and let God do the rest!

When you seek God first, you can leave your worries behind!

Poetry Corner

See the green meadow where the wildflower grows?
They're more beautiful than a king's royal clothes.
Don't worry about your needs—God already knows!

See the flocks of birds that sing, soar and glide?
They don't plant or reap (they couldn't if they tried)
But they live quite happily on what God provides.

Don't be afraid or worried or distressed.
Don't build up riches in a great treaure chest.
Seek God's kingdom first and trust God for the rest!

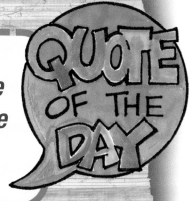

> "Where your treasure is, there your heart will be also."
> –Jesus Christ

Tired of worrying about where to store your valuables? Purses and wallets get holes, and robbers can steal from the bank, but Heaven's Savings and Loan is 100% safe. Every time you give to others and show God's love, you make a deposit in Heaven's Savings and Loan where your treasure will last forever!

A man came to Jesus because he wasn't getting along with his brother. Imagine that! In response, Jesus told the story of a man like I.M. Greedy. He wanted the people to learn from that story. What happened to the man in the story could happen to anyone who worries too much about money and not enough about things that are important to God. If we trust God to take care of our needs, we don't have to be greedy.

Go for the Godprint

Generosity: You might think it doesn't make sense when someone says, "Give so you can receive." But it's God's way. Everything we have comes from God. When we're doing what God wants then we might be surprised at how God gives just what we need. We can keep on giving to others because we know God will always take care of us.

What Digby Dug Up
The kind of story Jesus told about the rich man who was a fool is called a "parable." A parable is a simple story about real things that has a serious lesson about following God's way.

Café de Click

Have a generosi-TEA with your family. Set the table with a nice cloth or placemats and special dishes. Bake a package of refrigerated cherry turnovers. While they're baking, take a small tray outside and gather things God has provided, such as bird feathers, pretty rocks and leaves, pinecones or wildflowers. Arrange them on the tray and set them in the center of the table. Make tea or lemonade to serve with the baked turnovers. As you enjoy your treat, talk about these things.

• **What things does God provide every day that we hardly ever think about?**

• **How does knowing God provides these things help us be generous?**

Together plan three acts of generosity you could do as a family. Write them down and vote on which one to do this week. Tuck the other plans in your Bible to carry out when you're feeling down. You'll be amazed at how being generous lifts your spirits—it's a God thing!

God Talk

Take a prayer walk
around your neighborhood.
Pray for the people in each house you pass.
Ask God to help you show
his generosity in your neighborhood.
Remember, giving gifts of time and help
can be just as important as gifts that cost money.

The Best Seat in the House

I love a good party, don't you? And I get my share of them, believe me. My owner is a Pharisee, an important religious leader. People come to visit all the time. And it's always the same. Everybody goes for the best seat in the house. That's me.

I'm a plump, silky cushion. You can always find me at the place of honor, right next to the host. Anyone who sits on me gets lots of attention, not to mention the first chance at the food. And after the meal, the guest who sits on me can talk to the host as much as he

wants to. And who wouldn't want to—I'm the silkiest, most comfortable cushion. (I guess you could say I have a pretty soft life.)

Sometimes two guests race from the door to the table and collide when they get to me. Other times they politely move across the room, making conversation with other guests. But the whole time, they're thinking about how they can get to the best seat. No one wants to give up the best seat. I'm a real party guy and, trust me, it's the same every time.

I remember one time when a man came in with his best flowing robes on. He was so busy being proud of himself for getting the seat of honor that he didn't notice the gravy that dribbled all down the front of his robe. Thank goodness none of the gravy made it all the way down to me. It makes a nasty stain.

You would've laughed if you'd seen another Pharisee who got my spot. I don't mean to be rude, but this guy was stuck-up—literally! His nose was so high in the air that he missed his mouth and his vegetables went rolling up his sleeve. You should have seen him trying to get

that stuff out without being noticed. Suddenly it wasn't so great to be in the seat of honor with everyone watching.

Today was different though. I admit I was surprised. One of the guests was Jesus. He didn't like the way people were crashing around trying to get the best seat. So he told a story.

Jesus said that when you go to a wedding feast, for instance, you shouldn't try to get the best seat. Suppose you sit in that chair, and then the host comes and asks you to move. Suppose he meant for someone else to sit in the seat of honor. That's pretty embarrassing. Everybody's watching you, maybe even laughing at you. So you end up with the worst seat in the house instead of the best.

Jesus said, it's better to take the worst seat. Wouldn't it be great if the host came up to you and invited you to move up to a better place? Then you would be honored in front of everyone.

Now that would be a change, wouldn't it? I'd like to find out what it feels like to be empty until the host brings someone over to sit on me.

It's pretty clear to me what Jesus was trying to teach: If you try to put yourself in the spotlight, you end up humiliated. But if you let others go first and put them in the spotlight, you'll be honored. The big question is whether any of my owner's guests understand that. We'll find out at the next big party.

Go for the Godprint

Respectfulness: Do you ever have trouble letting someone else go first? What if someone else takes the cookie you wanted? Or what if someone else gets the best seat in the car? We can show respect for other people by letting them go first. Can you think of a way to let someone else go first today?

What Digby Dug Up
The dinner Jesus attended was on the Sabbath. This means the food was prepared the day before. Even a special party meal would be cooked ahead of time so the Jews did not have to work on the Sabbath by preparing food.

Jake's Mirth Quake

Play musical chairs—with a food twist. Pull all the chairs away from the table except one. In front of that place, put a plate full of goodies that everyone in the family enjoys. Now start the music. When the music stops, the person in front of the one chair politely offers the seat to another person. The person who sits down picks up the plate of goodies and offers it to someone else. Start the music again and play until everyone has had plenty of practice letting someone else go first—or until all the goodies are gone!

God Talk

Pick a chair in your living room
and call it the Prayer Chair.
Take turns inviting another member of the family
to sit in the Prayer Chair while you pray for that person.
Thank God for the special abilities he gives to each one in your family.

From
Luke
15:11-31

Prodigal Son

Scene 1

Son: Hey, Dad, I'm tired of all your rules and chores and not being trusted to think for myself.

Father: I'm sorry, son, but you're in my home, so it's my rules.

Son: Okay, then I want out. Give me my inheritance now instead of when you die, and I'll go out on my own.

Father: But son, I don't think you know how to be responsible with your money. You're not ready yet.

Son: I'm ready!

Father: But son, you don't know how hard it is out there.

Son: I know, and I'm ready.

Father: But son, you can't even drive a chariot yet.

Son: I know, I'm ready, and I can walk.

Father: Okay, son. Here's the money. *(Gives son money and they exit.)*

Scene 2

Son: Wow! Look at all this money! I'll budget my money carefully, but first I'm going to party!

Friend 1: Hey, you are really a fun guy. Could you loan me some money?

Son: Sure, I have plenty.

Friend 2: What about me? I want to buy lots of new clothes!

Son: Here, buy whatever you want!

Friend 1 and 2: You're the best friend we ever had! You're the greatest!

Waiter: Excuse me, but who is the one throwing this party?

Son: I am. Do you need any more food or drink? I've already bought enough for three days of parties!

Waiter: No, I am the waiter, and it's time for you to pay.

Son: No problem. Here's all I have left.

Waiter: This isn't enough! I'm throwing you out!

Son: Don't worry. I have plenty of friends. Hey, buddy, can you loan me a little money?

Friend 1: Who me? I don't even know you.

Son: What about you?

Friend 2: Never heard of you.

Waiter: Get out!

Scene 3

Son: I can't believe it. I lost all my money. I have no food or shelter. If I feed the pigs, the farmer lets me eat their leftovers. They don't leave much, either. I guess I wasn't as responsible as I thought. I didn't know I wasn't ready and my feet hurt. You know, my dad's servants are treated better than this. Maybe if I go back to my dad and tell him I'm sorry and that I'm willing to be one of his servants, he would let me come back home.

Scene 4

Father: When will I hear from my son? It's been such a long time since he left. Wait! Who's that coming down the road? Can it be? It's my son! Welcome home! I've been so worried about you. Give me a big hug!

Son: Oh, Dad, I thought you would be so mad at me. I am so sorry. I lost all the money you gave me. But don't worry—I just want to work for you as one of your servants.

Father: Nonsense! You've asked for forgiveness and I'm glad to give it. In fact, I'm going to throw a big party to welcome you back. I love you, son. I'm so glad you came home.

302

Go for the Godprint

Responsibility: The prodigal did some foolish things. But when he was ready to admit he was wrong and tried to make things right, he acted responsibly. Responsible people plan carefully, make wise choices, and accept what comes from the choices they make. God is like the father in the story. When we make bad choices, we can ask for and receive his forgiveness, then make a fresh start!

What Digby Dug Up

JEWISH LAW SAID THAT PIGS WERE UNCLEAN ANIMALS, AND GOD'S PEOPLE COULD NOT EVEN TOUCH THEM. TO HAVE A JOB FEEDING PIGS WAS A GREAT EMBARRASSMENT.

Café de Click

GET LIST:
CRACKERS, PEANUT BUTTER, MARSHMALLOWS,
COOKIE SHEET, CHOCOLATE SPRINKLES,
OVEN SET ON BROIL

When the prodigal son came home his father was so happy that he threw a party for him. He quickly forgave him for being irresponsible. God our Father is just as happy to forgive us. Here is a simple recipe that you can make and have a party of your own.

Spread your crackers with peanut butter and put a marshmallow on top. Place the crackers on a cookie sheet and put it under the broiler of your oven or toaster oven. Broil until the tops of the marshmallows are a little brown. Have an adult help you take them out. Put chocolate sprinkles on the marshmallows and enjoy!

As you eat, talk about these things.

• **Tell about a time you asked God's forgiveness for being irresponsible.**
• **Affirm each other for times you've acted responsibly.**

God Talk

Pray this responsive prayer together.
Lord, when I think I know what's best,
Help me turn around and come home to your love.
Lord, when I choose something that hurts me,
Help me turn around and come home to your love.
Lord, when I don't want to admit I'm wrong,
Help me turn around and come home to your love. Amen.

One Came Back

Ten men with leprosy suffered together.
They couldn't go back to their families–not ever.
They shouted "Unclean!" if folks came around;
People threw rocks when they came into town.

"Leprosy's awful," the first fellow said.
"My friends," sighed the second, "all act like I'm dead."
Number three said, "My family has turned me away."
"Mine too," said the fourth. "Now I've no place to stay."
"I miss my children," lamented the fifth.
"And their hugs and kisses," added the sixth.
The seventh one cried, "I can't feel my toes."
The eighth one complained, "There's a sore on my nose."
"My life is just wretched," number nine groaned.
"Not one person loves me," number ten moaned.

As the ten men sat beside the road talking,
Jesus himself came down the road walking.

"Look there! It's Jesus!" said man number one.
"Some people say that he's God's only Son."
"I've heard he's a healer," said man number two.
"Do you think he'd help people like me and like you?"
"Surely he'd help us," said man number three.
"He makes the lame walk and helps blind people see."
Man number four said, "I think we should go.
We must try to see him or we'll never know."

Five said, "Let's go now–no time to delay."
Six said, "But people will chase us away."
Said seven, "We'll have to stay back from the crowd;
We'll stand at the roadside and shout really loud."
Eight said, "Let's go, then. That sounds like a plan."
Nine said, "I can't wait to meet this great man."
Ten said, "We all could be healed today;
Don't stand there talking; let's be on our way!

Off toward the village the ten men stampeded.
"Jesus!" they called out in voices that pleaded.
"Master! Have pity on us!" they all cried.
Jesus heard them and turned; they waited wide-eyed.
"Go show yourselves to the priests," Jesus said.
The ten men obeyed. To the village they sped.

Man number one shouted, "Look! We've been healed!"
And took off running across a green field.
"I'm going home now, with no more delay,"
Said man number two as he raced on his way.
"Wait 'til my friends see I'm healthy and strong!"
Called out the third as he followed along.
Number four shouted, "I'm healthy again."
He took off following his first three friends.

Five ran toward home, his eyes brimming with tears.
"My children's voices will sing in my ears!"
"And I'll soon be getting sweet hugs and sweet kisses,"
Cheered number six, running home toward his missus.
"My toes! I can feel them! Look how they wiggle!"
The seventh man smiled as he jogged with a giggle.
Eight touched his nose. Sure enough–good as new!
He twitched it as he hurried on out of view.
"My troubles are over! I've got no more pain!"
Chortled the ninth as he ran down the lane.

The tenth, a Samaritan, started off with the pack,
Then thought of Jesus, turned around and came back.
Finding the Savior, the Samaritan knelt
At Jesus' feet, then said what he felt.
"Praise God! You've healed me! I'm well again!"
But Jesus said, "I healed not one man, but ten!
"Is it just you who've come back to thank God?"
The Samaritan answered by giving a nod.
Then Jesus said, "Rise and go on your way."
"Because of your faith you've been healed today."

Ten men were healed; just one showed his gratitude.
When God cares for you, what is your attitude?

Go for the Godprint

Thankfulness. What was the tenth man thankful for? He was thankful for what God had done for him. He wasn't in such a hurry to get on with his new life that he couldn't take time to tell Jesus "thank you." It's important to express our thanks to those who show God's love to us. "Thank you" meant a lot to Jesus and it means a lot to people today.

What Digby Dug Up

Leprosy is a skin disease that causes white patches on your body and can cause you to lose fingers, toes and other body parts. Today doctors know how to treat leprosy, but in Bible times the disease was so dangerous that people with leprosy had to leave their homes and friends and live outside of town.

Herbie's Hideaway

Use bear-shaped graham crackers to express your thanks. Sit around a table and count out ten crackers per person, to stand for the ten men Jesus healed. The challenge for the first five crackers is to thank God for something you've never thanked him for before. Take turns giving thanks and eating the crackers. For the second five crackers, the challenge is to thank family members around the table for things you don't usually say "thank you" for. Instead of eating your cracker, pass it to the person who's receiving your thanks. Talk about:

• **Why is it so important to say "thank you"?**

• **What happens when people forget to express their thanks?**

• **What's a special "thank you" surprise we can plan for someone who's important to our family?**

God Talk

Take turns acting out things to be thankful for
and let other family members guess what's being acted out.
After each correct answer, say together:
Thank you, Lord, for giving
The things we need for living.

Who Loves a Loser?

Who loves a loser? No one. That's what I used to think. And I was an out-of-luck loser, so I would know. At least I thought I was.

308

In the first place, I had a job that made me unpopular. I was a tax collector. That means I worked for the Roman government. I didn't have to. I was born a Jew, and I didn't care for the Romans any more than most Jews. But it seemed like the job would pay well. I could collect as much tax money as I wanted. As long as I paid the Romans their share, I got to keep the rest. So I had money, but I was out of luck in the friends department.

And then there's my height. I'm short. No other word describes me. I'm just plain short. I try not to let that bother me. Most of the time it doesn't matter. But there was one day that it did matter. I was out of luck because I'm short.

Jesus came to Jericho, the town where I live. I think he was just passing through. But I decided that I wanted to see this guy that everyone made such a fuss about. Wouldn't you know it, there was a crowd. A big crowd. A big crowd of tall people. Out of luck again. I couldn't see a thing!

I gave up stretching my neck and straining my toes and ran ahead of the crowd. I knew which way Jesus was going, and I knew of a sycamore fig tree right along the road. That's where I went, down the road and up the tree. Sycamores are great climbing trees. And I was right. That was the way Jesus came. Now I had a great view, the best around.

I just wanted to see Jesus. Imagine my surprise when he stopped right under my tree and looked up at me. "Zaccheus, come down immediately," he said. "I must stay at your house today."

I was the only guy up in that tree, and he had my name right. So I knew he was talking to me. I slid down right away and led Jesus off to my house. Suddenly it didn't matter that no one else liked me. Jesus liked me! He could have gone to any house in town, and he picked mine. We went home and had a great meal.

Now Jesus was the one who wasn't popular. The muttering mumbling people with the frowny faces weren't happy at all.

"He has gone to be the guest of a 'sinner,'" they said.

They were exactly right. That just what I was. I cheated my own people and thought nothing of it. All that mattered was that I was getting rich. No one had ever liked me before, so I didn't see the point in changing my ways. But it was different with Jesus. He loved me; I could see that. Maybe there was a point in changing my ways.

I stood up.

"Look, Lord!" I said. "Here and now I give half of my possessions to the poor, and if I have cheated anybody out of anything, I will pay back four times the amount."

I meant what I said. I wasn't an out-of-luck loser anymore. After meeting Jesus, I knew I was a real person, even if I wasn't like everyone else.

Jesus knew I meant what I said. He said to me, "Today salvation has come to this house, because this man, too, is a son of Abraham. For the Son of Man came to seek and to save what was lost."

That was me. Lost. And Jesus found me, loved me and saved me. I don't feel like a loser anymore. My story isn't about being a loser, it's about love. And what a difference it makes.

Go for the Godprint

Compassion: When a friend you care about is unhappy, it's easy to feel unhappy too. If someone you don't know very well is unhappy, you might think it's okay not to share the feeling. But that's the perfect time to share God's love. That's what Jesus did with Zacchaeus. How can you tell if someone is unhappy? What can you do to show God's love?

What Digby Dug Up

The Romans got the money for their great empire from all the countries under their control. The Jews did not like paying taxes to the Romans because they did not want to support the false gods of the Romans. But they were forced to pay taxes anyway.

Wally's Walkabout

Zacchaeus got a good look at Jesus and it changed his life. Take a new look at the people in your family. Instead of sitting and looking at each other, hang upside down on the furniture and look at each other. Or bend at the waist and look at each other upside down between your legs. Or stand up high and look down, like Zaccheus looked down from the tree. Talk about:

• **What looks different from your new perspective?**

• **How can seeing from a different perspective help us show God's love to each other?**

• **Think of some people outside your family you need to get a new perspective on. How can they know God's love through you?**

God Talk

If you have a good climbing tree in your yard or a nearby park, climb it together. While you sit in the branches, pray for God to help you love everybody, even people who are different.

Nicodemus

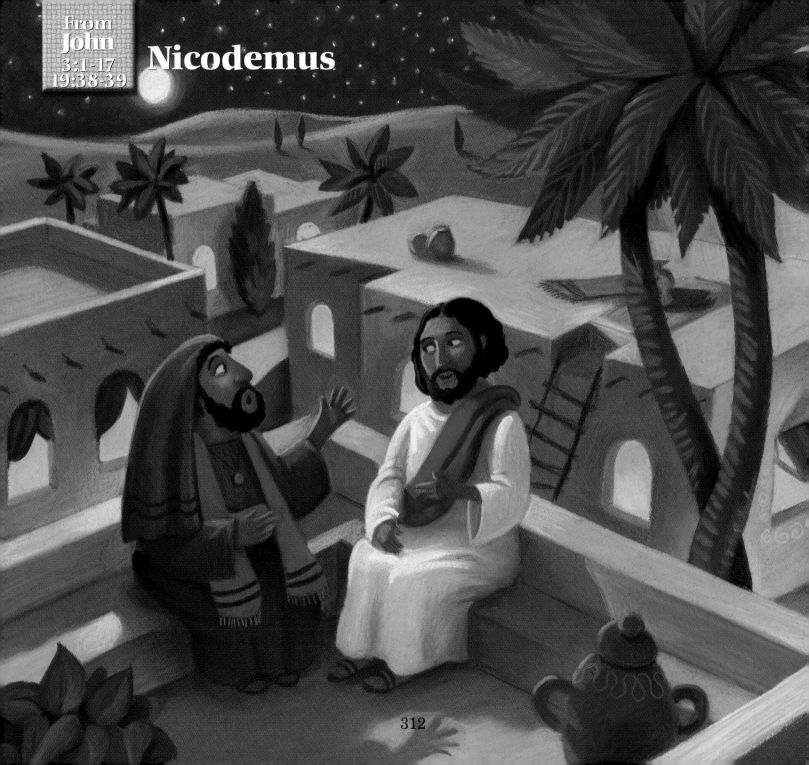

In this drama, Old Nicodemus tells the story of when he met Jesus; Young Nicodemus speaks as if he is still with Jesus.

Old Nicodemus: Greetings, everyone. My name is Nicodemus. I am a Pharisee, a teacher of the law of Israel, a respected citizen and a coward. At least I used to be. Yes, I admit it. You see, I knew Jesus when he was still here on earth. I was there to see his miracles and works of God. I wanted to talk to him, but I didn't want friends to see me with him. I wasn't ready to say I was a follower of Jesus. So I sneaked out one night. It happened like this. I went to Jesus and said:

Young Nicodemus: Teacher, I am sorry to come so late. I know you have come from God. No one could do the miracles you do without God's power.

Old Nicodemus: Jesus told me that no man can see the kingdom of God unless he is born again. I didn't understand.

Young Nicodemus: Born again? Like a baby? I don't know what you mean. I can't go back inside my mother's body. How can a grown man start all over again as a baby?

Old Nicodemus: Jesus explained that he wasn't talking about flesh, but about our spirits. Then I understood that he wasn't talking about our physical bodies turning back into babies. He was talking about our spirits being born from God. His answer made me ask more questions. How could this be?

Young Nicodemus: I know I haven't kept God's law perfectly. How can I be a child of God?

Old Nicodemus: Jesus reminded me that as a teacher of the law I should understand what he meant. But I didn't, so he explained. He said, "God so loved the world that he gave his one and only Son, that whoever believes in him shall not perish but have eternal life." Jesus said he didn't come into the world to bring punishment for sins but to save the world. I didn't understand then, but now I know Jesus was talking about when he would take our punishment by dying in the cross and rising again from the dead. Because of what Jesus did for us, we can have a new beginning—as if we had never sinned.

Young Nicodemus: Jesus, I want to believe in you. And I'm not just saying words. I really want to be your follower.

Old Nicodemus: I did become Jesus' follower. The proof came right after he died. While many of his other followers ran away and hid, I helped my friend Joseph of Arimathea take Jesus' body off the cross and carry it to the tomb.

Young Nicodemus: I'll follow Jesus no matter what the cost.

Old Nicodemus: The night I talked with Jesus changed me forever. Now that I'm old, I'm still looking forward to a life that never ends. I can't wait to see Jesus again. The next time it will be in heaven!

Go for the Godprint

Commitment: Nicodemus did more than just say he believed in Jesus. He made a commitment to him, even when his life was on the line. Choosing to follow Jesus means inviting him into your life, then living a life that serves God and honors him, no matter what.

What Digby Dug Up

Nicodemus was wealthy, a Pharisee and a member of the Sanhedrin, the Jewish high court. For Nicodemus to follow Jesus probably meant the other Jewish leaders would consider him a traitor.

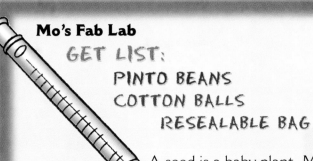

Mo's Fab Lab

GET LIST:
PINTO BEANS
COTTON BALLS
RESEALABLE BAG

A seed is a baby plant. Moisten a cotton ball with water. Don't make it too drippy. Take a bean and wrap the cotton around it. Place the cotton with the seed in a resealable bag. Seal the bag tightly and make sure there are no holes. Then put your bag in a safe place. Check your bag each day. Soon you will see your baby seed take on new life. You'll be able to watch what usually happens underground as a seed grows. You can watch for its roots and the leaf and stem. Talk about:

• **How are we like the seed?**

• **How can we be born again?**

• **What do you think it will be like to have life that lasts forever in heaven?**

God Talk
God wants to welcome you to his forever family!
Like Nicodemus, you must be born again.
Talk to Jesus in prayer. Ask him to forgive your sins.
Tell him that you believe in him and invite him into your life.

Jesus: The Bread of Life

"I am the bread of life."

Jesus was teaching a crowd of people in the synagogue in Capernaum when he said that.

Did you ever have to hear something more than once before you understood it? That's the way it was that day with Jesus and the people. First Jesus said he was the bread that God sent down from heaven. Then he called himself the bread of life. Then he said he was the living bread. Then he said again that he was the bread from heaven.

The people were shocked. How could Jesus be the bread of life? How could he be bread from heaven? The people knew that Jesus was born here on earth. His parents were Mary and Joseph.

The people missed the whole point of Jesus' teaching. When Jesus said he was the bread of life, he wasn't talking about food for our body; he meant that he had the spiritual food we need for our souls. People need food to live and grow physically. People need Jesus to live and grow in their relationship to God.

Bread of Life Food Pyramid*

A Guide to Daily Spiritual Nutrition

True Bread ← (John 6:32)

Jesus is the True Bread from Heaven. We have a sweet treat that the people in Jesus' day did not have—the words of Jesus written down for us to read. Take time every day to find out what Jesus wants you to know.

Eat richly.

Living Bread → (John 6:51)

Jesus is the Living Bread. He gave his own body when he died for us all. Because of what Jesus did, we can know God and live forever. Give thanks to Jesus for dying so we can live forever.

Eat abundantly.

← **Bread from Heaven** (John 6:58)

Jesus is the Bread from Heaven. Jesus didn't come to earth to do what he wanted to do. He came from heaven to do what God wanted him to do. Everyone who believes in Jesus can live with him in heaven forever. Get ready for heaven by praising God now!

Eat plentifully.

Bread of Life → (John 6:35)

Jesus is the Bread of Life. Anyone who comes to Jesus will never be hungry for spiritual food again. And anyone who believes in Jesus will never be thirsty for God again. When you eat food for your body, remember to eat food for your spirit, too.

Eat generously.

← **Bread of Life** (John 6:41)

Jesus is the Bread of Life. God gave his people manna in the wilderness so they would have food for their bodies. But the bread of life is even better than that. It never spoils or gets rotten, like the manna did. It keeps us alive in our spirits. Stay close to Jesus, and he will keep you satisfied.

Eat liberally.

Bread of God (John 6:33)

Jesus is the Bread of God, sent from heaven. God loved us so much that he sent Jesus to earth so we can know God. Jesus loved us so much that he came to do God's will. When he came to earth, he made a way for us to live a new life. Thank God for sending Jesus every day.

Eat constantly.

SOURCE: THE BIBLE, GOD'S DEPARTMENT OF SPIRITUAL HEALTH AND ETERNAL SERVICES.

The people Jesus taught in the synagogue remembered how God gave his people what they needed to stay alive in the wilderness for 40 years. When God gave us Jesus, he gave what we need to live in heaven forever. But we have to eat the bread of life. Because Jesus came from heaven to earth, we can know God–all day, every day.

Go for the Godprint

Commitment: When you choose to eat the bread of life and know Jesus himself, you make a commitment to "feed" on Jesus' words. You can find his words in the first four books of the New Testament: Matthew, Mark, Luke and John. Don't go hungry!

What Digby Dug Up

Bread was extremely important in the lives of Bible time people. It was the main source of food. People ate bread at every meal. Can you guess how many times the word "bread" is used in the Bible? The answer is hidden in the recipe. Just remember this order: sugar kneads flour.

Café de Click

Sweet Bread Recipe: 30 minutes preparation, 2 hours to rise, 40 minutes to bake. While you work, talk about how making this bread takes a time commitment.

1 cup light cream	2 packages yeast	5-**6** cups flour
3/4 cup sugar	1/4 teaspoon salt	4 eggs, beaten
1/4 cup butter	2 teaspoons vanilla	1 egg beaten + 1 tablespoon of water

1. Put the cream in a glass measuring cup and heat it in the microwave for 30 seconds. Add to it the sugar, butter and salt.
2. In a bowl, mix 1 1/2 cups flour and the yeast. Add the cream mixture and beat 2 minutes.
3. Add the eggs, vanilla and 1 more cup flour. Beat 2 minutes.
4. Sprinkle flour on a large cutting board or counter. Knead 6-**9** minutes, adding flour as necessary to make a soft dough.
5. Put the dough in a greased bowl, cover it, put it in a warm place and let it rise for an hour.
6. Punch the dough down! Put it back on the floured board and divide it into 3 equal balls. Place them in a cloverleaf design on baking sheet. Cover the dough and let it rise for one hour.
7. Brush the dough with the beaten egg. Bake at 425 degrees for 10 minutes. Reduce heat to 350 and bake for 30-35 minutes or until done.

Answer: 396

God Talk
We all "knead" to talk to God about what we "knead."
As you knead the dough for the bread, tell God how you "knead" him.
I "knead" you when I'm feeling… I "knead" you when someone…
The more you "knead" God, the softer you'll be!

Lazarus, Come Out!

Jesus didn't own a home of his own. When he traveled the countryside preaching, teaching and healing people, he would often stay with friends. Some of Jesus' closest friends lived in the town of Bethany. There was Mary, her sister Martha, and their brother Lazarus. Jesus loved this family, and they loved Jesus, too.

One day Lazarus got sick. Though Mary and Martha took good care of their brother, the next day he felt worse. They feared he would die and there was only one thing they could do to help him: they sent for Jesus.

When the messenger found Jesus and told him about Lazarus, Jesus said, "This sickness that Lazarus has won't end in death. Instead, God will get special honor from this." And instead of leaving right away, Jesus stayed where he was for two more days. Finally he said to his followers, "Let's go back to Judea." They discussed this journey for a little while, then Jesus told them, "My friend Lazarus is asleep, and I'm going to wake him up."

This statement confused Jesus' friends. Why should Jesus go wake Lazarus? They knew that a good sleep usually helps people get better. So Jesus explained further: "Lazarus is dead. Let's go to him."

By the time Jesus and his followers arrived, Lazarus had been buried for four days. Martha went out to greet Jesus when he arrived. "Lord," she told him, "if you'd been here, my brother wouldn't have died. But I know it's still not too late because God will give you whatever you ask."

Jesus answered her, "Your brother will be alive again." But Martha thought Jesus was talking about Lazarus going to heaven. So Jesus said, "I am the resurrection and the life. He who believes in me will live, even though he dies; and whoever lives and believes in me will never die. Do you believe this?"

"Yes, Lord," Martha responded. "I believe you are the Christ, the Son of God who was promised long ago."

Then Mary came to Jesus. She said just what Martha had said: "Lord, if you had been here my brother would not have died." Jesus knew how much Mary and Martha loved their brother. His heart was heavy and sad.

"Where is he buried?" Jesus asked.

When they got to the tomb, Jesus cried. Everyone noticed how much Jesus must have loved Lazarus.

Then Jesus did something that shocked everyone: he ordered the tomb to be opened. Martha explained that Lazarus had been in the tomb for four days. Dead bodies start to smell bad after just a short time. No one could believe Jesus wanted the tomb opened. But Jesus insisted, so they obeyed.

321

Then Jesus prayed, "Father, thank you for hearing me. I know you always hear me, but I want everyone else here to believe that it was you that sent me." When he finished praying he called out, "Lazarus! Come out!" And Lazarus did come out! He was still wrapped in the clothes that he'd been buried in, but he was alive!

You can imagine all the hugging and laughing that went on after that! Jesus showed his friends how much he cared for them. He also showed everyone that he was sent from God. He waited to heal Lazarus so that everyone would know that he had power not just over sickness, but over death, too!

Go for the Godprint

Compassion: In this story it seemed as if Jesus didn't care that his friend Lazarus was dying. Instead of going to help, Jesus waited two days. But Jesus did care about Lazarus and his sisters. He cried when they cried and he brought Lazarus back to life. Like Jesus, we show God's love when we're sad with those who are sad and when we do what we can to help them.

What Digby Dug Up

JOHN 11:35 IS THE SHORTEST VERSE IN THE WHOLE BIBLE. IT'S ONLY TWO WORDS LONG! LOOK IT UP TO SEE WHAT IT SAYS, AND THINK ABOUT WHAT THIS VERSE TELLS US ABOUT THE FEELINGS JESUS HAS.

GP Theater Company

Take turns making faces to show the feelings listed below. See if others can guess what emotion or feeling you're showing by the look on your face.

- Angry
- Embarrassed
- Shy
- Nervous

- Sad
- Happy
- Bored
- Tired

- Suspicious
- Scared
- Surprised
- Frustrated

After you've had fun making faces at each other, talk about:
- How should we respond when someone is feeling scared? Embarrassed? Happy?

- How do our actions help others feel better or make them feel worse?

- What can we learn from the actions of Jesus?

God Talk
This prayer is based on Psalm 145:9.
Lord, you show your goodness to everyone.
You have compassion on everyone you have made.

Jesus Says "I Am"

Jesus never had a classroom or a desk. No blackboard, no attendance chart, no computer, no grade book. But Jesus was the best teacher in the world. People followed Jesus everywhere to hear what he had to say.

Sometimes Jesus told stories that put pictures in people's minds.

Read the clues and find the picture stories Jesus told about himself. Start with this one:

I am something you would want in a dark closet if you were trying to read a secret message.

I am something you would be glad to find if you walked beside a long, high fence and you wanted to be safe on the other side.

That's a tricky one. Resurrection and life go together. Jesus said, "I am resurrection and life" (John 11:25). Jesus gives the kind of life that goes on even after we die. It lasts forever. Only Jesus can give us this kind of life.

Congratulations—you've done it again! The branch can't grow without the vine. Jesus said, "I am the vine; you are the branches" (John 15:5). If the branch stays connected to the vine, the fruit will be juicy and delicious. We show that we're connected to Jesus by doing what he asks us to do.

I am something that might look tangled and confusing, but as long as you see fruit growing on me you can be sure I'm healthy.

You found it!
The right road gets you where you want to go. Jesus said, "I am the way, the truth and the life" (John 14:6). Jesus wants us to go on the road that takes us to his Father—God. Jesus is the only way to get there.

I am something you can't see or touch, but anyone can have me and I never run out.

That's it! Swing me open on my hinges. A gate is the right way to go into a place. It's so much better than sneaking over the walls. Jesus said, "I am the gate" (John 10:9). Jesus is the gate because he opens the way to God. Anyone who trusts Jesus is safe in God's care.

Right! A light!
A light shows the right way to go in a dark place. Jesus said, "I am the light of the world" (John 8:12). Jesus is the light for the whole world because he shows everyone the right way to live. He shows us by the way he lived and the things he taught.

I am just what you need when you're on a car trip, if you want to get where you're going. And you need the right one for your life, too.

That's everything!
Jesus is the light,
the gate,
the resurrection and life,
the way and the truth,
the vine.

Most of all Jesus is love. He loved us enough to die for us so that we can know God. If you put your faith in him, you can

Walk in the light, and not stumble in the dark,
Go through the gate, and be safe in his care,
Share his resurrection and life, and never die,
Stay on the true way, and not get lost,
Be connected to the vine, and live a fruitful life.

Go for the Godprint

Faith: Jesus said he was a lot of things! Putting faith in Jesus means believing he really is all those things, even if you've never met him face to face. And it means that you choose to show you believe in Jesus by the way you live. What will you choose?

What Digby Dug Up

Matthew, Mark, Luke and John all wrote about Jesus' life. But only John told the "I am" picture stories. John told these true stories about Jesus so that people would believe in Jesus.

Herbie's Hideaway

What picture stories can you make up to share your faith in Jesus?
Take turns filling in the blanks in this sentence:

Jesus is like _____ because _____.

If you need some ideas to get started, try finishing these:

Jesus is like a cup of water because …
Jesus is like a field of grass because…
Jesus is like a warm, cozy blanket because…

Now try some on your own. You may want to have one person start the
sentence and someone else finish it. Or you might want to get out art supplies
and have everyone create a faith picture to share with the family.

God Talk

Choose two people in your family
to read the parts of this prayer,
or have one person read one part
and everyone else read the other part together.
Dear Jesus, the light of the world,
Thank you for showing your light to us.
Dear Jesus, the gate,
Thank you for showing us the way to a safe place.
Dear Jesus, the resurrection and life,
Thank you for offering us life that never ends.
Dear Jesus, the way, the truth and the life,
Thank you for showing us how to know God.
Dear Jesus, the vine,
Keep our branches strong and connected to you. Amen.

Mary's Oil

Mary is so excited. She is tingly all over!
The Savior of the world is only inches from her
hand. If she reaches out she can touch him. But
she doesn't. Jesus is not here to see her. He is a
guest of honor at a dinner in her hometown of
Bethany. Martha and Lazarus are there too. Yes,
Lazarus—the very man who was dead but now is
alive because of Jesus. Mary works all day to
help prepare this special meal.

Soon it's dinnertime. Mary eats as her sister, Martha, serves. Martha is a good cook. The lentil soup is well seasoned and the bread is filling and delicious. When she is done eating, Mary rises and offers Martha her place at the table. But it's hard to keep her mind on serving.

"What can I give to Jesus?" she wonders. "How can I show my respect to this man who is the Son of God and raises people from the dead? Serving food is not enough. I must do more."

As Martha finishes serving the last of the soup and bread, Mary tiptoes to the peg that holds her cloak. Reaching into the pocket she finds the small alabaster jar she put there early in the morning. The neck of the jar is long and thin and cool to the touch. Without waiting for permission (or even for Jesus to finish eating!) Mary reaches out and touches him.

Jesus turns.

With a swift motion, Mary breaks the neck of the jar on the table and then kneels. All eyes are now on Mary and the small alabaster jar. In the warm room, the wonderful scent fills the air. Mary rubs the sweet oil, drop by drop, into Jesus' feet. Then she wipes his feet with her long soft hair.

No one speaks. No one eats. Everyone watches. Mary continues to serve Jesus lovingly. The whole house smells of sweet perfume.

But a guest at the dinner, one of Jesus' disciples, is not at all happy. Judas Iscariot frowns at Mary. His voice is angry. "Why wasn't this perfume sold and the money given to the poor? It was worth a year's wages."

Mary's heart sinks. What has she done?

But Jesus smiles at her. "Leave her alone," Jesus tells Judas. "It was intended that she should save this perfume for the day of my burial. You will always have the poor among you, but you will not always have me."

Judas looks away.

Mary's heart sings. She knows she has served her Lord well.

Go for the Godprint

Reverence: As proof of Mary's faith and love for Jesus, she gave him the very best she had. The Bible does not tell us how Mary came upon such expensive oil. We do know that it was worth a lot of money. Mary could have sold the oil and bought herself many beautiful things. But she didn't. Instead she responded to Jesus' greatness and her deep respect for his power by using the oil (and her long hair!) to serve him.

What Digby Dug Up
Nard was the name of both the plant from India and the fragrant oil used to perfume Jesus. It was expensive, "…worth a year's wages," and often stored in small alabaster jars.

Izzy's Art Cart

GET LIST:
SMALL PIECES OF COLORFUL FABRIC
ZIP-TOP BAG, VANILLA BEAN
WHOLE CLOVES, DRIED DILL
ROSE PETALS, RIBBON

Mary gave Jesus a precious gift. It cost money and time. And she didn't save a drop for herself! Make sweet-smelling sachets to remind you of this story. Cut three 6-inch circles from the fabric. (Hint: Use a small desert plate to trace the circles.) In a sturdy zip-top bag, place a whole vanilla bean, a tablespoon of whole cloves, three teaspoons of dried dill and some dried rose petals. Seal the bag. With the heel of your hand or a block of wood, crush the spices and petals. Divide the crushed materials and place a small amount in the center of each fabric circle. Gather the fabric to make a "neck" and tie it with a ribbon.

• **Where can we keep one of these to remind us of Mary's gift to Jesus?**
• **Who can we share a sachet with so they can remember the story too?**

God Talk
Place a few drops of
scented bubble bath
in a basin of warm water.
Take turns washing each other's feet and
patting them dry with a towel.
While your feet are drying, take turns saying this prayer.
Fill in the blank.
Dear Jesus, you must become more important in my life.
You deserve the best that I can give. I will honor you by _____.

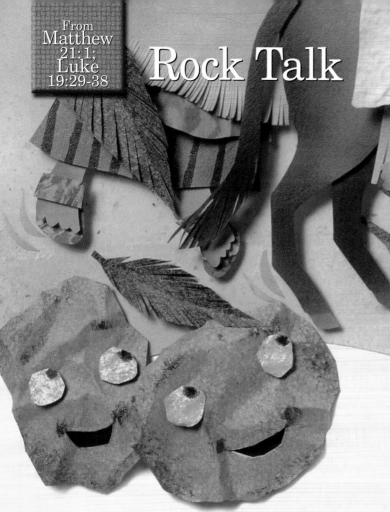

Rock Talk

You may want to make two "rock head" puppets to tell this story. Put eyes and mouths on two lunch bags. Stuff them with newspapers, tape them closed, then crumple the corners so they look like rocks.

Sandy: Rocky! Rocky! What is all the shouting about?

Rocky: It's Jesus! He asked his disciples to get a young donkey for him to ride.

Sandy: Where did they get it?

Rocky: Jesus told them to go to the house with the donkey and take it. If anyone asks them about it, he told them to say "The Lord needs it." He's going to ride it into the city!

Sandy: Oh, my, do you know what that means to the Jewish people?

Rocky: What?

Sandy: That means Jesus is letting the people know he is their king—a king who comes in peace. This is so exciting!

Rocky: No wonder the people are shouting praises to him. He is not just any king. He is the King of Kings!

Sandy: Wait a minute. What is that Pharisee saying to Jesus?

Rocky: He told Jesus to scold his disciples because they were making too much noise with their praises.

Sandy: What did Jesus say?

Rocky: He said, "I tell you, if they keep quiet, the stones will cry out."

Sandy: What! Us? We might get to praise Jesus? The rocks will cry out? Oh, I can't wait!

Rocky: Only if the humans stop praising him.

Sandy: But what if they do? Then it will be our turn.

Rocky: That sounds like work.

Sandy: Oh, come on, you've been sitting on your rock bottom for long enough. By the way, I've been meaning to tell you, you have moss growing on your backside.

Rocky: I think it gives me character.

Sandy: Well, I can't wait to see if those humans wimp out. He is so glorious and worthy of our praise! He's so awesome.

Rocky: Calm down. You'll start an avalanche.

Sandy: I'm sorry. I just can't help it. I'm so tired of sitting here day after day watching the rest of the world praise him. Even the trees can wave their branches and the birds sing. To cry out to praise him— what a privilege! The closest I came to wiggling around in praise of him was when a kid kicked me across the parking lot. Even then a chariot parked on me.

Rocky: I must admit, it would be pretty exciting. But we have a purpose too, you know.

Sandy: Like what?

Rocky: We are good examples of rocks, steady and solid. Some people describe Jesus as their rock, dependable and strong.

Sandy: Yeah, yeah, a real snore. Come on, don't you just want to shout and yell "Hallelujah!"? Praise Jesus! Uh oh, look. Now the people are waving something. What is it?

Rocky: Looks like palm branches.

Sandy: And they're taking off their coats and laying them on the ground. Now they're waving the branches and, and...Oh, no! They are still shouting praises to him as he rides down the street. They are doing it, praising him. Oh, pebbles! We missed our chance to praise him out loud so everyone can hear us.

Rocky: Well, maybe when he comes back next time we can do something.

Sandy: Yeah, maybe we can fall on someone.

Rocky: Sandy! Let's just sit back and listen to the humans praise him and be glad they didn't waste time getting to it.

Sandy: They do sound great! As a matter of fact, they rock!

Go for the Godprint

Worship: To worship God is to show we believe that God is worthy of our highest honor. It is to give him our attention by praising him and all that is good about him. When we praise God we feel close to him. Praising does not just have to happen in church. We can praise him anywhere and anytime. Rocky and Sandy considered it a privilege to praise Jesus on the first Palm Sunday. Be sure you don't waste your chance to praise him.

What Digby Dug Up

Zechariah 9:9, in the Old Testament, predicted that a king would ride into Jerusalem on a donkey.

IN BIBLE TIMES, THE DONKEY WAS AN ANIMAL OF PEACE, AS WELL AS THE RIGHT ANIMAL FOR ROYALTY TO RIDE. JESUS MADE ZECHARIAH 9:9 COME TRUE.

Izzy's Art Cart

In the drama the rocks did not get a chance to praise Jesus. If they could they might want to remind us to praise and worship God each day. Here is a way that they can. You can make Praise Rocks. Go out into your yard and look for some rocks. Smooth rocks will work best. Then take out your markers or paint and decorate your rocks in beautiful colors and designs. Leave some space to write praise words to God. Maybe you could use some of these words:

HALLELUJAH,
PRAISE GOD
AWESOME,
GLORY TO GOD

Put your rock in your room to remind you to praise and worship God.

God Talk

Look around your yard
or neighborhood for a "prayer rock."
Choose a rock that looks like it would praise God.
At your next family meal,
pass the rock around and ask everyone
to say something that praises God.

Fruit for Thought

Did you know that Jesus called you a branch? In fact, he called all his followers branches. He said it one evening in an upstairs room in Jerusalem. It was Passover, and Jesus was sharing the special Passover meal with his closest friends. Jesus knew it would be his last meal before he died, so he had important things to say.

Jesus said that he's the vine and his disciples are branches. His Father is the gardener who does the pruning. Pruning means cutting off parts of a living plant. Gardeners cut off dead, dying or unfruitful branches. Then they trim back the good, fruit-bearing branches. Pruning helps trees or vines grow better and produce more fruit. Pruning also helps to change the direction of branches that are growing the wrong way.

If you cut a branch off a tree, it will die. We must stay connected to Jesus to keep our spirits alive. But sometimes God needs to prune us to keep us going the right direction, to remove bad things from our lives and to help us bear more fruit.

Don't worry. You're not going to have apples hanging from your ears or grapes sprouting between your toes! The fruit you produce might be telling others about Jesus, praying for people, or showing love, patience, and self-control. (See Galatians 5:22–23 and 2 Peter 1:5–8 to read about other good fruit.)

Jesus taught a lot more about the vine and branches. See if you can guess what he said.

1. Every branch in me that does not bear fruit:
   a. bears vegetables.
   b. has worms.
   c. God takes away.

2. Just as a branch can't bear fruit when it's cut off a tree, you can't bear fruit if:
   a. you don't remain in Jesus.
   b. you don't drink lots of water and take vitamins.
   c. you don't roll around in the dirt once a day.

3. If you remain in me, you'll bear lots of fruit. Without me you can do:
   a. anything you want.
   b. nothing.
   c. only what your parents say you can do.

4. Anyone who doesn't remain in me:
   a. is thrown away like a dead branch, dries up, and is burned.
   b. bears dried fruit.
   c. eats prunes.

5. If you remain in me and my words remain in you, ask whatever you wish and:
   a. don't expect an answer.
   b. maybe I will help.
   c. it will be done for you.

6. If you bear much fruit my Father will be glorified and:
   a. people will like you.
   b. you'll prove you're my disciples.
   c. you'll have plenty to eat.

7. Just as the Father loved me, so I have loved:
   a. doing miracles.
   b. fishing.
   c. you.

8. You will remain in my love if you:
   a. pray a lot.
   b. attend church every week.
   c. keep my commandments.

9. I've told you all this so:
   a. you can be filled with my joy.
   b. you'll remember to eat fruit every day.
   c. you'll read the Bible instead of watching TV.

10. This is my commandment:
   a. go to bed on time.
   b. love one another as I've loved you.
   c. look both ways before crossing streets.

11. This is the greatest love:
   a. to give your life for a friend.
   b. to give nice greeting cards.
   c. to throw parties.

12. You are my friends if you:
   a. like me.
   b. say nice things about me.
   c. do what I tell you to do.

13. You didn't choose me. I chose you to bear fruit and your fruit will:
   a. rot.
   b. remain.
   c. win ribbons.

14. If you ask the Father anything in my name:
   a. he'll give it to you.
   b. you'll become a famous millionaire.
   c. he'll think you're me.

Answers:

1c, 2a, 3b, 4a, 5c, 6b, 7c, 8c, 9a, 10b, 11a, 12c, 13b, 14a

Go for the Godprint

Fellowship: Everyone who believes in Jesus can have a loving friendship with him. If we obey his command to love one another, we'll all be connected like branches to a vine. And our vine, Jesus, joins us to God. What can you do to stay attached to the vine?

What Digby Dug Up

THE BREAD USED AT THE LAST SUPPER DID NOT CONTAIN YEAST, SO IT WAS FLAT LIKE A CRACKER OR A MATZO. YOU CAN READ ABOUT IT IN EXODUS 12:8-15.

Mo's Fab Lab

Find a plant with tender leaves, like a philodendron or coleus. Bend the petiole of a leaf. (The petiole is the part of the leaf that looks like a stem.) Make sure that it's really bent or slightly broken and doesn't pop back up. Then break another leaf completely off. Put the leaf you broke off in a sunny spot. Later, check the two leaves to see what happened. When a leaf or a branch is cut off from the main stem, it can't get water or nutrients. First it will wilt, then turn brown and die. If we don't stay attached to Jesus, our spirits will be like dried up leaves.

God Talk

Find a stick or branch
to symbolize Jesus as the vine.
Put one hand on the stick
and the other on the person in front of you.
Form a circle that connects all of you to the symbol
for Jesus and to each other. Then pray this prayer together:
Heavenly Father, please prune out anything bad in my life.
Help me to grow straight and strong and bear good fruit for you.
Hold on tightly to me so I will always be part of your vine.
Amen.

Jesus Prays for You!

Jesus had a lot to say to his disciples at their last meal together. He washed their feet to show them how to serve each other. Then he told them to trust in God no matter what happened. He explained how he was the vine, and people who believe in him are branches–all part of the same plant. And then Jesus prayed. He had a lot to say to his heavenly Father, too.

Jesus looked toward the sky and prayed:

"Father, the time has come. You gave me the authority to give eternal life to the people you've given me. Eternal life is people knowing you, and knowing you are the only true God. I've done the work on earth that you sent me to do. Now, Father, let me return to you and to the glory I had even before the world began."

This was a prayer Jesus said for himself. He knew it would be agony to be killed, and he asked God to give him strength for what he had to do. Jesus also told God that he'd finished the work here on earth that God wanted him to do, and now Jesus wanted to return to heaven to be with God.

Jesus continued to pray, saying:

"I have shown people here on earth who you are. They know my power comes from you, and that you sent me. I pray for them. I won't be staying in the world any longer, but they'll still be in the world. I'm coming to you, Holy Father, so protect them with your power. While I've been here I've protected them. My prayer isn't that you'll take them out of the world, but that you'll protect them from the evil one. They've been sent out into the world to tell others about you. "

In praying these words, Jesus asked God to watch over his disciples, his closest followers, since Jesus would soon be returning to heaven. Jesus knew other people who didn't believe in him were going to make life hard for the disciples, and Jesus prayed for his close friends, asking God to protect them.

Jesus kept on praying:

"I'm also praying for people who will believe in me in the future after they hear the message of the disciples. I pray that they'll have the same love for you and for each other that we have, and that they'll obey you and your Word."

In this part of his prayer Jesus was praying for you! Jesus asked God to watch over all the people who would become Christians, even hundreds or thousands of years later. Jesus asked God to help Christians act lovingly toward one another so that when people who didn't know about Jesus saw their love they could learn about him.

When Jesus finished praying, it was time to go. He walked with his disciples to a favorite olive grove and waited in the Garden of

Gethsemane for the next part of God's plan to happen.

"Sit here while I go over there and pray," Jesus told his disciples. Jesus was troubled, because he knew what would happen that night. "Stay here and keep watch with me."

He walked a little further–about as far as you can throw a stone–and knelt down with his face the ground. He prayed, "Father, if it is possible, may this cup be taken from me. Yet not as I will, but as you will." Then he went back to see his disciples.

He found the disciples sleeping. "Why are you asleep? Get up and pray so you won't fall into temptation." Three times Jesus went off to pray by himself, and three times he came back to find his disciples sleeping.

Jesus wanted to do God's will, even when it was hard. He was ready to finish the work God gave him to do.

Go for the Godprint

Submissiveness: Jesus knew that it was going to be painful to die on the cross, but he also knew that was the only way to pay for the sins of people. He knew that it was all part of God's plan, and he trusted God. So he did what God wanted him to do, even when he knew it would be hard.

What Digby Dug Up

Jesus' prayer takes up all of John 17. This is the longest prayer by Jesus in the Bible.

Jake's Mirth Quake

Play a game like "Simon Says," but change "Simon" to the name of the person who's leading the game. Call out instructions like, "Touch your head! Hop on one foot! Say the alphabet!" These commands should be obeyed only when "Jenny says" (or the name of the family member giving the instructions) precedes the command. After you've played the game, talk about what "Jesus Says" we should do. What commands does Jesus gives us? Read John 15:12 to find the command that Jesus gave his disciples during their last meal. How can you carry out that command?

God Talk

When Jesus prayed, he prayed for himself,
for his followers, and for people
who would become his followers in the future.
Think of two other people besides yourself that you can pray for today.
Ask God to be with them and protect them.
You can pray the same thing for yourself.

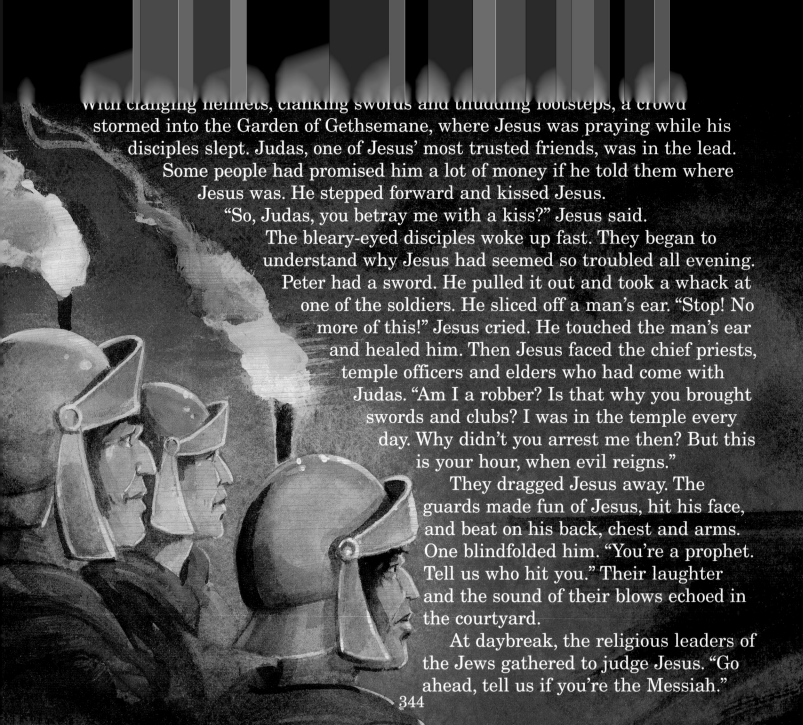

With clanging helmets, clanking swords and thudding footsteps, a crowd stormed into the Garden of Gethsemane, where Jesus was praying while his disciples slept. Judas, one of Jesus' most trusted friends, was in the lead. Some people had promised him a lot of money if he told them where Jesus was. He stepped forward and kissed Jesus.

"So, Judas, you betray me with a kiss?" Jesus said.

The bleary-eyed disciples woke up fast. They began to understand why Jesus had seemed so troubled all evening. Peter had a sword. He pulled it out and took a whack at one of the soldiers. He sliced off a man's ear. "Stop! No more of this!" Jesus cried. He touched the man's ear and healed him. Then Jesus faced the chief priests, temple officers and elders who had come with Judas. "Am I a robber? Is that why you brought swords and clubs? I was in the temple every day. Why didn't you arrest me then? But this is your hour, when evil reigns."

They dragged Jesus away. The guards made fun of Jesus, hit his face, and beat on his back, chest and arms. One blindfolded him. "You're a prophet. Tell us who hit you." Their laughter and the sound of their blows echoed in the courtyard.

At daybreak, the religious leaders of the Jews gathered to judge Jesus. "Go ahead, tell us if you're the Messiah."

344

Jesus answered, "But you won't believe me. From now on, the Son of Man will sit at God's right hand."

"Are you the Son of God?"

"Yes, I am."

The leaders were furious and took Jesus to Pilate, the Roman governor. They lied about Jesus. They said that Jesus fooled people, told them not to pay taxes and called himself a king.

Pilate looked Jesus over. "Are you the king of the Jews?"

"Yes."

Pilate turned to the Jewish leaders. He did not think Jesus would cause any trouble. "I don't see any reason to charge this man."

"But he makes trouble everywhere, from Galilee to Jerusalem."

"Oh, he's a Galilean?" Pilate said. "That's Herod's territory. Take him to Herod."

So the Jewish leaders took Jesus to Herod. Herod was glad to see Jesus, hoping he would perform a miracle. He asked Jesus one question after another. But Jesus answered all his questions with silence. So Herod and his soldiers made fun of Jesus. They dressed him in a fine robe and sent him back to Pilate.

Pilate decided to punish Jesus and release him. But the crowd cried, "Take him away! Let Barabbas go instead!" Barabbas was a murderer and troublemaker. The Jewish leaders hated Jesus so much that they would rather see a murderer go free. Pilate argued with them, but they insisted, "Crucify him! Crucify him!"

"Why? He doesn't deserve the death penalty."

They shouted louder and louder. Finally Pilate gave in. He released Barabbas and sent Jesus to be crucified. Jesus didn't fight them. He knew what was supposed to happen. And he knew that no matter how hard things got, his heavenly Father was with him. He let them lead him away.

Go for the Godprint

Perseverance: Even Jesus felt like the death he was facing would be hard for him. But dying was the only way he could save us from the punishment we deserve for our sins. Jesus prayed and God helped him through it. God will give you the strength you need too. When things get rough, will you persevere like Jesus did?

What Digby Dug Up

Gethsemane was a garden or a field or part of an olive grove on the southwestern slope of the Mount of Olives. Jesus went there with some of his disciples on the day before he died, after they had their last meal together.

Izzy's Art Cart

GET LIST:
PAPER, MARKERS OR CRAYONS, GLUE, DRY JELLO MIX IN VARIOUS COLORS, SALTSHAKERS

Sketch an outline of one of the parts of this story on a sheet of paper. Pour glue on the paper and spread it around with your fingers so that the whole picture has a thin coat of glue. Put the jello mix in salt shakers and sprinkle it onto the glue in your picture. Color the different parts of your picture with different colors of jello "sand." Let the picture dry, and then you can hang it. If everyone in the family draws a different part of the story, you can use your pictures to tell other people how Jesus followed God's plan, even though it was very hard to do.

God Talk
Kneel together like Jesus did
on the Mount of Olives and pray this prayer.
Lord, help us learn to pray like Jesus,
"Father, may your will be done."
Give us hope when we're discouraged.
Father, may your will be done.
Help us trust you when there's trouble.
Father, may your will be done.
Help us know your way is better.
Father, may your will be done.
Help us learn to live like Jesus.
Father, may your will be done.

One, Two, Three—Oops! Peter's Story Begins

Cockadoodledoo. Did you hear that? It's the rooster again, up at the crack of dawn. But you knew that. Some people think that's too soon!

I once heard the rooster crow too soon. I hadn't been to bed all night. But that's not why I didn't want to hear the rooster crow.

My story started the night before. I'm Peter, and I was with Jesus and the other disciples on the last evening before he died. We had a meal in a private upstairs room, and Jesus talked for a long time. He tried to tell us it was time for him to die, but we didn't want to believe it.

Jesus told me to stay on my toes, because there was trouble ahead. He was praying for me to be strong when the time of testing came, he said. I wasn't afraid of anything. I told Jesus, "I'd do anything for you, even die for you!"

I meant what I said. I couldn't think of anything better than being loyal to Jesus. But Jesus knew me even better than I knew myself. He told me, "Before the rooster crows today, you will deny three times that you know me." If only I had paid better attention.

Not long after that, we left our private room and went to the garden on the Mount of Olives to pray. Maybe you already know what happened there. Judas Iscariot led a large group of temple guards to Jesus, and the guards took him away. We were scared out of our minds. Most of the disciples went into hiding. I didn't want to be arrested, but I had to see what happened to Jesus. So I followed, but at a safe distance.

They took Jesus into the house of the chief priest. I couldn't go inside, but I could stay in the courtyard and wait.

It was a cold night. Someone started a fire. I stayed away at first, but the fire looked so comforting, so warm. I moved closer. And that's when she saw me. She was a maid, tired from her long day, just trying to keep warm like the rest of us. For some reason she noticed me. I saw her look at me, and I turned away. She looked at me again, closer this time. Then she shouted out, "This man was with him!"

"I don't even know him," I said. The words were out of my mouth before I thought about what I was saying. Are you counting? That's one.

348

There were so many people in the courtyard. Why should anyone notice me? But they did. It wasn't long before someone else said, "You're one of them."

Right away, I said, "No, I'm not!"

Are you counting? That's two.

Things settled down for an hour or so. I was still waiting to find out what was happening to Jesus. Suddenly someone stood up and pointed at me. "He's got to have been with Jesus. Listen to the way he talks. He's a Galilean."

"I don't know what you're talking about," I said.

That's three. Ooops.

I barely got the words out of my mouth before I heard the rooster crow. Just then, they were moving Jesus from one place to another. He looked right at me. And I remembered what he'd said while we were still in our private room. Do you remember?

One, two, three. He said I would deny knowing him three times before the rooster crowed, and I had. I ran out of there as fast as I could and cried my eyes out. Just a few hours ago, I'd said I would be willing to die for Jesus. Now look what I'd done!

I learned a big lesson about loyalty that night. The next time you hear a rooster, or even just read about one in a book, remember my story. You can learn to be loyal to Jesus without making the mistake I made.

Go for the Godprint

Loyalty: It's not always easy to show that you're loyal even when you say that you want to be. That's the problem Peter ran into. True loyalty to Jesus means that you show by what you do and say that you really want to serve him. Were you loyal to Jesus today?

What Digby Dug Up

The courtyard Peter was in probably was surrounded on four sides by buildings. Jesus may have been in a room that opened onto the courtyard. That's why he could see Peter at the moment that the rooster crowed.

Mo's Fab Lab

GET LIST: RED CABBAGE, STRIPS OF PAPER, VINEGAR, LEMON JUICE, DISHWASHING SOAP

Chop up half a red cabbage and boil 5 minutes. Remove the cabbage, leaving just the water. Dip strips of paper into water, and let them soak it up. Then lay the strips out to dry. Try to predict what will happen when you add a drop of vinegar, lemon juice and dishwashing soap to a strip of the cabbage paper. (Liquids that are acidic will turn red, and alkalis will turn green.) Can you tell whether a liquid is acid or alkali before you try the test? Talk about:

- **Putting a drop of each liquid on the paper shows what it really is. How is that like loyalty?**

- **How is your loyalty to Jesus put to the test?**

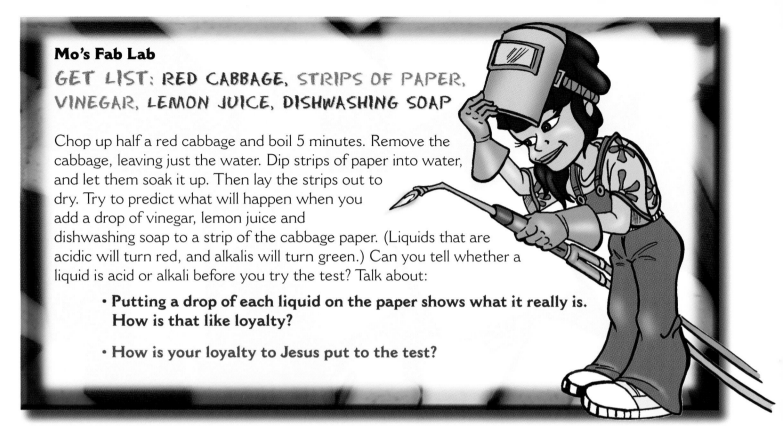

God Talk

One person reads the light printed lines.
Everyone else responds with the dark print.

When I feel like being mad and getting my own way,
I pledge allegiance to Jesus Christ.
When I want to keep the best things for myself,
I pledge allegiance to Jesus Christ.
When my friends want me to do something I know is wrong,
I pledge allegiance to Jesus Christ.
When I'm not sure what's going to happen next but I know God is with me,
I pledge allegiance to Jesus Christ.

Never Too Late to Forgive

Jesus' followers couldn't believe what they saw! Jesus was going to be nailed to a wooden cross and left to hang until he died. The Jewish high priests wanted him dead. Pilate, the governor, didn't think Jesus had done anything wrong, but he gave the high priests what they wanted. It wasn't fair at all. But it was really happening. Jesus' friends watched in horror as soldiers led Jesus to a place called the Skull. He even had to carry his own cross up the hill. Then soldiers nailed his hands and feet onto the cross.

Two other men also hung on crosses to die that day. They were criminals—robbers—who were being punished by death for what they had done. They were alongside Jesus, one on the right side and the other on the left.

Why didn't Jesus do something to help himself? Remember: Jesus is the Savior. He died for you and me. Look at your hands and feet. Imagine how painful it would be to have nails hammered through them! This is what happened to Jesus. He was nailed to his cross. Do you ever scream when you get hurt? Instead of screaming or crying, Jesus looked at the people who were killing him and prayed, "Father, forgive them. They don't know what they're doing." Jesus was willing to forgive even the men who were killing him! Why didn't Jesus do something to help himself? Because he was thinking about you and me. He forgives us, too.

After Jesus was nailed to the cross, the soldiers and other people stood around watching. The soldiers had Jesus' clothes, and they decided to play a gambling game to see who would get to keep them. They didn't care that Jesus loved them. They just wanted his clothes.

The leaders who hated Jesus laughed at him and made fun of him. They said things like, "Jesus saved other people. If he's really God, he can save himself now!" The soldiers joined in and said "If you're the king of the Jews, save yourself!" They made a sign and put it on Jesus' cross. The sign said, "This is the king of the Jews."

Why didn't Jesus do something to help himself? Because he was thinking about you and me. He took the punishment we deserve so that we can really know God.

Then one of the criminals on a cross beside Jesus joined in the mean insults. Even though he was dying, he yelled in an angry voice, "Save yourself and us. If you're God's Son, then save us." All around him Jesus heard voices mocking him and laughing at him while he was dying for them.

353

But the other criminal told this man to stop it. He said, "You should be afraid for what you're saying! We deserve to die here on crosses because we committed awful crimes. We're getting what we deserve. But Jesus hasn't done anything wrong."

The criminal who tried to protect Jesus from the rude insults turned his head toward Jesus. He said, "Jesus, remember me when you are in your kingdom." He believed that Jesus was God, and he was sorry for the wrong things he had done.

It was probably hard for Jesus to talk. But he answered with love in his voice. "Today you'll be with me in heaven." Jesus loved even a dying man who had done terrible things. He died for this man, and he died for you and me.

Why did Jesus forgive the criminal? Because the man wanted to know God. When we're sorry like the criminal was sorry, Jesus forgives us, too, and helps us to know God.

Go for the Godprint

Repentance: The second man who died next to Jesus knew he deserved to be punished for his actions, even if it meant dying. When he asked Jesus to remember him in heaven, he repented. In his heart he was truly sorry and wanted to change his ways. Are you sorry for something deep in your heart? You can tell God how sorry you are.

What Digby Dug Up

John 19:23 tells us that the garment the soldiers took from Jesus was seamless. It was made from one piece of cloth and was too valuable to tear. When the soldiers gambled to see who would get it, they did just what Psalm 22:17 said would happen :

"THEY DIVIDE MY GARMENTS AMONG THEM AND CAST LOTS FOR MY CLOTHING."

Herbie's Hideaway

Cut a strip of felt that is 1 inch wide and 8 inches long. Cut another strip 1 inch wide and 5 inches long. Glue the two strips together to make a cross. Write the letters **J-E-S-U-S** across the 5-inch strip. Make sure the first "S" is in the middle, where the strips of felt cross. Write **M-Y-S-A-V-I-O-R** down the longer strip, so that the "S" in the middle of "Jesus" becomes the "S" in "Savior." Keep your cross in a favorite book or in your Bible to mark your place and remind you that Jesus died on the cross to forgive your sins.

PAINT

GET LIST:
CRAFT FELT, RULER, SCISSORS, SQUEEZABLE GLITTER FABRIC PAINT

God Talk
Say this short prayer together.
"Jesus, thank you for being my Savior.
Help me to turn away
from things that are wrong and follow only you."

Hey! Where Did the Boulder Go?

"Hail, king of the Jews!"

The soldiers spat in Jesus's face. They didn't really think he was king of anything at all. He was a criminal—and the worst kind.

"Come down from the cross, if you are the Son of God!"

People passing by looked at Jesus in disgust.

"He saved others, but he can't save himself!"

Religious leaders made fun of Jesus. They dared him to call on God to rescue him.

Golgotha, the Place of the Skull, was an ugly place. The rocky hillside was shaped like a real skull. Soldiers nailed Jesus' hands and feet to a heavy wooden cross and dropped the cross into a hole in the ground. Execution by crucifixion was the worst punishment anyone could get in the Roman empire. And Jesus got it.

At noon Jesus was ready to die. Suddenly everything grew dark. It seemed like the middle of the night instead of the middle of the day. Jesus said, "It is finished." He cried out with a loud voice and then died. Jesus knew he was doing God's work by dying, even though he didn't deserve that punishment. And now he had finished his part of God's work.

At the very moment when Jesus took his last breath, the earth shook and split open. Even rocks broke apart. The curtain in the most holy part of God's temple was torn in half from top to bottom. Before Jesus died, ordinary people couldn't go to that holy place to be near God. But the curtain tore in two, and now God's people can be close to him anywhere, anytime.

The soldiers watching all of this weren't making fun of Jesus anymore. Now they were terrified! What did all this mean? Some of them started to change their minds. The soldier in charge looked up at Jesus on the cross and said, "Surely he was the Son of God!"

When evening came, a rich man named Joseph and his friend Nicodemus came and took Jesus' body. They wrapped his body in linen and put him in a cave. An enormous boulder sealed the tomb so no one could get in or out.

The next day was quiet. Because it was the day that the Jews worshiped God, no one was allowed to go to the tomb.

On Sunday, three women who loved Jesus hurried to the tomb. It was very early in the morning and still dark. They just couldn't wait any longer to put special spices on Jesus' body. But how were they going to move that enormous boulder? Imagine their surprise when they discovered that the stone had been rolled away from the tomb. They rushed inside, but Jesus wasn't there. Instead, they saw two angels gleaming like lightning with clothes as white as snow. "He is not here; he has risen!" the angels said.

The women ran as fast as they could to tell the good news to Jesus' disciples. Jesus is risen! "That's impossible!" the disciples thought. Peter and John got up and ran to the tomb to see for themselves. Sure enough, Jesus had risen! It wasn't long before people everywhere heard the good news. Many people even saw Jesus for themselves. He really had risen!

Jesus died so that God could show his power and bring him back to life. God is more powerful than anything, including death. When Jesus died and rose, he made a way for us to know God so that we can live forever too. We can be sure God is in control of absolutely everything.

Go for the Godprint

Hope: What can be more horrible than death by crucifixion? But if Jesus hadn't died, he would not have risen. And if he had not risen, we would not be able to know God and live with him forever. Because Jesus did die and rise again, we know for sure that God can bring good from anything. Hope is not iffy. It's a sure thing that God will take care of the future.

What Digby Dug Up

When Jesus was on the cross, someone offered him a drink, perhaps on the end of a long stick. When Jesus tasted it, he found out it had gall in it, so he spit it out.

GALL WOULD KILL THE PAIN. JESUS DID NOT WANT TO ESCAPE HIS PAINFUL DEATH. HE WANTED TO DO WHAT GOD WANTED HIM TO DO, RIGHT UP UNTIL THE END.

Izzy's Art Cart

GET LIST:

POTATOES (one for every two people)
PARING KNIFE
INK PADS
PAPER AND PENCIL

Cut the potatoes in half. Use a pencil to etch a different shape into the surface of each half potato. Choose shapes that represent different parts of the crucifixion-resurrection story, such as a cross, a cave, a boulder and an angel. With the knife, carefully cut away the potato around the etching lines to leave a raised shape. Press the raised portion of the potato into an ink pad and then stamp onto paper to create a story in potato pictures. Write a caption for each part of the story. Talk about:

• **What part of this story gives you the most hope?**

• **Why are you glad that Jesus died and then rose from the dead?**

God Talk

Make an acrostic poem with the letters
H-O-P-E.
Tell God four things that you can be hopeful
about because Jesus died and rose.
Use one letter from the word HOPE to begin each idea.

360

Stranger on the Road

One was Cleopas. We don't know the other man's name. But they have an amazing story.

Cleopas and his friend left Jerusalem and walked toward Emmaus, a little village a few miles away. They'd had the most incredible day and didn't know what to believe. Their friends were running around Jerusalem saying that Jesus was alive. Cleopas and his friend knew that Jesus had been killed three days ago. How could he possibly be alive? But that's what Peter and Mary and the others were saying.

A stranger joined them on the dusty road that afternoon. They didn't recognize him, but it was okay with them if he wanted to walk to Emmaus with them.

"What are you talking about as you walk?" the stranger asked.

Cleopas and his friend stopped walking and stood still. They couldn't believe the question.

"Are you just a visitor to Jerusalem?" Cleopas asked. "Why don't you know about the things that are happening?"

"What things?" the stranger asked.

"About Jesus of Nazareth," Cleopas answered. Then he told the stranger everything he knew. Jesus was a prophet with the power of God. But the religious leaders hated him and wanted to see him dead. They made sure he was crucified.

"We thought he was the one who would redeem Israel," Cleopas's friend said. "We hoped we could break free from being ruled by the Romans. We thought he would be the one to bring in God's kingdom. And then he died."

Cleopas told the rest of the story. Jesus had died. But now, three days later, some women they knew went to his tomb early in the morning—and he wasn't there! The women said he was alive. Their friend Peter said he was alive too. But Cleopas and his friend had not seen for themselves, so they weren't sure what to think.

The stranger shook his head. "How foolish you are." He started to explain a few things. He started at the very beginning and told the story of God's plan. He told them everything the prophets said hundreds of years before about the Messiah God would send. The holy writings even taught that the Messiah would suffer just the way Jesus had.

The stranger talked for a long time. Now they were near Emmaus. The stranger acted like he was going to keep walking, but Cleopas and his friend said, "Stay with us, for it is nearly evening; the day is almost over." So the stranger went in the house to stay with them.

The evening meal was served. The stranger picked up the bread, thanked God for it, broke it and started to give it to Cleopas and his friend. Suddenly their eyes popped open and they knew who this stranger was. It was Jesus himself!

As soon as they knew who he was, he disappeared. They jumped up and ran back to Jerusalem. They found Jesus' followers gathered together and burst into the room saying, "It's true. The Lord has risen." They told everyone what had happened and how they knew it was Jesus when he broke the bread.

Go for the Godprint

Preciousness: Can you imagine what it must have been like for Cleopas and his friend to suddenly realize that Jesus had been with them? Jesus cared enough about them to make sure they knew the truth. And he cares for you the same way. He's with you wherever you are.

What Digby Dug Up

The Bible says that when Cleopas and his friend went back to Jerusalem, they found the "Eleven" (Luke 24:33). That's what Jesus' 12 disciples were called after Judas betrayed Jesus.

GET LIST:

- CARDBOARD
- FELT OR FABRIC
- LOOSE PLAIN PAPER OR
- CONSTRUCTION PAPER
- GLUE
- MARKERS
- PAINTS
- GLITTER
- WIDE RIBBON OR
- HEAVY STRING

Cut two pieces of cardboard the same size. Cut felt or fabric pieces about one inch wider and one inch longer than the cardboard. Center the cardboard on the felt, wrap the edges around and glue them down. Now you have a front and back cover for a scrapbook. Decorate the front cover with paint, glitter or other art supplies. Use a marker to make a title that says "Jesus is With Me." On the paper, trace your feet and hands. Measure them, and write down your size and age and other interesting information about yourself. You can add pages to this scrapbook anytime. Draw or keep pictures of important times when you know Jesus is with you. You can wrap the scrapbook with the ribbon or string and tie a bow. Just unwrap it when you want to add pages or remember how Jesus was with you.

God Talk

Jesus surprised Cleopas and his friend
by being with them when they didn't expect it.
Play a game of "Hide and Seek."
Every time the seeker finds someone who is hiding,
name a different way that you know Jesus is with you.

Thomas's Surprise

Dear Journal,

So much has happened in the last few days. I'm not sure what's going on. Some guards came and took Jesus away. They beat him up, whipped him, made fun of him and told lies about him. I thought Jesus would defend himself, but he didn't. When I thought things couldn't get any worse, they nailed Jesus' hands and feet to a wooden cross, put the cross in the ground, and left Jesus hanging there until he died. It was the saddest day of my life! Jesus was killed.

Some friends took his body down, wrapped it up in cloths and put it into a tomb—it was a hole in the side of hill. They covered the hole with a huge rock and left soldiers there to guard it.

A few days later, Mary Magdalene went to visit the grave really early in the morning. When she got there, she saw that the big rock had been moved away! She ran and got my friends, Simon Peter and John, who were also close friends of Jesus. Together they ran back and searched inside the tomb. They found the strips of cloth used to wrap Jesus' body, but the body was gone. John thinks he understands something about Jesus from all this. But I just don't get it! What is going on?

Dear Journal,

I think my friends are going crazy. A bunch of them were together the other night, talking about Jesus and crying because he's gone now. They had the door locked because they were afraid of the people who killed Jesus—we don't know if they might come after us next! They tried to tell me that all of a sudden Jesus was right there with them! They say he said, "Peace be with you!" then all this other stuff about the Father sending him and now he was going to send them. Send them where? And then he went on about the Holy Spirit and forgiving people. I can't believe it! They keep saying, "Thomas! We saw the Lord!" But I think they're losing their minds! I said, "Unless I see the nail marks in his hands and put my finger where the nails were and put my hands into his side, I will not believe it!"

Dear Journal,

Well, things have gotten stranger still, but now I'm the happiest man on earth. Jesus really is alive! My friends weren't crazy! They were telling the truth! We were all at the house together talking about Jesus and what we're going to do next. The doors were locked tightly to keep us safe.

And then it happened. Jesus was right there with us! Jesus knew what I'd said about not believing, because he walked right over to me and showed me his hands and his side. He said to me, "Put your finger here; see my hands. Reach out your hand and put it into my side. Stop doubting and believe." At first I was kind of embarrassed that Jesus knew what I had said, but then I didn't care because he really is alive and I saw him with my own eyes! I said, "My Lord and my God!" to let him know I was a believer now.

Jesus realized that I believed because I had seen him. He said that the people who are able to believe without seeing him will be truly happy. I wonder who they will be?

366

Go for the Godprint

Confidence: It can be hard to believe in something you can't see. But Jesus is as real today as he was to Thomas 2,000 years ago. And just as Jesus understood the doubts Thomas had, he understands our doubts today and helps us have faith. If you ever have doubts, talk to Jesus about them.

What Digby Dug Up

Jesus said, "Peace be with you" to his disciples. This was an ordinary greeting, as common as saying "Good morning" today.

PEACE BE WITH YOU

Mo's Fab Lab

What's something invisible that you know is real? How about air? We can't see air, but we know it's there. Explore the reality of air with some experiments. Blow up a balloon and feel the sides; you can feel the pressure of the air. Pop the balloon; you can hear the release of the air in the bang. Stand in front of a fan; you can feel the power of the wind lifting your hair and cooling your face. Watch a video about hurricanes or tornadoes and discuss the immense power of air to change things forever. What else can air do even though we can't see it? When you've finished with your experiments, think of other things we cannot see but know are real. Love is invisible, and so are happiness, trust, friendship and kindness. How do we know these are real? How can knowing these are real help us have confidence that Jesus is real?

God Talk

In a family prayer time, take turns finishing this sentence. "Lord, help me to know you are real when I _____."

Fish 'n' Tips: The Rest of Peter's Story

It had been a long week. Everyone was thinking about Jesus. He'd been killed, but now he was appearing to different people. We never knew when to expect him.

"I'm going fishing," I said to my friends.

Thomas and Nathanael looked at one another and shrugged their shoulders. "We'll go with you," they said. It was late in the day, but we made our way to the Sea of Galilee. A few more disciples joined us, including John.

We gathered our nets and jumped in the boat. First we paddled to deeper water, then we dropped the nets, hoping to catch fish underneath. After the nets floated down through the murky water and nestled on the sandy bottom, everyone strained to lift the wet cords. Each time the nets were raised, we gathered, ready to rejoice over the catch.

Time after time we followed the same routine. And time after time we came up with nothing. There was no rejoicing.

The night dragged on. We were disappointed, of course, and then we started to get tired and hungry. Finally the sun began to rise. It was early in the morning when one of my friends heard a voice. "Friends, haven't you any fish?"

We didn't recognize the man calling out to us from the shore.

"No," we called back, heads hanging low.

"Throw your net on the right side of the boat, and you will find some," the man told us.

We looked at each other and scratched our heads. Why would the right side of the boat be any better? Hadn't we tried the right side hours ago? But since there were no fish in the boat, we decided to take the stranger's advice.

When the net was cast and drawn back up, we could hardly pull the heavy weight. There were so many fish! The nets bulged from all sides and looked like they would burst open.

"It is the Lord!" John said. That's all I needed to hear. Before anyone could take another breath, I was in the water, swimming toward shore where my Lord stood. My friends in the boat hauled the nets closer to the boat and made their way to shore.

When we all got to shore, we saw Jesus and a fire with fish and bread laid out for breakfast.

"Bring some of the fish you've caught," Jesus said.

I climbed back in the boat and helped drag our enormous catch onto shore. The cords held each fish tightly. Later we found out we had caught 153 large fish—a great catch.

"Come and have breakfast," Jesus said, waving us closer.

Jesus broke the bread and passed it around. He offered each of us pieces of fish, and we all ate until we were full.

Jesus turned to me and said, "Do you love me more than these?"

I looked around the circle of fishermen and answered, "Yes, Lord; you know that I love you."

Then Jesus said, "Feed my lambs." He went on to ask a second time, "Do you truly love me?"

"Yes, Lord; you know that I love you," I answered.

"Take care of my sheep," Jesus told me.

Jesus asked me a third time, "Peter, do you love me?"

All of a sudden, I felt really sad. I remembered the three times I had said I didn't even know Jesus. Now Jesus was asking me the same question—three times. I was ashamed and wondered if Jesus still loved me.

"Lord, you know all things; you know that I love you," I said.

"Feed my sheep," Jesus encouraged me.

Now I understood. Jesus challenged me to help people in need and maybe even begin a church. Even though I had let Jesus down, he forgave me. It was my job to follow the Savior's commands. My love for Jesus was all I needed to do my best for God. I wouldn't fail him again.

Go for the Godprint

Purposefulness: God is forgiving and patient. Although human beings mess up, God never does. He has a plan for each of his creations. Keep in mind that you can serve God any time and anywhere. You won't let him down if you love him and try your best to follow his Word.

What Digby Dug Up

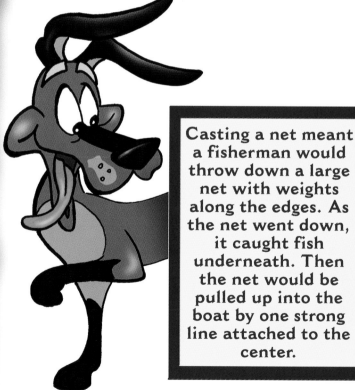

Casting a net meant a fisherman would throw down a large net with weights along the edges. As the net went down, it caught fish underneath. Then the net would be pulled up into the boat by one strong line attached to the center.

Mo's Fab Lab

GET LIST:
HOT WATER, RED FOOD COLORING, SALT,
ICE CUBE, MIXING BOWLS

Mix two cups hot water, four drops red food coloring and two cups salt in a jar or mixing bowl. Stir well so the salt dissolves completely. Put an ice cube in a separate mixing bowl. Talk about:

• **How is sin like an ice cube?** (It makes us cold, hard people who aren't any fun to hold or snuggle up to.)

• **When Jesus died on the cross, what happened to our sin?** (Because Jesus died, God forgives our sins. It's like they were never there.)

Slowly pour the red liquid over the ice cube and watch it disappear! Share a sin you need to be forgiven for or mention someone you need to forgive. Pray for forgiveness and thank Jesus for all he's done to wipe out all the times we mess up.

God Talk

Go around the table
and have each family member
talk about a favorite breakfast food.
Or prepare a special breakfast for everyone
to share and set an extra place setting
to represent Jesus' presence.
Now imagine sitting with Jesus around the fire
and have each person finish these prayer starters:
Jesus, I need to be forgiven for _____.
But, Lord, I will try to live for you by _____.

371

Into the Clouds

This is D.J. Lipz for I Witness radio KBJC, Jerusalem. We now take you to the Mount of Olives at the edge of town where my fellow reporter, Ima Noyze, is standing by. Ima, bring us up to date on the recent strange turn of events with Jesus of Nazareth.

Ima: D.J., If you recall, Jesus of Nazareth was nailed to a cross and died over a month ago. Just three days after his death, Jesus' body turned up missing. Then reports started coming in that several people had seen Jesus—alive! Remarkable, but true. Jesus often met with his followers after he came back from the dead. Peter, a former fisherman, is one of Jesus' closest friends. He's here with me now. Peter, can you tell us what Jesus was like after his death? Was he out for revenge?

Peter: No, Ima. It wasn't like that at all. Jesus let us know he wasn't going to be in the area for long. He gave us special instructions.

Ima: What kind of instructions?

Peter: He told us to stay here in Jerusalem until we received the promise from God that he'd told us about. He explained that John the Baptist had baptized with water, but we were going to be baptized with the Holy Spirit.

Ima: What does that mean?

Peter: I don't know yet, but I'm sure we'll find out! Jesus always knows what's going to happen. I've learned to trust what he says.

Ima: Did Jesus tell you anything else?

Peter: Yes. After the Holy Spirit comes, we're supposed to go all around the world telling people about Jesus. I can't wait!

Ima: Thank you, Peter. Now back to you, D.J.!

D.J.: Thank you, Ima. Many of the local religious leaders have tried to cast doubts on Jesus' rising from the dead. But yesterday Jesus' followers claimed that Jesus had disappeared into the sky! Andrew, one of the men who was with Jesus at his disappearance, is with me in the studio today. Andrew, what really happened? Is Jesus hiding somewhere?

Andrew: No, D.J., Jesus was taken into heaven. He was talking with us when suddenly he started floating upwards! He floated right up into the clouds until he disappeared!

D.J.: What did you do?

Andrew: We stood there just staring into the clouds for a while. Then we looked around and saw two men in bright white robes. They said, "Why are you standing here looking up into the sky? Jesus was taken up into heaven, and he'll come back the same way."

D.J.: What does that mean?

Andrew: I don't understand everything myself. But I know this: Jesus had finished the work that God gave him to do. And so he went back to heaven. Now we—his followers—need to tell everyone in the world about him. When we've done our work and when the time is right, Jesus will come back.

D.J.: Well, folks, there you have it. Several reliable witnesses support this report that Jesus has ascended into heaven. There's a strong feeling here that we haven't heard the last of Jesus or his band of loyal followers. We'll continue to monitor their activities here in Jerusalem. This is D.J. Lipz. Join us again next week on KBJC, I Witness radio, Jerusalem.

374

Go for the Godprint

Purposefulness: What's your job? To go to school? To make friends? Even while you're working on the job of growing up, remember that God uses kids to get his work done. Jesus had a purpose for coming to earth and didn't return to heaven until he finished the job. In the same way, God wants us to be faithful each day to obey him and use our lives to bring honor to him.

What Digby Dug Up

Jesus went up to heaven 40 days after he rose from the dead. During those 40 days, he showed himself to hundreds of people so that everyone would know he was really alive.

Mo's Fab Lab

GET LIST:
HELIUM BALLOON
PERMANENT MARKER

Can you imagine how incredible it must have been to watch Jesus disappear into the sky? Reenact the scene with your family and a helium balloon. Purchase an inflated, solid-color helium balloon. Stand outside in a circle and read Acts 1:1-11. Discuss:

- **What job did Jesus give his followers?**

- **How can we carry on that job in our family?**

Pledge to carry out the work that Jesus has for your family to do. Then sign your names on the balloon and let it go. Because helium is lighter than the air around us, it will rise. Sing a favorite praise song to Jesus as it floats away. Then get to work—the work Jesus has for you to do!

God Talk
Gather an assortment of items
that represent kinds of work that family members do,
such as a kitchen utensil, a gardening tool, a briefcase,
a school textbook, cleaning supplies, even a computer.
Let everyone select an item to hold.
Take turns asking God to help you do his work wherever you are.

Tongues of Fire

We waited. Sometimes we wondered what we were waiting for. But Jesus had told us to stay in Jerusalem and wait, so that's what we did.

When Jesus died, we crashed into the pit of despair. After three years of following him and listening to him teach, we were on our own. It seemed like it had all been for nothing.

That was Friday. On Sunday, we found out he was alive again! We were so excited, we could hardly keep our feet on the ground. But how long would he be with us? Jesus showed himself to a lot of people in the weeks after his resurrection. Then, 40 days after he rose from the grave, we stood and watched him rise into the sky and disappear from sight.

But before he left, he told us to wait. "Wait for the gift my Father promised," he said. "You'll be baptized with the Holy Spirit."

So we waited for another ten days. The feast of Pentecost came, 50 days after the Passover time when Jesus had been killed. Jerusalem was full of people again. Jews lived all over the Roman world, but Pentecost was one of those times when Jerusalem was crowded. Pentecost was the end of the spring grain harvest, and it was a time to celebrate and be thankful. Anyone who could come to the festival made the trip. Jews came to Jerusalem from faraway empires, hundreds of miles away. Rome was over a thousand miles away, but people came from there. If you walk through the market streets at Pentecost, you hear dozens of different languages.

Our group of believers had grown every day since Jesus was raised from the dead. On the day of Pentecost, 120 of us gathered. And waited. Jesus had promised the Holy Spirit. We didn't know when or how the Spirit would come. But we wanted to be ready.

Suddenly the house shook with a gale-force wind. No, it was even worse than that. This was no summer breeze, no spring fluttering of leaves, no winter bluster. It was a wind like we'd never seen before or since. It blew through the house powerfully, like it was coming straight from heaven, and filled up every nook and cranny of the place.

The next moment, flames burst out. But nothing burned. We saw tongues of fire in the air. They settled on each of us. And we were filled with the Holy Spirit. This was what Jesus had promised! This was what we had spent ten days waiting for.

Suddenly everyone started talking. But if you tried to understand us, you might have had trouble. We were talking in languages that we didn't even know! We had never studied these languages, never practiced them. But now we couldn't stop speaking.

The wind and the fire and our speaking made such a ruckus that people came running from all over Jerusalem. These were the people who had come from far away for the feast. Imagine their surprise when they heard us talking—and could understand us.

"Aren't all these men Galileans?" they asked.

"How is it that we hear them talking about God in our own languages?"

Peter got up to explain. He told everyone that what was happening was exactly what the prophet Joel had said would happen when God poured out his Spirit on the earth. It was right there in the Scriptures the whole time. And now it had come true.

More than 3,000 people believed in Jesus that day. After that, we met together for meals and to worship God. God's Spirit made us bold to tell our friends and family and even strangers about Jesus. And every day, God brought more people to our group.

Jesus told us to wait. And we waited ten days. And nothing has been the same since.

Go for the Godprint

Discipleship: The thousands of people who believed in Jesus on the day of Pentecost wanted to learn more about Jesus, so they could live the way he wanted them to live. What have you been learning about Jesus recently? Can you think of someone who needs to know the good news about Jesus?

What Digby Dug Up

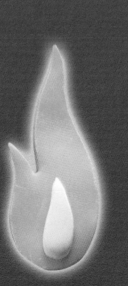

The Day of Pentecost is also called the Feast of Weeks (Deuteronomy 16:10), the Feast of Harvest (Exodus 23:16) and the Day of First Fruits (Numbers 28:26). Along with Passover and Feast of the Tabernacles, it is one of the three biggest festivals in Judaism.

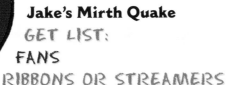

Jake's Mirth Quake

GET LIST:
FANS
RIBBONS OR STREAMERS

Bring all the fans you have in your house together in one room. Tie streamers or ribbons to the grate in front of each fan. Turn the fans so they face each other and sit in the middle of the fans. Now set the fans on high speed. Watch the streamers. Put your face up close to a fan, and talk right into the blowing air. What does your voice sound like? Talk to each other and see if you can understand each other. Talk about:

• **What do you imagine it was like to be in the room on Pentecost?**

• **How can we remember that the same power of the Holy Spirit is with us today?**

God Talk
How many languages can you name?
Can you say any words in languages
besides the one your family uses?
Pray together and thank God for showing at Pentecost
that he sent his Spirit into the world.
Ask him to help you use your tongue to tell someone else about Jesus.

Stephen's Rap

Hey, there! This is Stephen.
    I'm up here with God in heaven.
But when I lived back down on earth,
    I was one of seven—
The apostles who were chosen to lead
    and spread God's word.
No matter what it cost me,
    I made sure that it was heard.

The story starts with Abraham
    who went when God said "Go!"
He started out for points unknown—
    a land that God would show.
He packed his goods and followed God
    without hesitation
And came here down here to Canaan-land
    to start a holy nation.

God's story is for all of us,
    for me and for you,
Because our God who ruled in the past,
    rules the future too.

Abraham believed God's pledge
    that Sarah would have a boy,
And after waiting many years,
    Isaac brought them joy.
Then Jacob followed Isaac
    and had a dozen sons,
And Jacob's precious Joseph
    became God's chosen one.

As a slave in Egypt-land,
    Joseph found God's grace.
Got in good with Pharaoh,
    and governed the whole place.
For seven years he stored up food,
    so there would be enough
Then shared it with his family,
    though their treatment had been rough.

In Egypt Joseph's family
    kept growing through the years
'Til Pharaoh saw how large they were
    and acted on his fears.
Pharoah made them all his slaves;
    he worked them day and night
Until God sent in Moses
    to make everything all right.

Moses worked God's miracles
    to set the people free,
They fled into the desert
    and escaped by the Red Sea.
God gave them Ten Commandments
    which many folks ignored.
They bowed before a golden calf
    and did not obey the Lord.

For 40 years they wandered
    in the barren desert sand.
Then Joshua took them all
    into the promised land.

They trusted in the Lord again,
    and drove the others out.
God's power won their battles;
    walls fell at their shout!

David made the nation great,
    then Solomon his son.
God's prophets wrote and told about
    the coming Righteous One.
But people killed the prophets,
    and they murdered Jesus too.
And when they turned their hate on me,
    I knew that I was through.

Angry people yelled and dragged me
    to the edge of town,
They dropped their coats and threw their stones
    until they knocked me down.
I knew they could not hurt my soul
    so I still told God's story,
Until I looked up to the sky
    where I could see God's glory.

"Lord Jesus, take my spirit now,"
    I knelt and cried aloud.
"And don't hold this against them," I said,
    praying for the crowd.
And then I was in heaven
    with the Savior I adored.
I stayed true until the end
    to Jesus Christ, my Lord.

God's story is for all of us,
    for me and for you,
Because our God who ruled in the past,
    rules the future too.

Go for the Godprint

Conviction: Steven was determined to share the story about God's plan for his people. Some people didn't believe Steven's story—especially the part about Jesus being "the Righteous One," God's own Son. Even when people threatened to stone Steven to death, he kept sharing God's story. How can your faith become as strong as Steven's?

What Digby Dug Up

Steven basically gave his listeners a lesson in Bible history.

To read more about the characters in Steven's story, check out the stories listed below.

PJ's Good to Go

Interview as many relatives as you can about their faith. Start with the family members who live with you, then e-mail family members who don't live nearby. Ask each family member the following questions. Write down the answers and compile them in a folder or notebook as a record of the ways God has worked in your family's faith life.

- **What's the first Bible story you remember hearing?**
- **When did you first decide to follow God?**
- **Tell me about a time when you stood up for your faith.**
- **Tell me about a prayer God answered.**
- **Tell me about someone whose faith you admire.**

God Talk
Gather your family together.
Have each family member bring an item
that represents one way
they'll trust God about the future.
For example, you might bring a pencil
as a reminder to trust God at school.
A can of soup might remind you to trust God
to provide food for your family.
After all family members have shared how they want to trust God,
put all of the items in a box.
Pick a date in the future. Write on the box,
"Do not open until (the date you picked).
When the date arrives,
open the box and talk about the ways God has helped your family.

Saul Becomes Paul—*A New Man*

It was a terrible time for Christians. Jesus' followers were being imprisoned and killed by those who wanted to stop Jesus' fame from spreading. A man named Saul was one of the most-feared enemies of Christians. He took the lead in tracking Christians down and arresting them. Follow these events in the life of Saul to see how God changed his heart.

In Jerusalem, Saul threatens followers of Jesus, saying he will kill them.

Saul gets permission to go to the city of Damascus and arrest Christians there too.

On the way to Damascus, a bright light flashes around Saul and he hears a voice.

Saul falls to the ground and the voice asks, "Saul! Why are you persecuting me?"

Saul asks, "Who are you?"

The voice answers, "I am Jesus, the one you're persecuting. Now go into the city. You'll meet someone there who will tell you what to do next."

Saul gets up, but suddenly realizes he's blind !

find the house of Judas, and ask for Saul. Saul had been told in a dream that you will come and lay your hands on him so he can see again."

Ananias is afraid because he's heard of Saul arresting Christians.

God says, "I've got an important job for Saul. He's going to tell many people about me."

Ananias obeys God and finds Saul. Saul suddenly can see again!

The people traveling with him lead him to Damascus.

For three days Saul can't see, and he doesn't eat or drink.

God speaks to a follower of Jesus named Ananias who lives in Damascus. "Go to Straight Street,

Saul believes in Jesus and is baptized as a Christian—even though just a short time ago he was the enemy of Christians.

Saul begins to preach in Damascus, saying, "Jesus is the Son of God."
People know Saul's heart is changed.
People in Damascus who don't believe in Jesus decide to kill Saul because of his message about Jesus.

Christians help Saul escape by putting him in a basket and lowering it through an opening in the city wall.

Saul goes back to Jerusalem and tries to join other Christians. They're afraid of him. Barnabas helps others believe that God has changed Saul's heart.

Saul begins preaching about Jesus all around Jerusalem.

Barnabas and Saul, who was also called Paul, travel to other cities and countries telling people everywhere about Jesus.

Go for the Godprint

Commitment: When Saul hated the Christians he gave all his time and energy to arresting them and killing them. He was committed to what he believed. But when God changed Saul's heart, Saul gave all his time and energy to telling others about Jesus. He was now committed to God. Can you think of a way that you can give your energy and time to God?

What Digby Dug Up

Shortly after Saul became a Christian, he changed his name to Paul. Paul, who had been so mean to Christians when he was Saul, ended up writing several books of the Bible!

Mo's Fab Lab

GET LIST:
JAR OF WATER, BLUE FOOD COLORING,
CELERY STALK WITH LEAVES, KNIFE

Mix the water and food coloring in the jar. Stand a celery stalk in the jar. Make sure you keep the leaves on it. Put the jar near a window and leave it for a few hours. The blue water will slowly rise in the veins of the stalk, turning the leaves blue. Slice across the stalk and see for yourself how the celery's color is changed from the inside out. Talk about:

- **How is a change on the inside different from a change on the outside only?**
- **How is this like the change God can make in our hearts when we decide to believe in him?**

God Talk
If God can change a heart like Saul's,
God can change the hearts of others,
too—no matter how hateful they are now.
Pray for someone who is full of hate or who hurts Christians.
This could be someone you know, or a world leader,
or someone who spreads a message of hate.
Pray that God will change this person's heart
so the person will know the love and forgiveness of Jesus.

Stronger than Chains

It was a good time for Christians; it was a bad time for Christians. Good, because more and more people believed in Jesus every day, and the apostles did great miracles of healing. Bad, because the religious leaders and King Herod were out to put a stop to Christianity. They wanted to banish the name of Jesus and never hear of him again.

Herod came from a long line of mean kings. And he seemed more than glad to carry on the tradition of being mean. He had James, the brother of John, put to death. This made the Jewish leaders happy. Herod thought, "Hmm—I put one of the Christian leaders to death, and now the Jewish leaders like me. I could do it again and they would like me even more!" So he had Peter arrested.

That was a bad thing. The Christians were frightened for Peter, who was one of their greatest leaders. So they gathered to pray.

King Herod was mean, but he wasn't dumb. He knew that Peter had done great miracles. And he knew that God did incredible things when the Christians prayed. So he put Peter under heavy guard and chained him with two chains.

King Herod didn't know that the power of prayer is stronger than soldiers and chains. But he was about to find out.

It was the night before Peter's trial, and all through the prison, not an inmate was stirring. Peter lay fast asleep on the floor. Suddenly a light pierced the cold darkness. It was an angel! He nudged Peter and said, "Quick, get up and get your clothes on!"

As Peter rose, his chains fell off. The guards didn't see or hear a thing as their famous prisoner dressed to leave. Peter followed the angel out of the prison. When they came to the heavy iron gate, it swung open for them and they kept walking. Suddenly the angel disappeared as quickly as he had come.

Peter looked around the quiet streets of Jerusalem. Then it dawned on him. *This is really happening! This isn't just a vision or a dream. The Lord sent his angel to rescue me from Herod's clutches. I'm free!*

388

So Peter set off for the house where he knew his friends would be praying. When he arrived, he knocked at the outer gate. Most of the people didn't hear the knock—they were too busy praying for Peter. But Rhoda, the servant girl, ran to the door.

"Who is it?" she asked.

"It's Peter!" came the answer through the door.

Rhoda recognized Peter's voice. She gasped and ran to tell everyone the news. "Peter is at the door!" she exclaimed. And that was precisely where she'd left him!

The people who were praying thought Rhoda must be out of her mind. Then they heard it. *Pound! Pound! Pound!* Peter stood stranded in the street, still knocking.

It was a mad dash for the door. They pulled it open, and sure enough—there stood the man they'd been praying for.

"Peter!"

"How did you get here?"

"Praise God!"

"It's a miracle!"

Peter couldn't get a word in edgewise. He finally motioned for everyone to hush and explained how the angel had led him out of prison.

Astonishing. Miraculous. Marvelous. And true. The power of prayer broke chains, dulled the senses of the guards, opened gates and foiled the plans of a nasty king.

The God who answered the prayers of Peter's friends is still listening. Have you talked to him lately?

Go for the Godprint

Community: King Herod surrounded Peter with guards. Peter's friends surrounded him with prayer. The situation seemed impossible, but it wasn't. There are lots of hard things in life that we can't fix—but we can pray. When difficult things happen we can stand together and wrap people up with our prayers. When you're hurt or sick or scared, there's nothing better than knowing that people are praying for you. Be a partner in prayer. And remember: God hears us and anything can happen!

What Digby Dug Up

When Rhoda told the others Peter was outside, they told her she was crazy. They didn't believe what she said until they saw Peter with their own eyes. Can you think of another person in the Bible who wouldn't believe in something until he'd seen it with his own eyes? You can find his story on page 364 or in John 20:24-29 in your Bible.

Izzy's Art Cart

GET LIST:
ALPHABET BEADS
12-INCH LENGTHS OF TWINE OR A SHOELACE

Have a party with your friends and make P.U.S.H. bracelets together. What does P.U.S.H. mean? **"Pray Until Something Happens!"** Tie a knot three inches from one end of the twine or shoelace. Slide the **"P"** bead up to the knot. Tie a knot close to this first bead, then add the **"U"** bead. Knot again. Do this for the remaining beads. Drape the bracelet comfortably around your wrist and ask someone to tie the ends so the bracelet is loose enough to slide on and off easily. Trim the ends to about an inch. When you all have your bracelets on, make a pact to pray for each other. Remember Peter and his prayer friends and keep believing that God can make great things happen!

God Talk
In this Bible story it seemed impossible
for Peter to get out of prison,
but God did the impossible! What seems impossible to you?
What about an unkind person learning to love?
The freedom of Christians being mistreated in other countries?
Someone who's very sick being made well?
Even though these things seem impossible, pray for them. Nothing is impossible with God!

An Open Door

A preacher who can't preach is like a soggy potato chip or a backboard with no hoop—what's the point?

That's probably how Paul felt as he traveled through Phrygia and Galatia. He was there to preach about Jesus, but in city after city God told him: not here, not today. Well, if not here, where? If not today, when? Paul and his companions kept traveling and obeying what God told them. But their mission was a mystery.

Then, one night Paul dreamed about a man in Macedonia. The man in his dream stood and begged, "Come over to Macedonia and help us." Mystery solved! Paul and company sailed for Macedonia the very next day.

After putting to shore in Neapolis, they traveled overland to Philippi, the leading city in Macedonia. Knowing that the people who worshiped the true God would probably gather by the river to pray, they headed for the riverbank. Then God told Paul: preach!

Paul was more than ready. He found a group of women and told them the good news about Jesus. He told them that Jesus was God's Son who had come to earth just as the prophets foretold hundreds of years before. He told how Jesus preached and healed people. He told that Jesus died a terrible death on a cross, and that Jesus' death paid the price for the sins of the world. He told how Jesus rose again, appeared to many of his followers, then went to heaven. And he told his own story—how he had killed Christians until God spoke to him and changed his life.

The women listened carefully—especially one named Lydia. God spoke to Lydia's heart and she believed in Jesus.

Lydia was a business woman. She sold purple cloth which was used for the finest clothes. She gladly welcomed Paul and his companions to stay at her comfortable home. Having a place to stay made it easy for Paul to keep on telling about Jesus. The group of believers grew into one of the most wonderful churches that's named in the Bible.

Years later, Paul wrote a letter to the church at Philippi. Here's what he said.

I thank my God every time I remember you. In all my prayers for all of you, I always pray with joy because of your partnership in the gospel from the first day until now, being confident of this, that he who began a good work in you will carry it on to completion until the day of Christ Jesus.

It is right for me to feel this way about all of you, since I have you in my heart; for whether I am in chains or defending and confirming the gospel, all of you share in God's grace with me.

God can testify how I long for all of you with the affection of Christ Jesus.

And this is my prayer: that your love may abound more and more in knowledge and depth of insight, so that you may be able to discern what is best and may be pure and blameless until the day of Christ.

(Philippians 1:3-10)

Paul's letter to the Philippian church is filled with love and joy. That letter has brought encouragement and wisdom to Christians for two thousand years.

The church at Philippi started with the help of a gracious lady who shared her home with God's messengers.

Maybe you live in a big, comfortable house like Lydia did. Maybe you live in a small apartment. Whatever your home is like, God can use it help build his kingdom. Open your door and open your heart. Who knows what God will do?

Go for the Godprint

Friendliness: Lydia showed her love for God by being friendly toward Paul and his companions. Think about your relationship with God. Your friendship with him can help you reach out and do good for others the way Lydia did. Can you think of someone you can be friendly to?

What Digby Dug Up

Do you know who was the first one in the Bible to show hospitality? It was God himself! He put Adam in the Garden of Eden and provided everything he needed—even a wife!

PJ's Good to Go

Fold a simple boat from a blank sheet of paper. Let each family member write on your "friend-ship" the name of someone who needs a friend. You might list a new person at school, a new family on your block, a family that has visited your church or someone whose family is facing tough times. Brainstorm ways you can show friendship and hospitality to each of the people you listed. Here are some ideas to get you started.

- Make it a point to smile and call the person by name.
- Ask that person three questions about himself or herself.
- Send a friendly note or e-mail.
- Plan to have lunch or go on a walk together.
- Share a treat.

One person's friendship can make a big difference.

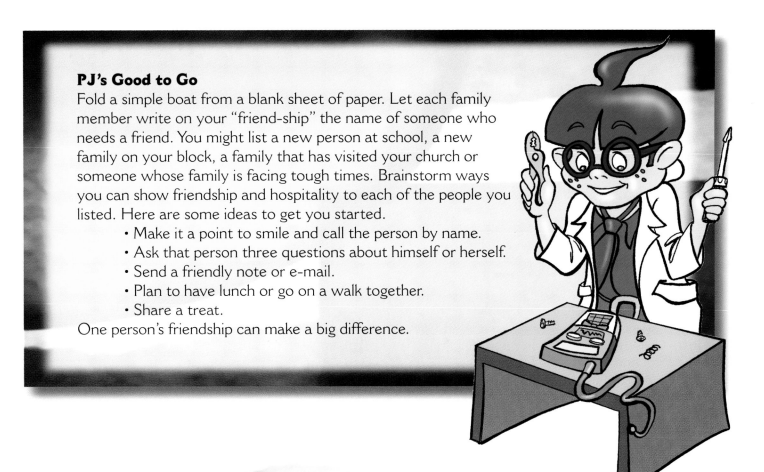

God Talk

Keep the "friend-ship" you made as a prayer reminder.
Put today's date on it. Pray each day for the people you listed.
Ask God to help your friendship get growing!
Check your progress in one week, in one month and in two months.
How has God grown your friendship?

Paul and Silas: JAILBIRDS IN PHILIPPI

It was quite a day in Philippi! Paul and Silas had to cast out a nasty demon from a slave girl who was following them. And then… *(You guess.)*

A: EVERYONE IN PHILIPPI REJOICED THAT THE GIRL WAS FINE. THEY HAD A LITTLE PARTY FOR PAUL AND SILAS, WITH POMEGRANATES AND FIGS FOR REFRESHMENTS.

B: THE OWNERS OF THE SLAVE GIRL GOT MAD. THEY LIKED HAVING A SLAVE WITH A DEMON. THE DEMON COULD MAKE THE GIRL TELL THE FUTURE. THE ANGRY OWNERS DRAGGED PAUL AND SILAS TO THE CITY JUDGE.

It would be nice if "A" were the answer, but God had a little something different in mind. The judge didn't like Paul and Silas, so he let the guards tear off their clothes. When they were just about naked, the guards beat them with sticks. Ouch and double ouch.

Next, a jailer locked Paul and Silas in a cell. He wanted to make sure they couldn't run away, so he put their feet in stocks, which are not a thing like *stock-ings*, but are thick wooden blocks. And then…?

A: PAUL AND SILAS DIDN'T CARE ABOUT THE CUTS OR THE STOCKS. THEY DIDN'T MIND BEING IN JAIL. THEY TRUSTED GOD AND SANG SONGS (PROBABLY A LOT LIKE "KUM BA YA") ABOUT HOW WONDERFUL GOD IS.

B: PAUL AND SILAS THOUGHT GOD HAD FORGOTTEN THEM. THEY TOOK THINGS INTO THEIR OWN HANDS. WHEN THE JAILER CAME INSIDE THE CELL TO GIVE THEM FIGS AND POMEGRANATES, PAUL TRIPPED HIM, AND THEN SILAS GRABBED THE KEYS. THEY UNLOCKED THEMSELVES AND RAN AWAY.

Okay, this time it's "A." (You knew that from the picture, didn't you?) Paul and Silas were singing and praising God. The Bible doesn't say if they were on key or not, or if the song really was "Kum Ba Ya," but it does say the other prisoners listened. The Bible also says that about midnight, something strange happened. What do you think it was?

A: AN EARTHQUAKE SHOOK THE JAIL. ALL THE DOORS FLEW OPEN AND THE LOCKS ON THE STOCKS CAME OFF.

B: A SNAKE SLITHERED INTO THE CELL AND BIT PAUL WITH ITS SHARP, POISONOUS FANGS, BUT PAUL DIDN'T DIE.

Wouldn't "B" make a great story? We'll, it's true! But it's a different story. See page 400 for that one. This time, it's "A"—the earthquake ending. The jailer heard the noise from the earthquake and woke up. He saw the open doors and he…

A: THOUGHT ALL THE PRISONERS HAD ESCAPED. HE DREW HIS SWORD. IF THERE HAD BEEN ANY LIGHT, THE SWORD WOULD HAVE GLEAMED SILVERY WHITE. INSTEAD, THE JAILER HELD THE DEADLY TIP TO HIS BODY, AND JUST AS HE WAS ABOUT TO THRUST IT, PAUL SHOUTED, "DON'T DO IT! WE'RE ALL HERE."

B: SAW AN ANGEL OF THE LORD WHO SAID, "BE NOT AFRAID." THE ANGEL WAS SILVERY WHITE BECAUSE ANGELS DON'T NEED LIGHT TO GLEAM.

"B" would be great in a movie for the lighting effects, but "A" is the answer. The jailer was so worried the prisoners were gone that he was going to kill himself. When he heard Paul, he was overwhelmed with joy and fell in front of Paul and Silas. "What must I do to be saved?" he asked.

Paul answered, "Believe on the Lord Jesus and you shall be saved, you and the wife and kids."

So, the jailer took them straight home, and everybody was happy to believe in God. The jailer washed their yucky wounds. And finally, Paul and Silas got their little party. The jailer gave them food. It might even have been figs and pomegranates!

Go for the Godprint

Confidence: From this story we know that:
A: God will help us when bad things happen.
B: Trusting in God when you are in a bad place, like jail, makes people sit up and take notice.
C: You can do anything with God's help.

The answer: A and B and C.

You can't miss with God.

What Digby Dug Up

The "sticks" that were used to beat Paul and Silas were actually a bundle of rods. Sometimes the bundles had an ax inside them. The ankle holes in the stocks were far apart. When a prisoner was locked in them, his legs were spread uncomfortably apart.

Herbie's Hideaway

Sing this song together to the tune of "America" commonly known as "My Country, 'Tis of Thee."

If God wants me to share
His true love everywhere
I feel I must.
He will not let me fall.
He's with me through it all.
He'll help me to stand tall.
His Word I trust.

Talk about:

• **Can you think of a time when God did something powerful for you?**

• **How can remembering that help you be more confident the next time you're in a tough spot?**

God Talk
Gather a pile of clean, smooth rocks
(five or six) and some acrylic paint.
On each rock, paint a picture or a word
that represents a family prayer request.
Set the rocks along a walkway or near a door.
Pray for the requests painted on the rocks whenever you pass them.
Remember, Psalm 31:3 says, "You are my rock and my fortress" (NIV).

A Rough Ride

Paul had gotten into a lot of trouble for telling people about Jesus. Now he was a prisoner. He had to sail to Rome, Italy, to let Caesar decide what should happen next. On the ship, a centurion named Julius was making sure Paul did not escape.

Paul did go a-sailing,
A-sailing on the sea.
Paul began his journey,
A-bound for Italy.

The ship made many stops. First Sidon, then Myra. Julius made Paul switch ships. The new ship stopped off of Crete in a place called Fair Havens. It was getting on toward winter, and Paul wanted to stay at Crete until better sailing weather. But Julius and the captain of the ship wanted to sail on.

The ship a-sailed slowly.
The wind blew very strong.
They landed at Fair Havens.
The trip was going wrong.

A northeastern wind came and took the ship away. The sailors couldn't fight it. They were afraid the ship would be torn to splinters, so they wrapped rope around it to make it stronger. The weather got so bad the sailors couldn't see the sun or stars for weeks. To lighten the ship, they threw all the extra stuff off the ship.

The wind kept assailing;
It blew the ship off track.
It almost hit a sandbank,
For weeks the sky was black.

An angel appeared to Paul and told him that no one would die as long as no one left the ship. Paul cheered everyone up with this news.

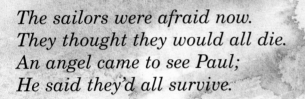

The sailors were afraid now.
They thought they would all die.
An angel came to see Paul;
He said they'd all survive.

When the sailors realized the ship was close to land, they wanted to leave it. They lowered the lifeboat and were about to get in. But Paul warned the ship's officers and told them that if anyone left, God would no longer protect their lives. The officers, being wise, stopped the sailors from leaving by cutting the ropes to the lifeboat. It floated away with nobody in it.

Sailors dropped the lifeboat.
They wanted off the ship.
The officers stopped them
And set the boat adrift.

Again Paul spoke to the crew and urged them to eat. No one had touched any food for fourteen days. After they ate, the sailors felt happier and began throwing more extra things off the ship, including some grain. The next day, they saw the shore. The ship couldn't get close enough to land safely, so everyone would have to swim ashore. The soldiers guarding the prisoners thought Paul and the others would try to escape, so they wanted to kill them. But Julius stopped the killing. Everyone swam or floated to shore in safety. God kept his promise. No one died.

The ship stopped a-sailing.
The sailors spotted land.
Everyone swam safely.
God's power is so grand.

The island they landed on was called Malta. The ship's people were wet and cold. Paul was helping gather wood for a fire to warm everyone when a poisonous snake bit his hand. But God saved Paul. All the people of Malta were amazed that he lived. The next day Paul went to stay at the village leader's house. A man was sick there, and Paul prayed for him and healed him. Then all the sick people of Malta came to see Paul. He healed them, too. Paul and the sailors stayed on Malta three months. Then Paul left for Rome.

Paul wound up on Malta.
He stayed on the island.
God saved him from dying
When a viper bit his hand.

Go for the Godprint

Compassion: Paul cheered up the sailors during the storm, he helped save their lives, and he healed the sick people of Malta. Can you think of someone that you could cheer up? When times are hard, can you remind others that God really, truly, forever cares?

What Digby Dug Up

The name of the island Malta means "refuge," and many a sailor had been washed up on its shores, thankful for safety. The place where the sailors tried to leave the ship is now known as "St. Paul's Bay." Paul had been shipwrecked before and spent a day and a night floating at sea (2 Corinthians 11:25).

Mo's Fab Lab

GET LIST:
PLASTIC DISPOSABLE PLATE,
BALLOON, KNIFE OR SCISSORS

Make your own sailboat with a plastic dinner plate and a balloon. Poke a hole in the center of the dinner plate. Blow up the balloon and pinch the end closed. Stick the end through the hole without letting the air out. Now knot it. (The knot should be on top of the plate, and the balloon underneath.) Float the boat in a bathtub or wading pool. The boat is flat enough to carry small waterproof toys, such as plastic people. While you play, talk about:

• **List all the good things that happened to Paul, even through stormy times.**

• **What good things have happened to you during stormy times?**

• **How can you show God's love to someone else having a tough time?**

God Talk
Pray this prayer in parts:
Parent: When I am sailing—
Child: Guide me where I am to go.
Parent: When I feel like I'm drowning—
Child: Help me not to struggle, so you can pull me out.
Parent: When life is a storm—
Child: Help me not to make waves, but peace.

Fruit of the Spirit

Learning to be like Jesus is something we can do every day. God's Spirit in our hearts teaches us and helps us. Galatians 5:22 tells us nine ways we can be like Jesus. Look for the answer to each of these riddles. When you find the answer, the next riddle will be right below it! Start with this one:

This is much more than hearts and warm feelings. This means caring as much about others as you do about yourself. It means being nice and wishing the best for people no matter how they treat you.

This Fruit of the Spirit is

_____

Great! That's it. Jesus tells us to "love one another." Jesus can work in your heart and help you love people who seem unloveable.

Long faces don't belong on God's people! Because we know that God works out everything for the best in our lives, we can face each day with a smile. Oh, boy!

This Fruit of the Spirit is

_____

Happiness comes and happiness goes. Joy is deeper and stronger. Pray for the joy that comes from being one of God's people.

"It's my way or the highway." That's not God's way. Jesus solved people's problems and told them how to get along. Winning an argument isn't the best thing—winning a friend is!

This Fruit of the Spirit is

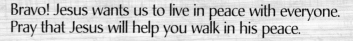

_____

Bravo! Jesus wants us to live in peace with everyone. Pray that Jesus will help you walk in his peace.

Things don't always happen as quickly as we'd like them to. Sometimes God has a good reason for us to wait. But he is always at work. He makes things happen in his time. God's Word tells us to wait on the Lord.

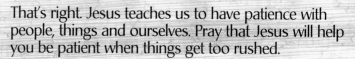

This Fruit of the Spirit is

_____

That's right. Jesus teaches us to have patience with people, things and ourselves. Pray that Jesus will help you be patient when things get too rushed.

When you see someone who needs help, are you ready to jump up and give it? Are you glad to share what you have with friends? Do you like to do things that make other people happy?
Then you know this one.

This Fruit of the Spirit is

_____

Superb! Speaking kind words to others and acting in a kind way is what Jesus wants us to do. Pray that Jesus will help you be kind to others.

It's not always easy to do the right thing. That might mean obeying, or sharing, or giving up your turn. You can do the right thing because you have to or because you want to. It's so much better to do the right thing with a smile and a happy heart.

This Fruit of the Spirit is

_____

Excellent! Goodness helps you and everyone around you have a better day. Ask Jesus to help you find ways to show his goodness to others.

This means sticking with something you believe in, even when it's hard. Being loyal to God is the best of all. He shows the way for us to follow. Our job is to believe he knows what's best and do what he asks.

This Fruit of the Spirit is

_____

Way to go! One way Jesus showed faithfulness was by doing things he knew God wanted him to do, even when it was hard. Pray that he will help you to be more faithful.

This one is soft, easy, not rough, polite. This is the way you hold a little baby or your grandmother's favorite teacup. And it's the way you treat other people's feelings.

This Fruit of the Spirit is

_____

Yahoo! Pray that Jesus will help you to be gentle with others.

You want to reach and touch that pretty vase in the store, but you don't. You want to shout at the friend who just took your toy, but you don't. You want to throw your clothes on the floor, but you don't.

This Fruit of the Spirit is

_____

Good job. We show self-control when we put others' needs before our own. Pray that Jesus will help your self-control grow each day.

Love, joy, peace, patience, kindness, goodness, faithfulness, gentleness and self-control. These are nine ways we can be more like Jesus—the Fruit of the Spirit. We can't make these things happen on our own. We need God's Spirit at work in our hearts. God wants this for you! Open your heart and ask God to change it to be more like his. Then get ready for bushels of blessings!

Go for the Godprint

Integrity: Have you ever bitten into a piece of chocolate only to find out that the inside was not what you expected? Imagine if someone could look at the inside of you. God can. Believing in Jesus makes you a new creation. Integrity means that on the outside you act like the new creation that you are on the inside.

What Digby Dug Up!

Jesus was a friend to people most people would laugh at, be mean to, or ignore. He was friends with tax collectors, people with terrible diseases and even enemy soldiers. He wanted everyone to know that he loved them—even bad people and mean people. This was one way Jesus showed he had integrity.

GP Theater Company

As a family, brainstorm a dozen or so situations in which a person must choose whether to act with integrity or not. Some examples might be: to cheat or not to cheat on a test; to tell the truth or a lie; to share an extra snack or not. Write each idea down on a separate slip of paper, fold it in half, and put it in a bowl. Divide into equal teams. Take turns acting out these situations. Both teams will act out each situation. However, one team will act it out showing integrity, and the other team will act it out not showing integrity. Briefly discuss the choices that were made before you go to another situation.

God Talk

Cut up a variety of fruit
into bite-size pieces
and put them in one big bowl.
Give everyone a fork.
With each bite of fruit you take,
finish this short prayer by filling in the blank
with a fruit of the Spirit from Galatians 5:22.
Lord, fill me up with the fruit of _____
so I can be more like you.

Stand Up Against Evil

In the book of Ephesians, Paul wrote about battles that Jesus' followers must fight and about the battle gear God gives us to help us win.

The enemy is after us,
(And he's not flesh and blood).
Dark forces strange, invisible
Surround us like a flood.
But we won't dodge or run away.
No—we'll stand and fight,
Put on the armor of the Lord
And conquer in his might!

Let's stand up against evil.
  (*Stand up.*)
God gives us what we need
  (*Bend arms up like a strong man.*)
To fight off Satan's army.
  (*Hold out shield.*)
In God's strength, we'll succeed.
  (*Lunge with sword.*)

When Satan tries his tricky schemes
Our belt of truth's around us,
And righteousness protects our hearts
When enemies surround us.
Our feet stand firm on solid rock;
We will not turn away.
God's peaceful gospel forms our shoes.
We're ready, come what may.

Let's stand up against evil.
  (*Stand up.*)
God gives us what we need
  (*Bend arms like a strong man.*)
To fight off Satan's army.
  (*Hold out shield.*)
In God's strength, we'll succeed.
  (*Lunge with sword.*)

For fiery arrows flying fast
We'll take faith as our shield.
Our helmet of salvation
Will make the devil yield.
Our trusty sword, the Word of God,
Can strike at any hour.
The final blow is frequent prayer
With Holy Spirit power.

Let's stand up against evil.
(Stand up.)
God gives us what we need
(Bend arms like a strong man.)
To fight off Satan's army.
(Hold out shield.)
In God's strength, we'll succeed.
(Lunge with sword.)
YEAH!
(Wave sword in air for victory.)

Go for the Godprint

Courage: It's tough living for God when people around us take drugs, lie, steal or do other wrong things. When we choose right instead of wrong, they might make fun of us or try to get us in trouble. Evil comes from the devil, and we can't fight him alone. But with God's limitless power, we can stand up against danger and persecution.

What Digby Dug Up

The Roman army conquered much of the world in Bible times because it had the best equipment and the best trained soldiers. God gives us the equipment and training we need for the battles we face.

Jake's Mirth Quake

GET LIST:

WIRE HANGERS, PANTYHOSE, SHOWER SCRUBBIES OR WADS OF PAPER

God gives us the shield of faith as part of our spiritual armor. Make mini-shields to see how a shield can protect you. Bend a wire coat hanger into a circle. Stretch pantyhose over the circular frame. Pull the hose tightly near the "hook" of the hanger and knot it. Bend the hook towards the back of your mini-shield to form a handle. Choose sides and battle it out using shower scrubbies or wads of crumpled paper. Talk about:

✔ HOW DO WE WIN WHEN WE CAN'T SEE OUR ENEMY?

✔ WHAT TOOLS DOES GOD GIVE US TO WIN?

✔ WHAT CAN WE DO TO BATTLE EVIL?

God Talk

Gather several blankets.
Read Ephesians 6:10–18 aloud as a family.
Each time body armor is mentioned,
spread a blanket across the floor.
Before reading verse 18,
"And pray in the Spirit on all occasions
with all kinds of prayers and requests…,"
kneel on the protective blankets and finish by "praying for all the saints"
who do battle for Christ around the world.

411

Humility of Christ

When Paul was Saul, he hated Christians. But when Saul became Paul, he became one of the greatest leaders of the Christians. (You can read about that amazing story in Acts 9:1–19 or on page 384.) Paul traveled around as a missionary to start churches. Later, he wrote letters to many of the churches he had helped start.

One of the places Paul visited was the city of Philippi. (You can read about some of the things that happened there on page 392 and 396. After he left, Paul wrote a letter to the church at Philippi to teach the Christians there what it means to be like Jesus.

Paul taught the Philippians not to do anything out of selfishness. When people think only of themselves, the church can't work together. Instead, Paul told them to think of other people before themselves. Working together to care for the problems of other people follows Christ's example.

Paul wrote:

> *Your attitude should be the same as Christ Jesus:*
> *who, being in very nature God,*
> *did not consider equality with God something to be grasped,*

Jesus is God's Son. He has a right to the same glory and power as God the Father. But Jesus set that aside for a while when he became human. Instead of insisting on being equal to God, Jesus did what his Father wanted him to do.

> *but made himself nothing,*
> *taking the very nature of a servant*
> *being made in human likeness.*

Jesus was born as a human baby. He was not born into a rich and powerful family. He was born to a young couple staying in an animal stable. Jesus was still God, but he became human, too. He entered our world as a person so he could save all the people in the world. He came to serve other people, not to get glory for himself.

> *and being found in appearance as a man*
> > *he humbled himself*
> > > *and became obedient to death—even death on a cross!*

Jesus didn't come into the world to do what he wanted to do, but to do what God wanted him to do. He gave up what he deserved so he could obey God and serve others. Obedience was not an easy road to take. It led to the cross, where Jesus died.

413

therefore God exalted him to the highest place
and gave him the name that is above every name,
that at the name of Jesus every knee should bow,
in heaven and on earth and under the earth,
and every tongue confess that Jesus Christ is Lord
to the glory of God the Father.

Jesus gave up his right to glory. And once his work on earth was finished, God gave him the glory he deserved. God took him back up to heaven. Someday everyone in heaven and earth will know that Jesus Christ is Lord. Even the people who don't want to admit it will bow to Jesus. And Jesus will give the glory to God.

Go for the Godprint

Humility: Can you congratulate someone else on doing a great job even when no one congratulates you? Being humble, like Jesus was, means not worrying about getting lots of attention and privileges yourself, even if you deserve them. God is the one who gives us our talents and abilities—it's right to use them for his glory, not for our own.

What Digby Dug Up
The words of Philippians 2:5–11 are a hymn that was sung in the early Christian church.

THESE FEW WORDS REMINDED THE CHRISTIANS OF THE MIRACLE OF JESUS BECOMING HUMAN AND DYING FOR THE SINS OF ALL PEOPLE.

Jake's Mirth Quake

Bragging and humility are opposites. Play a fun game of Brag Tag with your family and friends. Instead of running in this game, you'll walk with your ankles pointed out and your toes pointed in. The oldest person is "It." When It tags someone, he or she must brag about that person. It might say, "This is a great young man who is fantastic at making friends," or "This is the most helpful, encouraging Mom on the block!" Keep playing until everyone has been bragged about. Then talk about:

- **What do you think when people who brag about themselves?**

- **How does it feel when someone else brags about you?**

- **Why is it important to brag about other people instead of about ourselves?**

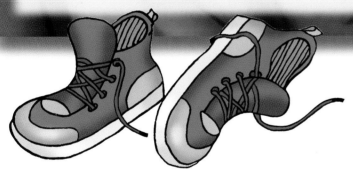

God Talk
"May the mind of Jesus
go with me everywhere I go."
Repeat that sentence prayer together
until everyone can say it.
Then take turns calling out all the places
that members of your family go during the day.
After each place is mentioned, repeat the prayer together.